Critical Essays on Emile Zola

Critical Essays on
World Literature

Robert Lecker, General Editor
McGill University

Critical Essays on Émile Zola

David Baguley

G. K. Hall & Co. • Boston, Massachusetts

Library of Congress Cataloging in Publication Data
Main entry under title:

Critical essays on Emile Zola.

  (Critical essays on world literature)
  Bibliography: p. 191
  Includes index.
  1. Zola, Emile, 1840–1902 — Criticism and interpretation —
Addresses, essays, lectures. I. Baguley, David.
II. Series.
PQ2538.C69 1986   843'.8   85-21915
ISBN 0-8161-8826-2

Pour
F.W.J. Hemmings
et
Henri Mitterand
zolistes, maîtres, amis

CONTENTS

INTRODUCTION

Zola and His Critics

There will never be a day when criticism will be of one mind about him, when he will no longer be a question, and will have become a conclusion.

William Dean Howells

When, toward the end of his career, after a long spell away from the profession, Zola turned briefly once again to journalism and published a second series of articles in *Le Figaro*, he entitled one of his pieces "The Toad" and used the occasion to direct some rather heavy-handed irony against his critics.[1] The title refers to the French expression "avaler un crapaud," which usually translates as "to swallow an insult." "Every morning," Zola writes, "for thirty years now, before I start to work, I swallow my toad as I open up the seven or eight newspapers that await me on my desk. As I eagerly scan the columns, I am sure that it is there, and rarely do I fail to find it." He goes on to claim that he has come to rely upon his daily dose of insults to give him courage to continue his work — Zola subscribed unreservedly to the "hard-knocks" formula for success — and that he welcomes, too, the regular delivery of the piles of articles and reviews that his editor, Charpentier, sends him, "a whole swamp, the toad-hole itself, in all its frightful pullulation." For several years he has thought of collecting together "a delicate choice of the compliments" that the critics have paid him. It would be called "Leurs injures" (Their insults). But the flow never stops. With some typical Zolaesque expansiveness, he adds that his attic in his country house at Médan is full of the creatures: "Decidedly, the deluge is endless, the heavens have opened, it is raining toads." Yet for all their stupidity, viciousness, intolerance, and folly, these "putrid flows of invective" are the very signs, according to Zola, of his vitality as a writer. In an opportune version of the *cogito* he argues: "The proof is infallible. I am still attacked, therefore I still am." So, in a no less typical rhapsodic vein, he concludes: "Fall then, fall for ever on my house, beneficent rain of toads! Continue to bring me the courage to face my fellow men without being seized by despair."

1

Zola's attitude is clearly a way of coming to terms with the extraordinary incongruity in his career between, on the one hand, his unprecedented popular success and serious literary aims, and, on the other hand, the manner in which critics in his own country relentlessly hounded him. Of his success, publishing figures speak for themselves. In a period of fierce competition in the publishing industry when a writer was most fortunate to have a second edition (of usually a thousand copies) printed, several of Zola's novels had already run to well over a hundred editions in France by the time of his death (1902); and, more recently, in the pocket book French editions of his novels ("Livre de poche") for instance, almost ten million copies were printed between 1953 and 1972. But even such impressive figures give a limited idea of Zola's readership, for his novels regularly appeared, of course, in newspapers and journals both before and after their publication in volume form, and were also widely read, despite institutional controls, in public libraries.[2] As for the critics' offense against his works — and sometimes against his person — Zola was often bemused by it, though, as we have already seen, it was not entirely unwelcome. In June–July 1887, for example, he wrote to his Dutch correspondent J. Van Santen Kolff, then resident in Berlin, about the furore in that city over the play *Thérèse Raquin*, a work apparently well received in Italy, Spain, and Portugal: "Is it then a question of latitude? So what! The main thing is to stir up the crowds. Only indifference kills. You have to be execrated to be loved."

Yet Zola received more than his fair share of execration and his works, during his lifetime at least, provoked the most extreme of reactions, usually unfavorable. A controversial figure, his public image was far removed, as he and his friends quickly pointed out when the attacks began, from the reality of the retiring, sedentary, kindly, sensitive, and nervous bourgeois writer, bound to his desk and his routines for much of the year in his country retreat. But, even from a distance and even behind a cloak of scientific neutrality, he was always a provocative writer. "The bourgeois reader must be made to feel," he wrote in his preliminary notes for *Germinal*, "a shudder of terror." And, throughout his career, in the various campaigns in which he was involved — for Manet and the Impressionists in the sixties, for the Naturalist novel and theater in the seventies and eighties, for Dreyfus at the turn of the century — he proved to be a doughty fighter who pulled no punches. His very success provoked jealousy. His frankness called forth recriminations. His work was too bold to be ignored, too pertinent to be marginalized, and too challenging to be recuperated by a bourgeois society whose illusions and delusions he constantly defied in his representations of it. He was accused of writing crude books for profit, then condemned for writing virtuous books, like *Le Rêve*, to cull official favour. As Colette Becker writes: "Zola quickly became a star. The newspapers and illustrated journals followed his comings and goings; he was photographed on a bicycle, at Médan, or on a locomotive . . . Street vendors took possession of his person: they sold pipes in the shape of his head, postcards showing him with his heroes and heroines . . . His death [from asphyxiation due to a blocked chimney] was even used for publicity in Germany — and in France! — by the manufacturer of an apparatus that could be adapted to chimneys to ensure their proper functioning."[3]

But the surest evidence of Zola's fame was the extent to which he became, after Sarah Bernhardt, so it seems, the most caricatured personality of his age. From the time of the stage adaptation of *L' Assommoir* (January 1879), which first inspired them, and subsequently on any significant Zola occasion like the publication of *Nana, Pot-Bouille, La Terre, La Débâcle*, or his numerous attempts to get elected to the French Academy, or during his trip to Lourdes in 1892 and, most ferociously, during the Dreyfus Affair, the caricaturists never tired of lampooning the stocky, bearded figure with his pince-nez and his high, furrowed brow, either in compromising postures with his own characters or engaged in what they considered to be an appropriate occupation: as cesspool cleaner or rag and bone man.[4] Chamber pots and pigs most frequently recur in these images; Zola is variously shown on, in, emptying, or dipping his quill in the former, and usually riding the latter. In a striking variation on the theme in *Le Sans-Souci* (25 June 1881), the head of a huge pig is shown gazing into a trough at its reflection which has taken on the form of Zola's familiar face. The imagery of the trough was, alas, no less a constant of written Zola criticism!

In the light of all this and in retrospect, the tone of Louis Ulbach's somewhat hysterical review of *Thérèse Raquin* seems less eccentric than one might at first have supposed. His article, "Putrid Literature," was the first significant critical reaction to Zola's works in France and it anticipates a number of later trends: the vehemence of the language, the polemical stance, the focus on the pathological elements in the work, the attack on a certain type of literature and on an emergent literary movement that was yet (but very soon) to find its name, and opposition from the political left as well as the right, for Ulbach was a staunch Republican. The article provoked a reply from Zola, then, in turn, a response from Ulbach, in the pages of *Le Figaro* (31 January and 6 February 1868). Indeed, Zola's famous preface to the second edition of *Thérèse Raquin* (dated 15 April 1868) is a part of the same polemic. In that equally anticipatory text Zola claims, as he will so often do in the future, that his work has been misread, that he has serious scientific aims, which he is compelled to explain himself since the critics have failed to do so; and it is in this preface too that Zola uses for the first time in a prominent context[5] the term *naturalist* to apply to the writer's art.

It is usually considered that the controversy occasioned by the appearance of *Thérèse Raquin* was an isolated incident, uncharacteristic of the almost total complicity of silence that accompanied the publication of Zola's early novels, until the sudden onslaught of the critics in 1877, outraged by the physiological realities and crude language of *L' Assommoir*. However, in a study of the critical reception of his works before *L' Assommoir*, Robert Lethbridge has shown that the polemic over Zola's novel of working-class life in Paris was also the culmination of a prolonged debate and echoed complaints that had already been leveled against earlier works.[6] Nevertheless the clamor was unprecedented and, even before the volume appeared, critics were vigorously denouncing the novel in its serialized version. Albert Millaud wrote in *Le Figaro* (1 September 1876): "It is not realism, it is filth; it is no longer crudity, it is pornography"; B. de Fourcaud in *Le Gaulois* (21 September) called the novel "the most complete collection of turpitudes" that he had ever come across. When the first edition was published in January 1877 — to be followed by thirty-seven more that year — the battle raged again. Though there were admirers of the work, charges of scatology, perversion, plagiarism, were made in a rush of articles, brochures, pamphlets, parodies, caricatures, and songs.

Though adumbrated by the response to *Thérèse Raquin* and extreme in its intensity, the critical reaction to *L' Assommoir* set a pattern for the reception of Zola's works in France that would recur through the years: a combination of public outrage and popular success; attacks from critics of both the left and the right, for the novel was condemned by Republican commentators as a calumny of the people; expressions of appreciation from fellow writers, frequently conveyed in private letters;[7] the fact that almost all the criticism on Zola and his works in France during his lifetime was motivated by some such publishing event, there being an almost total lack of general assessments of his art; the readiness of the novelist himself to intervene and defend his work — thus the preface to (the volume) *L' Assommoir* is a reply to the critics of the feuilleton and, to a considerable degree, even Zola's later theoretical writings were prompted by criticisms of his fictional works; finally, a developing solidification of opinion, the emergence of myths, legends, and, above all, received opinions that would crystallize into a public image and a tradition of unexamined views. Less than three years later, in an article defending *Nana* against similar charges — once again before the book had appeared — Zola would declare: "For ten years, the same article has been written against me, with the result that, when I am sent a newspaper, I only need to look at the signature. There! no need to read it; I know already what the article contains."[8]

Though an older generation of realist writers like Flaubert, Edmond de Goncourt, and Champfleury, was unimpressed by *L' Assommoir*, the merits of the novel and the violence with which it was attacked caused a younger group to rally around Zola: in January 1877 Léon Hennique delivered a public lecture to defend the novel; two months later, J.-K. Huysmans published a laudatory series of articles in a Belgian newspaper,

L'Actualité, then had them issued as a pamphlet in Paris soon after; Paul Alexis, Henry Céard, and Guy de Maupassant would add their voices in defense of Zola's work in France and abroad. Thus what contemptuous critics dubbed "Zola's tail" and what literary historians would call the "Médan group" asserted its existence. Though the group was less cohesive and lasting as a unit than has often been supposed, a concerted sense of purpose grew out of the battle over *L'Assommoir*, and the novelist's disciples, as Alain Pagès has shown in his article on "The Myth of Médan," certainly worked, not only at defending Zola against the abuse of the critics, but also at dispelling certain myths and creating others, at advancing the Naturalist cause, at the very least until April 1880, when they published, together with Zola, a collection of stories, *Les Soirées de Médan*, as a gesture of solidarity.

But for all this outcry and indignation in the press, more formidable opponents of Zola's art were beginning to assert themselves at this time. The *Rougon-Macquart* novels and the theory of the "experimental novel" had nothing to recommend themselves in the eyes of France's literary Establishment, the critics with Classical convictions, the guardians of France's own "great tradition," the arbiters of taste associated with the French university (and, in particular, the Ecole Normale Supérieure), who wrote for serious reviews like the *Revue des Deux Mondes*. Unlike the ephemeral outbursts in the daily press, the monolithic opposition of literary officialdom had longer lasting effects and more influence, perpetuating prescriptive judgments through the authority of academic institutions. There was, it has been convincingly argued also, an important political dimension that explains why Zola was anathema to the ruling, "rightist" critics, for the novelist's works provoked reactionary fears and undermined bourgeois myths based upon the related repression of the human body and the lower classes.[9] One of the most authoritative voices belonged to Ferdinand Brunetière, whose article on *The Experimental Novel* is one of the more significant of a number of exchanges in a long polemic with Zola. It is remarkable how Brunetière's charges — bad style, crude language, absurd theories, excessive description, lack of complex, human characters, unhealthy preoccupation with all that is base in man and nature, then a grudging acknowledgment of a certain poetic "power" — are echoed in the works of other academic critics. Thus Gustave Lanson will later blame Zola for his scientific pretensions, for the "psychological indigence" of his characters, but tentatively recognize, nevertheless, his novels to be "poems, heavy and crude poems, but poems."[10] Emile Faguet, in an obituary general assessment — to give another example — takes up the very same arguments as Brunetière and concludes that the novelist was a second-rate Romantic, crude, misanthropic, pornographic, but a poet with a special talent for depicting crowds, a "barbarous poet," a "vulgar Hugo," a "rude demiurge," a "kind of strange demon half-way between Prometheus and Caliban."[11] In the same article, Faguet expresses some surprise that Jules Lemaître, another fine and educated mind like Brunetière, should have been so indulgent in his judgment of Zola's talents, despite his natural repugnance. Yet Lemaître's interpretations, with his famous definition of Zola's work as "a pessimistic epic of human animality," have often been considered a landmark in the history of criticism on the writer, for the early appreciation that they contain of his ability to depict collective forces and for the rare sensitivity that they show to features of the novelist's art. Some of the arguments of the academic critics are still in evidence, but we can see how this renegade academic critic broke with the censorious "criticism of faults" in the Classical manner and was more inclined to follow his own tastes and impressions even against prevailing views. Indeed he was to become associated with Anatole France as the main exponent of an "impressionistic" form of literary commentary that did much to liberalize the higher reaches of the French institutions of criticism still bound by traditional dogma.

Still, ten years after the storm over *L'Assommoir*, Zola's work was a subject of controversy. In 1887 it was the turn of *La Terre*, his novel of peasant life. Of numerous protestations the most blatant appeared in *Le Figaro* on 18 August, signed by five young writers, Bonnetain, Rosny, Descaves, Margueritte, and Guiches, a kind of "anti-Médan group," and quickly baptized "The Manifesto of the Five," a swingeing attack on Zola's recent novel, work, ideas, art, and person. It was felt to be a particularly "low blow" for several reasons: the abusive terms of the attack; its collective nature; the pretense that a set of disciples was turning against their master — though, as Zola promptly pointed out, he barely knew them — and that a new generation of writers was rejecting Naturalism — though, as was also pointed out, their accomplishments and prospects were very modest; finally, the suspicion, which was not without justification, that Zola's *confrères*, Edmond de Goncourt and Alphonse Daudet, had urged on his detractors — though they both denied it. Brunetière used the occasion to declare "the bankruptcy of Naturalism" in the *Revue des Deux Mondes* (1 September), while Anatole France called Zola's novel the "Georgics of Debauchery" and its author "one of those unfortunate people about whom one can say that it would have been better if they had never been born" (*Le Temps*, 28 August).

Nevertheless, the commotion over *La Terre*, as Auguste Dezalay has noted, marks a turning point, even a terminal point in at least the fiercest forays of the battle between Zola and his (literary) critics: "No doubt, people had progressively grown accustomed to reading Naturalist novels, and perhaps all the resources of pharisaic indignation had been exhausted."[12] No doubt also, Zola was being progressively considered less as a threat in the capacity of leader of a subversive literary movement and more as a distinctive artist, almost a literary institution in his own right. Certainly when, in 1891, the energetic journalist Jules Huret, a convinced

Darwinian, conducted his well-known survey on literary evolution in *L'*
Echo de Paris by interviewing sixty-three men (and one woman) of letters,
the consensus among both enemies and friends was that Naturalism was
already as good as extinct, but that Zola himself had survived the
struggle.[13] His greatest battle was, of course, still to come, but it was to be
in the political arena, and naturally, at the time of his death, the flood of
homages was rendered more often to the defender of Alfred Dreyfus than
to the author of the *Rougon-Macquart*. Thus Anatole France was invited
to honour the writer at his graveside on 5 October 1902. Though singing a
very different lament since the days of *La Terre*, he still chose to focus
more on the glory of the man and his recent action than on the qualities of
his life's work, in a famous, resounding speech of which we have translated
certain extracts:

> Gentlemen, when his work was seen mounting up stone by stone,
> its greatness was measured with surprise. It was admired; it caused
> astonishment; it was praised and it was blamed. Praise and blame were
> uttered with equal vehemence. At times (as I myself know), sincere, yet
> unjust reproaches were leveled against the powerful writer. He was both
> violently attacked and defended. And his work went on growing.
>
> Today, now that we can discover its colossal form in its entirety, we
> can also recognize the spirit with which it is imbued. It is a spirit of
> kindness. Zola was good. He had the greatness and the simplicity of the
> magnanimous. He was profoundly moral. . . .
>
> This sincere Realist was an ardent Idealist. His work can only be
> compared in its grandeur to Tolstoy's. They are two vast ideal cities built
> by the lyre at the two extremes of European thought. They are both
> generous and pacific. But Tolstoy's is the city of resignation. Zola's is the
> city of work. . . .
>
> Let us not pity him for having endured and suffered. Let us envy
> him. Rising above the most prodigious accumulation of insults that
> stupidity, ignorance, and malice have ever created, his glory reaches
> inaccessible heights.
>
> Let us envy him: he has brought honour to his country and to the
> world by his immense work and by a great act. Let us envy him; his
> destiny and his heart brought him the greatest of fates: *He was a*
> *moment of human conscience.*[14]

Critical reactions to Zola's works abroad were initially quite varied
from country to country, though not in the extreme, for, as F. W. J.
Hemmings indicates, there was generally a "pattern of development
uniform almost everywhere, with variations in pace and stress: first, a
campaign of detraction on the part of traditionalists, followed by the
launching of translations, then a phase of violent argument between the
old guard and a group of younger critics and writers favoring certain of
Zola's innovations, and finally, the production of works in more or less
conscious imitation of his masterpieces."[15] Generally also, an enthusiastic

intermediary emerged to introduce Zola's works to his or her fellow countrymen and women, like Michael Georg Conrad in Germany, George Moore in Britain, or Emilia Pardo Bazán in Spain. There were, however, considerable regional variations. Zola was enthusiastically read in Russia, it appears, even before he was well known in France, yet he had little impact on Russian literature. His theories were taken most seriously in Germany (and Holland), inspiring poets and dramatists as well as novelists, whereas elsewhere they were scornfully dismissed. Derivative movements like *verismo* in Italy were sometimes inspired by his works and in several countries any literature based on deterministic premises, or depicting the life of the lower classes, unreserved in its use of the common language or in the representation of sexual mores tended to be ascribed to his influence and to the spread of pernicious Zolaism. "Hostility to Zola's novels," F. W. J. Hemmings adds, "was nowhere more marked than in the Anglo-Saxon countries."[16]

The story of Zola's introduction into Britain is not without its contradictions and ironies. As in France and elsewhere, *L' Assommoir* and *La Terre* figured prominently in the adventure. It was, in fact, the publication of *L' Assommoir* in France that prompted the first significant public reaction in England, Swinburne's "Note on a Question of the Hour" in the *Athenaeum* (16 June 1877), in which the brandy-swigging initiate into the "birchen mysteries," the disciple of de Sade and taunter of the Vice Society, the so-called English Baudelaire, expressed his sense of moral outrage—not a little inconsistently—at Zola's novel. Then it was also a reading of *L' Assommoir*, but more especially of Zola's articles in *Le Voltaire* in 1879 (part of the future *Roman expérimental*) that inspired George Moore's dramatic conversion to Naturalism—he was prone to dramatic conversions—during his stay in Paris. The event is recounted in his *Confessions of a Young Man* (1888), the very text in which disparaging remarks on Naturalism by a less enthusiastic Moore later led to a break in his good relations with Zola.[17] But the links and parallels between the French writer and his self-confessed (if temporary) disciple are particularly significant. The issue of the first English translations of Zola's novels, for example, and the publication of Moore's own Naturalist novels were part of a vigorous effort to break the near monopoly of the circulating libraries, Smith's and Mudie's, which bought three-volume novels (usually romances) from publishers and lent them to readers, exercising thereby a powerful control and moral censorship over the publishing industry in Britain, to the obvious disadvantage of the realistic and naturalistic tendencies. Hence the fact that, even though the first Zola translation published in England was a "three-decker," issued by the firm of Tinsley Brothers,[18] thereafter the enterprising publisher Henry Vizetelly brought out a string of seventeen Zola novels in various cheaper or illustrated *one-volume* editions between 1884 and 1889. Similarly, when the circulating libraries banned *A Modern Lover* (also published by Tinsley Brothers in

1883), Moore turned to Vizetelly for his uncompromisingly Naturalist novel, *A Mummer's Wife* (1885), published a scorching attack on Mudie's, the pamphlet *Literature at Nurse, or Circulating Morals* (Vizetelly, 1885), and set about abetting the spread of Zola's novels in Britain. As is well-known, when French realist texts began to flood the market — in however bowdlerized a state — the authorities intervened. Vizetelly's translation of *La Terre* (The Soil) in 1888 led to a debate in the House of Commons during which the M.P. for Flintshire, Samuel Smith, expressed the considered view that Zola's novels were "only fit for swine, and those who read them must turn their minds into cesspools." Eventually Vizetelly was prosecuted (twice) and imprisoned for three months for publishing "obscene libels" as a result of the successful campaigns of the National Vigilance Association, successor to the Vice Society, against "Pernicious Literature."[19] Thereby the curious situation arose in which Zola's novels were read by the English in drastically expurgated translations, some of which were even banned in Britain and her dominions, while the French originals still circulated freely and inviolably in the country.

Judging by the ferocity of their denunciations, most of the critics, we can assume, read their Zola in the original. In this field the literary historians have culled a rich harvest of their remonstrances and their vilifications. Of major, obsessive concern was the corrupting influence of Zola's fiction on innocent English youth. According to one concerned Victorian, who read a couple of pages of a Zola novel on display in a book shop, "the matter was of such leprous nature that it would be impossible for any young man who had not learned the Divine secret of self-control to have read it without committing some form of outward sin within twenty-four hours after."[20] "Leprous," Enid Starkie remarks, "was the favourite term of abuse against any literature coming from France."[21] The Poet Laureate himself, for whom, it was reported, the name of Zola was synonymous with sewage, penned some elegant couplets on the theme, with Zola's work (and perhaps Moore's also) in mind:

> Feed the budding rose of boyhood with the drainage of your sewer;
> Send the drain into the fountain, lest the stream should issue pure.
> Set the maiden fancies wallowing in the troughs of Zolaism, —
> Forward, forward, ay, and backward, downward too into the abysm![22]

Yet, even though such attacks had far from abated when Zola in person paid a visit to London in 1893 as a guest of the newly founded Institute of Journalists, he was honoured and fêted with receptions and fireworks!

The more reflective and temperate English critics found other causes for complaint, objecting to Zola's works on aesthetic and philosophical grounds: his cold impersonality, his materialism, his inhuman determinism, his narrow pessimism, his lack of a redeeming idealism. But, by the 1890s, some favorable opinions began to surface. Edmund Gosse, in 1892, expressed admiration for Zola's attempt to give "a large, competent, and profound view of the movement of life" and E. C. Townshend argued for a serious consideration of Zola's genius.[23] But the degree to which Zola ever received critical acceptance in Victorian Britain remains difficult to gauge. Whereas Decker writes that, by 1900, "even Zola" had found "a large audience of sympathetic readers," Frierson concludes that only "a relatively small group of literati" really accepted French naturalistic literature.[24]

Havelock Ellis was certainly among the leading Victorian literati, but his exceptional study of "Zola: The Man and His Work," which was first published in the *Savoy* in 1896, the year of the founding of that advanced journal by Arthur Symons and Aubrey Beardsley, is clearly the product of a man with wider tastes and interests — doctor, criminologist, anthropologist, sociologist, and, of course, sexologist — a francophile, Victorian polymath, who energetically opposed moral restraints on literature, promoted the works of foreign writers in England and sought to foster the "new spirit" in his age. This "born pioneer," as Phyllis Grosskurth calls him,[25] had recently translated, with the help of his wife, Edith, Zola's *Germinal* for the Lutetian Society (1895), which issued translations of foreign works (including six Zola novels) for private distribution in limited editions, to avoid Vizetelly's fate. His essay on Zola, in Decker's estimation, is "typical of the erudite, balanced, and sympathetic criticism that was to stamp his work as modern in the sense that it combined the most conclusive aspects of all that was known in contemporary science, aesthetics, and ethics."[26] And it is doubtless no coincidence that Ellis should emphasize in his article Zola's irony in terms similar to those employed ten years earlier by Professor Thomas Davidson in a very different context. The two men had had a close association in London, working together toward the founding in 1883 of the Fellowship of the New Life, which later became the Fabian Society.[27] In the spring of 1886, the outspoken Scottish philosopher and journalist, the "Wandering Scholar" as he was known, gave an address at the informal summer school, held annually between 1879 and 1887 on the farm of Bronson Alcott at Concord (Massachusetts), where many a distinguished American philosopher would speak on the favorite topics of transcendentalism, Hegelianism, and educational theory. Davidson caused a stir by placing Zola in the exalted company of Aristotle, Plato, and Christ, a bold move at the best of times, but decidedly reckless at a time when Zola's reputation in the United States was no better than his reputation in Britain. But the incident was not without significance. In the first place it shows the volatile nature of opinion in the United States. In his thorough study of Zola's reputation and influence there, Albert J. Salvan points to the diversity of tendencies, the "profound uncertainty" ranging from "an immediate and violent antipathy" to an "unexpected show of tolerance" such that constant tendencies, however "satisfying to our sense of logic," are hard to discern.[28] Nevertheless, 1886, the year of Davidson's lecture, was perhaps a turning point, according to Salvan's study, when the tendency became less to blame Zola's immorality than to question his supposed pessimistic views.[29]

Not that there had been or still was a lack of moral outrage. As usual, *L'Assommoir* started it off. As in Britain, the American translations were drastically cut, expurgated, even modified versions of Zola's texts, but they still managed to give offense. They were rapidly incorporated into an active industry of popular literature, "dime-novels" with alluring titles. Malcolm B. Jones writes that "between 1878, the date of the first American translation of any work of Zola, and 1900 thirty-one American publishers brought out, counting duplications and new editions when it is possible to ascertain these, something like one hundred and eighty books of this author."[30] Morality was again the major concern of the critics, who tended to view Zola's works as a form of contamination. "We would as soon," one of them wrote about one of Zola's texts, "introduce the small pox into our homes as permit this unclean volume to come in contact with the pure-minded maidens and ingenuous youth who form their chiefest ornament." *Pot-Bouille* was denounced as "the microscopic examination of a pailful of sewage" in an article entitled "Zola's Stink-Pot" and a critic in the *Critic* expressed a widely held opinion of the novelist himself: "Like his predecessor the Marquis de Sade, he seems to be following the path which leads to madness."[31]

By the 1890s however, there was, it seems, a growing acceptance of Naturalism, notwithstanding Brunetière's attempts to discredit Zola's influence during a successful lecture tour of the United States in the spring of 1897 and the claim that the critic's denunciations had delivered a "knock out" blow to the novelist's reputation.[32] The high moral seriousness of his later works and his role in the Dreyfus affair were sufficient rehabilitation for some. By the time of his death serious critics and writers like Harry Thurston Peck and William Dean Howells were far more circumspect in their views. The latter, for example, describes Zola as an "epic" and a "classic" writer, whose works are often indecent, but never immoral, "an artist, and one of the very greatest"; "but even before and beyond that he was intensely a moralist, as only the moralists of our true and noble time have been."[33] In general, as Albert J. Salvan writes, "Zola's success parallels the expansion of journalism in America and it is because the public found in the novelist's work documents full of life rather than the result of the critics' literary discernment that his success was so complete."[34]

It is clear that in its most rudimentary outline the abiding pattern of response to Zola during the novelist's lifetime was threefold: tremendous popular success, (usually) vigorous denunciation by the professional critics, and a recurrent strain of expressions of esteem from fellow writers, even those who did not share his aesthetic views, but admired his robust talent. Flaubert, for example, despite his scorn for Zola's theories, privately enthused over several of the *Rougon-Macquart* novels that he lived to read. Mallarmé, as we have noted, wrote letters of appreciation and publicly expressed his admiration for Zola in Huret's survey. Some writers, like Anatole France and Mark Twain,[35] overcame their initial aversion to Zola and changed their views, mainly as a result of the Dreyfus affair. Henry James, roughly speaking, followed this course, though his early distaste for Zola's works was mixed with admiration and his later approbation is greatly qualified. In a review of *Nana* in the *Parisian* (26 February 1880), he acknowledges in Zola "an artist" whose work "deserves a great deal of respect and deference," but deplores the "singular foulness of his imagination," the "unclean vessel" into which it is poured, and the "melancholy dryness of his execution, which gives us all the bad taste of a disagreeable dish and none of the nourishment." By August 1903, in a general study for the *Atlantic Monthly*, he has more respect for the French writer, but carefully weighs his judgments as well as his words. He admires, marvels at Zola's monumental, methodical (if blinkered) achievement, his "capacious vessel," his "gregarious" art, which he considers to have produced "the most extraordinary *imitation* of experience that we possess" and which, for all its lack of taste, is "great at congruous subjects."[36]

When, for fifty years (1903–1952), Zola lapsed into almost total disregard by the critics, there were still novelists and poets, no doubt less inclined than most to accept unthinkingly prevailing views, who continued to read and comment perceptively on his works. When reviewing one of the few books published on Zola during this period, *Le Groupe de Médan* by Léon Deffoux and Emile Zavie (1920), Albert Thibaudet wrote in *La Nouvelle Revue Française* that Zola's was a "great work," but one that was "read no more";[37] he was referring no doubt to the critics, for the general public still continued to buy the novels. But at least one critic of the *N.R.F.* read Zola. On 17 July 1932, André Gide wrote in his *Journal*: "I consider the present discredit of Zola a monstrous injustice which says little for the literary critics of to-day." Other distinguished writers too, like Aragon, Cocteau, Jules Romains, even Valéry, deplored the critics' neglect of Zola's works, celebrated his achievements, acknowledged, in some cases, his influence and commented on his art. In 1933 Céline paid homage to the novelist and defender of Dreyfus at one of the annual "pilgrimages" to Médan, which contributed to keeping Zola's memory alive during these lean years and have continued to do so down to our own day.[38] The novelist Henri Barbusse, an uncompromising realist like the author of *La Débâcle* and a militant communist, also spoke at Médan, in 1922, and, ten years later, published an important book on Zola, which was widely read and translated into several languages.[39] But what was arguably the finest study by another writer of Zola and his works came from abroad: the long essay by Heinrich Mann, of which an extract has been translated and reprinted in this volume, showing the central place of the earth in the French novelist's poetic vision and celebrating his social conscience.[40]

Zola, then, fared much better — to use Albert Thibaudet's categories (from *Réflexions sur la critique*, 1922) — with the "criticism of artists" than with "university criticism" and the spontaneous, "spoken" criticism of the press. But in these inter-war years especially, in an age of intense political debate, his novels and political act naturally engaged comment from a more committed form of criticism, an ideological criticism, particularly from the left. The polemical edge that was always a characteristic of what was written about Zola became more political than moral. The article by Georg Lukács, "The Zola Centenary," written in 1940 when the clashing ideologies had already gone to war, is the best-known Marxist assessment of Zola, if only because it came from the pen of the so-called "Marx of aesthetics." The essay is valuable, however, less for its topicality than for the way in which it articulates an already firmly established and seemingly self-perpetuating set of arguments against Zola and Naturalism by Marxist critics, a tradition that can be traced back to Plekhanov, Gorki, and Lafargue, and even to that famous letter of Engels to Miss Harkness (of April 1888), in which Balzac is appraised as infinitely greater than "all the Zolas past, present and future."[41] The recurring charges are that Zola's Naturalism is a debased form of the great Realist tradition, represented in France by Balzac; that it mechanistically assimilates society to a biological model and passes over its inherent contradictions; that, except perhaps in *Germinal*, it fails to depict the class struggle and offers instead a Darwinian vision of competing social species; that it espouses a fatalistic and static worldview; that it is excessively preoccupied with peripheral detail, facts, description, documentation, failing to represent characters who convey social, as opposed to physiological or pathological significance; that, politically, its message is reactionary, preferring, however implicitly, reformist solutions as in *L'Assommoir* or idealized, utopian illusions as in the novelist's last series, the *Quatre Evangiles*. Not that there has been unanimity, by any means, among Marxist critics over Zola's place in their scheme. In his biography Barbusse represents Zola as a "force of nature" rather than as a "man of ideas," a fighter rather than a dialectician, but a writer who was "instinctively right," a "socialist without knowing it, even when he denied it," and a great writer, whose work is to be built upon rather than decried.[42] And Jean Fréville, in a later study, even though he systematically takes up the familiar criticisms of "the master of Naturalism" in (chapter 2 of) his analysis, defining Zola as a "bourgeois democrat, the prisoner of his class prejudices", ends by hailing "the indomitable fighter linked by his books and by his acts to the history of France, the gatherer of storms raining fire and brimstone on bourgeois society, the glorifier of work whose immense production is a hymn of love as well as an indictment."[43] Yet, despite such shows of enthusiasm from certain Marxist critics — and, no doubt, from the bulk of Marxist readers —

the strictures expressed by Lukács, for all their dogmatism, are thoroughly representative of the orthodox view.[44]

It is regrettable, though perfectly understandable in view of the date (1940), that Lukács's mainly negative assessment is the only study of any significance to have emerged from the centennial anniversary of Zola's birth. Twelve years later, on another anniversary occasion, the situation would be very different. Marcel Girard begins a general survey of Zola's standing in 1952 in the following manner:

> Fifty years after his death, Emile Zola has not found peace. Neither the peace of glory, nor the peace of oblivion. Something equivocal still clings to the immense celebrity of his name. Cultured people read him, or dare not admit that they have not read him; but they often speak of him with their noses in the air: "It's a bit crude, isn't it?" His rather uninspiring personality is not well known or admired. His work stirs up passions that we would think had died out. Until quite recently he was dogged by hate; whereas, for some people, he was the object of a display of enthusiasm that, to be frank, was often more inspired than it was intelligent and effective. Like the coffin of his "old friend" Flaubert, that was lowered all askew into his tomb, Zola has entered into posterity all awry.[45]

Girard goes on to deplore the critics' neglect of Zola, their disdain for the profundities in his works, the lack of rigorous studies of his novels in other than their secondary aspects, and the fact that foreigners seemed to value his achievements more highly than the French. Yet in the same year occurred the beginnings of a remarkable renewal of interest in Zola's works, expressed not only in ceremonial gestures at the time of the anniversary, of which there were plenty, but in the publication of serious critical studies of the writer. In a letter to Paul Brulat, dated 20 December 1895, Zola himself, in Stendhalian fashion, had predicted this turn of events: "Nobody reads me, of that there is no doubt, at least with intelligence; and I suspect that, twenty or fifty years after my death, I shall be discovered." As it happened, the more cautious estimate proved to be correct.

To avoid the impression that a kind of *annus mirabilis* came about, it must be pointed out that, well before 1952, there was a steady stream of academic studies of Zola and his works. But, thereafter, on the tide of university expansion, a veritable swell occurred,[46] and a prestigious tradition of historical scholarship was soon established. Of the mass of monographs and scholarly studies that have appeared since the "Zola revival" began, the early critical and biographical studies by Angus Wilson (1952) and F. W. J. Hemmings (1953) — both subsequently revised (1964 and 1966) — are of special interest to the English-speaking reader, while the latter's more recent biography (1977), the best of the genre, offers a welcome complement to the earlier work, which has become the standard of Zola criticism.[47] Inspired by the example of Guy Robert's masterful study of *La Terre*[48] and encouraged by the availability in the Bibliothèque Nationale in Paris of almost all the novelist's working notes (including outlines, plans, character sketches, documentary notes, manuscripts, proofs, etc.), the tracing of the overt genesis of his novels rapidly became a specialty of Zola criticism.[49] These "sources-to-reception" histories of individual texts provided invaluable material for – and, in turn, as far as the later ones are concerned, were likewise informed by – the amply annotated and now standard critical edition of the *Rougon-Macquart* novels, prepared by Henri Mitterand in five volumes of the Bibliothèque de la Pléiade series (1960–1967). But, in more than thirty years of intensive historical scholarship, all aspects of Zola's life and works have undergone rigorous scrutiny and studies have appeared on his minor as well as major works, on his activities ancillary to novel writing, his art criticism, his theater, literary criticism, journalism, social and political ideas, his role in the Dreyfus affair, his influence abroad, and the films that have been inspired by his works. This period of concentrated activity has also given rise to a fifteen-volume edition of Zola's complete works, edited by Henri Mitterand (again) for the Cercle du Livre Précieux and published by Tchou (1962–70). Far from abating, this tradition of cumulative historical scholarship is continuing to produce ever more detailed and sophisticated studies of Zola's life, works, and reputation, as in Colette Becker's series of articles on the writer's early years or in such investigations as our sample article by Alain Pagès on "The Myth of Médan," studies that not only add to our fund of knowledge about the writer and his accomplishments, but also put to the test of historical fact many of our preconceptions about him. Indeed, what has already proven to be a fine achievement of this tradition is currently underway: an eleven-volume edition of Zola's correspondence, including hundreds of previously uncollected letters, prepared by two international teams of scholars based at the University of Toronto and in Paris, editing a considerable mass of texts. Each volume contains an impressive wealth of annotations, historical and biographical studies, chronologies, bibliographies, and indexes, all in all an attempted collaborative enterprise of erudition whose usefulness extends well beyond the immediate needs of the Zola scholar, creating the record of a whole age.[50] As Henri Mitterand persuasively argues in his preface to the third volume, this monumental undertaking of historical research is by no means outmoded, but is gaining a new relevancy now that formalist and exclusively text-centered approaches to literature are tending to give way to studies that relate the literary work to other forms of discourse, to contemporary institutions and ideologies, to reader expectancies. This edition will be a bridge between the old and new literary histories.

If, in this way, research on the historical contexts of Zola's works held a special place during the years of resurgent interest in the author of the *Rougon-Macquart*, the texts themselves did not by any means go neglected. It is true that—to use the traditional categories—there was, and has been, comparatively little research on Zola's style, or rather "styles": impressionistic, popular, scientific, epic, biblical, didactic, polemical, etc. But a vigorous strain of *thematic* criticism, in the broadest sense of the term, has traced and interpreted recurrent motifs and myths in the full range of Zola's works, John C. Lapp's *Zola before the "Rougon-Macquart"* being a noteworthy case in point.[51] Not only has this tradition of thematic studies, dating back at least to Marcel Girard's exemplar of an article on the "universe of *Germinal*,[52] revealed in Zola's works an unsuspectedly rich, complex, and profound textual creation, a subtle fabric of fable beneath the facts, but, emphasizing by its very nature the immanent analysis of texts and looking naturally toward contexts of explanation in human sciences other than positivistic history, it has served as an important vehicle of transition between the more traditional studies and the newer critical readings, between what Henri Mitterand defines, in his article "The Narrator's Fantasies," as the second and third ages of Zola criticism.

As we know, this transition in other fields was marked by bitter confrontations in the sixties, but a spirit of peaceful coexistence and collaborative effort has usually prevailed among the practictioners of conflicting methodologies in their application to Zola's works. The early Barthes study of *Nana*, which we may have usefully exhumed, is by a critic, of course, who was in the thick of the methodological fray. His brief article is conventional enough to be attributed to the general tendency of thematic studies that has just been defined, but there are enough hints of the bolder Barthes to leave us dreaming of what might have been the contents and consequences of a volume *Sur Zola*. However, typical of the prevailing spirit in Zola studies and yet symptomatic of the more fiercely contended issues elsewhere was the polite polemic in the columns of the *P.M.L.A.* between two distinguished American Zola critics "Concerning Color in *Germinal*" (June 1964). Prompted by an article by Philip Walker on the theme in the same journal,[53] Elliott M. Grant expressed his reluctance to accept symbolic interpretations of Zola's texts, arguing for an integral realism and for the authority of the author's expressed intentions. In reply, Philip Walker, whose influential early study "Prophetic Myths in Zola"[54] was the first of a series of stimulating articles that explore the novelist's mythopoeic art and visionary universe, argued for true account to be rendered to Zola's "shadowy poetic side." By 1971, in her article on Zola and *la nouvelle critique*, another American critic, Naomi Schor, could report that "in a few short years—since 1952 to be exact—the dark side of Zola's work has been brought to light. The Fatal Woman, the triangle, the voyeur, the underground, the elements, the cycle have become familiar notions to a whole new generation of scholars."[55] Furthermore, the same critic, two years earlier, edited an important special number of *Yale French Studies* (1969) devoted entirely to Zola, which delves into such themes as fire, the look, the labyrinth, and in which an excerpt of Michel Butor's study of Zola (reproduced below) appeared in English for the first time. Butor's compelling reading of Zola is at once one of the most eminent products of the thematic tradition, giving a refreshing view of the typically Zolaesque motifs of alcohol and heredity, and a testimony to the abiding interest and challenges that the experimental novels of another age continue to offer to the newest of novelists and critics of our own.

In the ethos of vigorous eclecticism that characterizes the contemporary discipline of literary criticism and in the state of constant methodological reevaluation that France's critics have so often inspired since the sixties, it is hardly surprising that the current trend in Zola criticism is towards a lively diversity. The old, author-centered dichotomies have been largely exploded. Thus the two Zolas that it was once fashionable to define and contrast — the recorder of facts and the creator of myths, the depicter of "slices of life" and the artistic temperament, the positivist and the poet, the man of science and the personality, the Realist and the Romantic — have become a host of Zolas, as each critical approach redefines its subject and refines its models. The so-called "structuralist" and "post-structuralist" tendencies — terms that, of course, denote a multitude of approaches for some (and of sins for others) — have had the great positive effect of, on the one hand, thoroughly analyzing Zola's texts in their previously unacknowledged "literariness" and, on the other hand, breaking down disciplinary barriers, aligning Zola's works with the informing principles of allied fields of inquiry like linguistics, anthropology, psychoanalysis, to explore their systematic configurations. Surprisingly to those who have regarded Zola's novels as dated, they have proven to be an ever fertile terrain. The very rudiments of the novelist's art have, in fact, gained a new relevance. Thus heredity itself, as Butor has remarked, is a "syntax," a vast network of similarities and differences that structure the novelist's series, and the famous genealogical tree, an organic model with its multiple ramifications. For the English reader there is fortunately available a fine example of the most enterprising of contemporary Zola criticism, renewing the thematic trend, analyzing with insight individual texts, and illuminating Zola's works with concepts and strategies derived from other fields. In *Zola's Crowds*[56] Naomi Schor takes up a tried Zola theme which becomes a "structuring theme," informed by detailed analyses of individual (and refreshingly lesser-known) works and by the methods of structural semantics, anthropology, stylistics, and psychoanalysis, to fathom such fundamental patterns as the myth of origins, the individual-crowd opposition, and the scapegoat motif.

We can only make rapid mention of the other main directions that Zola critics are now pursuing and the major studies that they have produced. Michel Serres, in a brilliant book, adopts an epistemological approach, delineating on the basis of a study of *Le Docteur Pascal* the circulation of "energies" in Zola's works according to the metaphors and operations of thermodynamics and mechanics.[57] Auguste Dezalay, in an equally impressive book, borrows musical analogies for his "rhythm-analysis" of Zola's series, an exhaustive study of repetition and variation in the *Rougon-Macquart* novels.[58] In his monumental investigation of mythical expression in the novelist's works, in which a long-standing constant of Zola criticism is critically and exhaustively reexamined, Roger Ripoll writes: "However bizarre this degree of unanimity might be when we think of all that divides them from each other, modern critics of all persuasions are agreed with Zola's contemporaries in proclaiming that the author of the *Rougon-Macquart* is a creator of myths."[59] Indeed, "Zola and Myths" is the title of Jean Borie's Freudian interpretation of the novelist's work as a single phantasmic project, a "mythical anthropology" in its dynamic evolution from the "novels of nausea," with their submission to primordial matter, to the "novels of redemption," with their sublimated, radiant visions.[60] An Oedipal Zola emerges too in the intriguing analyses of Philippe Bonnefis, who employs an epistemological and a psychoanalytical approach, in his articles like "Oedipus at Médan" and more fully in his recent book,[61] to detect and explore the implications of what he calls Zola's *concupiscentia nominum*, an obsession with names and the unnameable in his works.

As one might expect in view of the nature of the novelist's art, a more substantial body of criticism deals with the social rather than the psychological dimensions of Zola's works. Though he duly acknowledges the private obsessions and personal fantasies in the novelist's works, F. W. J. Hemmings, in an incisive general study reproduced in this volume, emphasizes the innovations and achievements of Zola the social writer. In his book *Zola and the Bourgeoisie* (and in his article below), Brian Nelson highlights in Zola the satirist of his own class and of the moral (dis)order of the society that he represents in his fiction, whereas Françoise Naudin-Patriat brings the expertise of the political scientist to a study of the social and economic order of the *Rougon-Macquart* series.[62] The more consciously theoretical "socio-critics" of France, notably Claude Duchet and Henri Mitterand, have rigorously analyzed the verbal structures of Zola's fictional discourse and related them to the ideology of his age, as in the latter's influential study of *Germinal*, which appears in translation below. As Sandy Petrey, an American exponent of the same approach, has shown in a very useful critical introduction to their works,[63] even though contemporary socio-criticism may arrive by different methodological routes at conclusions similar to those of an earlier form of social criticism based on an extrinsic analysis of Zola's representation of history and society (as in Lukács's article), socio-critical principles point the way to challenging new perspectives on the "sociality" of his fiction. There have also been in recent years, as one might also expect, important examples of a more purely formalist approach, as in Neide de Faria's analysis of narrative strata and schemata in selected novels of Zola's main series, or in the skillful analysis by the Quebec critic Jacques Allard of the hidden geometry and the spatial structures of *L'Assommoir*.[64] Significantly, one of France's leading narratologists, Philippe Hamon, constantly refers to Zola's fiction to illustrate the laws of a narrative poetics that he is in the process of elaborating, and he has made the novelist's characters the central focus of a recent book.[65]

Finally, in diverse manners, critics have shown their versatility in pluralistic readings of individual texts, as in Jacques Dubois' study of *L'Assommoir* and Patrick Brady's essays on *L'Oeuvre* and *Germinal*.[66] And, as Naomi Schor's contribution to this volume and Chantal Jennings's book *L'Eros et la femme chez Zola* (Paris, 1977) show, contemporary debates on feminist issues have by no means passed Zola by. Furthermore, in a time of systematic transcoding and of sensitivity to the permeability and interdependence of different types of discourse, critics have been far less dismissive of Zola's own attempts to ally the science of his day to the art of his novels. The French philosopher Alain de Lattre, for example, has published an earnest study of Zola's aesthetic ideas, traditionally held in low esteem as embarrassingly naive, and the novelist's "metalanguage" is undergoing serious revision, if not a full rehabilitation.[67] "And their work goes on growing."

In the conclusion of his recent biography F. W. J. Hemmings fancifully wonders "what the ghost of Zola, if one may suppose so obdurate a materialist to have been granted any form of spectral survival, would make of the mind-boggling manifestations of modern academic appraisal. Would he be gratified," his biographer adds, "or would his sturdy good sense cause him to recoil in horrified amazement and flit back to whatever Elysian fields he now roams?"[68] To pursue the interesting fantasy, we can assume, no doubt, that, whatever his views would be on contemporary critical debates, if he were granted a long enough stay to explore them, he would scan the shelves of books and journals in some well-stocked library or consult the files in one of the centers established in his name in Paris or Toronto with a sense of wonder, and, one hopes, of vindication, at the quantity and diversity of the studies that his life's work has generated, particularly in the last thirty years. No longer would he be able to complain that his works were not seriously read or that the same article was constantly being written about him. And he would marvel too, no doubt, at the scarcity of "toads."

There is every indication that Zola's work will continue to command the attention of critics of every persuasion. Indeed, such is the vitality of current Zola criticism that calls for synoptic studies may well be premature, or even out of tune with our times. As Malcolm Bradbury has written of the ethos of modernism: "No one position in the culture seems, in a world that is constantly creating new contexts for knowledge, a sufficient standpoint from which to acquire an overview. Synthesis thus becomes available only at the extreme or with reference to a point in the future, envisioned perhaps utopianly or perhaps apocalyptically. In art and philosophy as in science it becomes necessary to maintain a sense of eclecticism, an openness to change."[69] Such is the present openness in the field of Zola studies — and such is the danger of foreclosure in a cumulative view of research — that it is safer to state that much will be done than to attempt to define what needs to be done. Nevertheless, there *is* a constant need for retrospection so that diversity may thrive. Furthermore, though the heated polemics, moral, political, literary, have long since petered out, certain preconceptions, even a certain stigma, still attach to Zola's name, for it quickly came to signify — and for the uninformed may still do so — a certain unrefined type of literature, to be scornfully dismissed with an unreflective response. Within the constraints imposed by the series, by the feasibility of translations, and, above all, by the availability of texts and of space in which to include them, this book attempts to present to the reader in English a selection of Zola criticism in which both the issues of the past and the practices of the present are illustrated and represented.

In addition to the authors and editors who generously gave me permission to reproduce materials in this volume, I wish to thank the following people, who, in various ways, contributed to the preparation of the book with advice, translations, and practical help: F. W. J. Hemmings, Henri Mitterand, Brian Nelson, Janice Best, Barbara Gough, Dolorès Signori, Deborah Smith, Kathleen and Natasha Baguley. I am also grateful for the financial support provided by the Faculty of Arts of the University of Western Ontario and the Social Sciences and Humanities Research Council of Canada.

University of Western Ontario   DAVID BAGULEY

Notes

1. Emile Zola, "Le crapaud," *Le Figaro*, 28 February 1896. The eighteen articles, dating from December 1895 to June 1896, were collected together in the volume *Nouvelle campagne* (1897) and are to be found in vol. 14 of the *Œuvres complètes* (Paris: Cercle du Livre Précieux, 1969). There is no English translation.

2. See the excellent study of Zola's reading public by Colette Becker, "L'audience d'Emile Zola," *Les Cahiers naturalistes*, no. 47 (1974):40–69.

3. Colette Becker, *Les critiques de notre temps et Zola* (Paris: Garnier, 1972), 7.

4. For a good selection see the following illustrated studies: John Grand-Carteret, *Zola en images* (Paris: Juven, 1905), and Pierre Baudson, "Les romans de Zola et la caricature de leur temps," *Gazette des Beaux-Arts* 94 (September 1979):69–94.

5. Though not, F.W.J. Hemmings has shown, on the first occasion, as it is often

claimed. See his article "The Origins of the Terms *naturalisme, naturaliste*," *French Studies* 8 (April 1954):109–21.

6. Robert Lethbridge, "L'acceuil critique à l'oeuvre de Zola avant *L'Assommoir*," *Les Cahiers naturalistes*, no. 54 (1980):214–23.

7. Stéphane Mallarmé and Paul Bourget, for example, wrote letters expressing their admiration for the originality of *L'Assommoir* on February 3 and 2 respectively. See *Les Rougon-Macquart*, tome 2, edited by Henri Mitterand (Paris: Bibliothèque de la Pléiade, 1961), 1563–67.

8. Emile Zola, *Le Voltaire* (28 October 1879); the article has been reproduced by Henri Mitterand in vol. 12 of the *Œuvres complètes*, 597–602. Cf. Zola's comment to J. Van Santen Kolff in a letter of 22 January 1888, on a batch of articles that the latter had sent him: "I have the feeling that I am always reading the same article about me."

9. See Sandey Petrey's extended review of Jean Borie's book *Zola et les mythes*: "Obscenity and Revolution," *Diacritics* 3 (Fall 1973):22–26.

10. See his *Histoire de la littérature française* (numerous editions), part 7, book 3, chapter 5.

11. Emile Faguet, "Emile Zola," *Minerva* (Paris) 4 (15 October 1902):493. The article was issued the following year as a short book: *Zola* (Paris: Eyméoud, 1903).

12. Auguste Dezalay, *Lectures de Zola* (Paris: Armand Colin, 1973), 35.

13. Huret's interviews appeared between 3 March and 5 July, then were collected into a volume: *Enquête sur l'évolution littéraire* (Paris: Charpentier, 1891), which has recently been reedited with notes and a preface by Daniel Grojnowski: (Vanves: Les Editions Thot, 1982). It was on this occasion that Zola's faithful friend and disciple, Paul Alexis, sent his famous dissenting message by telegramme: "Naturalism not dead. Letter follows."

14. Anatole France, from *Vers les temps meilleurs. Trente ans de vie sociale* (Paris: Emile-Paul Frères, 1949):1:117–20.

15. F.W.J. Hemmings, "The Present Position in Zola Studies," in *The Present State of French Studies: A Collection of Research Reviews*, ed. Charles B. Osburn (Metuchen, N.J.: The Scarecrow Press, 1971), 604. This article first appeared in *French Studies* 10 (April 1956):97–122.

16. For details see the articles by Hemmings and Lethbridge as well as the reference works by Baguley and Nelson listed in the bibliography. On the broader question of the spread of Naturalism, an international group of researchers is currently working, under the auspices of the International Comparative Literature Association and under the direction of Yves Chevrel, Janina Kulczycka-Saloni, and Halina Suwala, on a general study of the impact of Naturalism on the literatures of the world using European languages as their medium. See their preliminary publication: Yves Chevrel, ed., *Le Naturalisme dans les littératures de langues européennes* (Université de Nantes, 1983); see also Yves Chevrel's recent book *Le Naturalisme* (Paris: Presses Universitaires de France, 1982).

17. See the critical edition of Moore's book by Susan Dick: (Montreal and London: McGill-Queen's University Press, 1972), 241–43.

18. Emile Zola, *The Ladies' Paradise [Au Bonheur des Dames]*, trans. Frank Belmont (London: Tinsley Brothers, 1883).

19. For more detailed accounts of these events see the books by Becker (pp. 350–82) and King (chapter 5) listed in the bibliography below; also Clarence R. Decker, "Zola's Literary Reputation in England," *P.M.L.A.* 49 (December 1934):1140–53 — reprinted in *The Victorian Conscience* (New York: Twayne, 1952); William C. Frierson, "The English Controversy over Realism in Fiction (1885–1895)," *P.M.L.A.* 43 (June 1928):533–50; W.E. Colburn, "Zola in England, 1883–1903," (Ph.D. diss., University of Illinois, 1952); and the account by Henry Vizetelly's son in Ernest A. Vizetelly, *Emile Zola, Novelist and Reformer* (London: Bodley Head; New York: J. Lane, 1904).

20. Quoted in Frierson, "English Controversy," 539.

21. Enid Starkie, *From Gautier to Eliot: The Influence of France on English Literature; 1851–1939* (London: Hutchinson, 1960), 106.

22. Alfred, Lord Tennyson, "Locksley Hall Sixty Years After" (1886). See Frierson, "English Controversy," 536, and Decker, "Zola's Literary Reputation," 1148. "The Troughs of Zolaism" is the chapter heading of William York Tindall's study of French realism in Britain, *Forces in Modern British Literature 1885–1956* (New York: Knopf, 1947), chapter 5.

23. Edmund Gosse, "The Tyranny of the Novel," *National Review* 19 (April 1892):170; E.C. Townshend, "Towards an Appreciation of Emile Zola," *Westminster Review* 143 (January 1895):57–65. Gosse's article is reprinted in *Questions at Issue* (London: Heinemann, 1893).

24. Decker, "Zola's Literary Reputation," 1153; Frierson, "English Controversy," 549.

25. Phyllis Grosskurth, *Havelock Ellis: A Biography* (Toronto: McClelland and Stewart, 1980), 116.

26. Decker, "Zola's Literary Reputation," 1151.

27. See Grosskurth, *Havelock Ellis*, 62–69.

28. Albert J. Salvan, *Zola aux Etats-Unis* (Providence, R.I.: Brown University, 1943), 11–12. This book has been reprinted twice: Paris: Le Cercle du Livre, 1958, and New York: Kraus Reprint Corporation, 1967.

29. Ibid., 88.

30. Malcolm B. Jones, "Translations of Zola in the United States Prior to 1900," *Modern Language Notes* 55 (November 1940):520–21.

31. These views were expressed in *Harper's New Monthly Magazine* 59 (July 1879):309; in *Literary World* 13 (3 June 1882):175; and in *Critic* 3 (10 March 1883):104. See Salvan, *Zola aux Etats-Unis*, 39, 68, 71.

32. Salvan, *Zola aux Etats-Unis*, 99.

33. William Dean Howells, "Emile Zola," *North American Review* 175 (November 1902):587–96. This article is reprinted in *Prefaces to Contemporaries: 1882–1920* (Gainsville, Fla.: Scholars' Facsimiles & Reprints, 1957), 89–102, and more recently in Sidney D. Braun and Seymour Lainoff, eds., *Transatlantic Mirrors: Essays in Franco-American Literary Relations.* Boston: Twayne, 1978), 145–54.

34. Salvan, *Zola aux Etats-Unis*, 124.

35. See Sydney J. Krause, *Mark Twain as Critic* (Baltimore: Johns Hopkins Press, 1967), 260–83.

36. Both articles are reprinted in Leon Edel, ed., *The Future of the Novel* (New York, Vintage Books, 1956). The later study has been frequently reprinted: in the *Art of the Novel* (1948), *The House of Fiction* (1957), *Selected Literary Criticism* (1963), and *Documents of Modern Literary Realism* (1963). Partly because of the availability of this essay, partly for technical reasons, and partly because of its prolixity, it has not been included in this volume.

37. Albert Thibaudet, "Réflexions sur la littérature," *N.R.F.* 15 (1 December 1920):923–33.

38. Céline's speech "Hommage à Zola" has been translated into English by Milton Hindus in *New Directions in Prose and Poetry* 13 (1951):60–64. Nowadays the speeches of the "pilgrimage" to Médan each October are published in *Les Cahiers naturalistes* the following year.

39. Henri Barbusse, *Zola* (Paris: Gallimard, 1932); the English translation, by M.B. and F.C. Green, appeared the same year (London: Dent, 1932).

40. On this study see David Roberts, "*Wirklichkeit oder Gedicht*: The Zola Essay of Heinrich Mann," *Forum for Modern Language Studies* 6 (July 1970):243–54.

41. See Karl Marx and Friedrich Engels, *Literature and Art: Selections from Their*

Writings (Bombay: Current Book House, 1956), 35–38. On Marxist criticisms of Zola, see J.H. Matthews, "Zola and the Marxists," *Symposium* 11 (Fall 1957):262–72.

42. Barbusse, *Zola*, 249–64.

43. Jean Fréville, *Zola, semeur d'orages* (Paris: Editions sociales, 1952), 160.

44. Several critics have recently written commentaries on the Lukács article. See, for example, Brian Nelson "Lukács, Zola and the Aesthetics of Realism," *Studi francesi* 24, no. 71 (May–August 1980):251–55; Ira N. Shor, "The Novel in History: Lukács and Zola," *Clio* 2 (1972):19–41; Patrick Brady, "Lukács, Zola, and the Principle of Contradiction," *L'Esprit créateur* 21 (Fall 1981):60–68.

45. Marcel Girard, "Situation d'Emile Zola," *Revue des Sciences humaines*, no. 66 (April–June 1952):137–56.

46. Statistically, according to the two volumes of bibliography of Zola criticism by D. Baguley, for the years 1952 to 1980 some 2,700 books and articles dealing directly with Zola have appeared.

47. For further details see the selected bibliography of English studies on Zola below.

48. Guy Robert, *"La Terre" d'Emile Zola: Etude historique et critique* (Paris: Les Belles Lettres, 1952).

49. For examples written in English see Richard B. Grant, *Zola's "Son Excellence Eugène Rougon": An Historical and Critical Study* (Durham, N.C.: Duke University Press; London, Cambridge University Press, 1960); Elliott M. Grant, *Zola's "Germinal": A Critical and Historical Study* (Leicester University Press, 1962; 2d ed. rev., 1970); Martin Kanes, *Zola's "La Bête humaine": A Study in Literary Creation* (Berkeley: University of California Press, 1962); Robert J. Niess, *Zola, Cézanne, and Manet: A Study of "L'Œuvre"* (Ann Arbour: University of Michigan Press, 1968); on *Germinal* also there is Richard H. Zakarian, *Zola's "Germinal": A Critical Study of its Primary Sources* (Geneva: Droz, 1972); an early example is Helen La Rue Rufener, *Biography of a War Novel: Zola's "La Débâcle"* (New York: King's Crown Press, 1946).

50. The edition is copublished by the Presses de l'Université de Montréal and the C.N.R.S. of Paris. By the summer of 1984 four volumes appeared, covering the years 1858 to 1883 of Zola's life.

51. John C. Lapp, *Zola before the "Rougon-Macquart"* (Toronto: University of Toronto Press, 1964); then in a French translation: *Les Racines du naturalisme: Zola avant "Les Rougon-Macquart"* (Paris: Bordas, 1972).

52. Marcel Girard, "L'univers de *Germinal*," *Revue des Sciences humaines*, no. 69 (January–March 1953):59–76.

53. Philip D. Walker, "Zola's Use of Color Imagery in *Germinal*," *P.M.L.A.* 77 (September 1962):442–49.

54. Philip Walker, "Prophetic Myths in Zola," *P.M.L.A.* 74 (September 1959):444–52. See also his article below and his recently released book: *"Germinal" and Zola's Philosophical and Religious Thought*, Purdue University Monographs in Romance Languages (Amsterdam and Philadelphia: John Benjamins, 1984).

55. Naomi Schor, *L'Esprit créateur* 11 (Winter 1971):20.

56. Naomi Schor, *Zola's Crowds* (Baltimore and London: Johns Hopkins University Press, 1978).

57. Michel Serres, *Feux et signaux de brume: Zola* (Paris: Bernard Grasset, 1975). For a very useful review and study of this book in English, see David Bell, "Serres's Zola: Literature, Science, Myth," *Modern Language Notes* 94 (May 1979):797–808.

58. Auguste Dezalay, *L'Opéra des Rougon-Macquart: Essai de rythmologie romanesque* (Paris, Klincksieck, 1983).

59. Roger Ripoll, *Réalité et mythe chez Zola* (Lille: Université de Lille III, 1981), 1.

60. Jean Borie, *Zola et les mythes, ou de la nausée au salut* (Paris: Seuil, 1971).

61. Philippe Bonnefis, *L'Innommable: Essai sur l'oeuvre d'Emile Zola* (Paris: S.E.D.E.S., 1984).

62. Brian Nelson, *Zola and the Bourgeoisie* (London: Macmillan, 1983); Françoise Naudin-Patriat, *Ténèbres et Lumière de l'argent: La Représentation de l'ordre social dans Les Rougon-Macquart* (Université de Dijon, 1981).

63. Sandy Petrey, "Sociocriticism and *Les Rougon-Macquart*," *L'Esprit créateur* 14 (Fall 1974):219–35.

64. Respectively: *Structures et unité dans "Les Rougon-Macquart" (La poétique du cycle)* (Paris: Nizet, 1977); *Zola, le chiffre du texte: Lecture de "L'Assommoir"* (Montreal: Les Presses de l'Université du Québec; Presses Universitaires de Grenoble, 1978).

65. Philippe Hamon, *Le Personnel du roman: Le Système des personnages dans "Les Rougon-Macquart" de Zola* (Geneva: Droz, 1983).

66. Jacques Dubois, *"L'Assommoir" de Zola: Société, discours, idéologie* (Paris: Larousse, 1973); and Patrick Brady, *Le Bouc émissaire chez Emile Zola* (Heidelberg: Carl Winter, 1981).

67. Alain de Lattre, *Le Réalisme selon Zola: Archéologie d'une intelligence* (Paris: Presses Universitaires de France, 1975). See also the articles by Henri Mitterand, "Textes en intersection: *Le Roman expérimental* et *Les Rougon-Macquart*," *University of Ottawa Quarterly* 48 (October–December 1978):415–28, and Alain Pagès, "En partant de la théorie du roman expérimental," *Les Cahiers naturalistes*, no. 47 (1974):70–87.

68. F. W. J. Hemmings, *The Life and Times of Emile Zola*, (London: Elek, 1977), 184.

69. Malcolm Bradbury, *The Social Context of Modern English Literature* (Oxford: Blackwell, 1971), 16.

Articles and Essays

Putrid Literature
Ferragus [Louis Ulbach]*

A monstrous school of novelists, established several years ago, claims to substitute the eloquence of the charnel-house for the eloquence of the flesh, calls upon our most surgical of curiosities, groups together victims of the plague to have us admire their sores, finds its direct inspiration in cholera, its master, and fills our minds with pus.

The cold slabs of the morgue have replaced the sofas of Crébillon; Manon Lescaut has become a sordid kitchen-maid, forsaking the grease for the mud of the streets. Faublas needs to kill, to watch his victims rot in order to conjure up visions of love; or else, by whipping high-class ladies, he acts out the writings of the marquis de Sade (without ever having read them!).

Germinie Lacerteux, Thérèse Raquin, La Comtesse de Chalis, and many other novels not worth mentioning (for I am not trying to hide the fact that I am providing them with publicity), will prove what I am stating.

I am not questioning the intentions, which are good, but I am hoping to show that, in an era which is so blasé, perverted, lethargic and sick, the best of intentions get off track and try to correct matters by means which only serve to corrupt. They look for success in order to have an audience, and they hang out dirty laundry like flags to attract the passers-by.

I respect the writers whose works I am about to trample underfoot: they believe in social regeneration, but in making their little pile of mud, they only mirror themselves in it, before they sweep it away. They want other people to sniff it and everyone see himself reflected in it; they have an affected taste for their own task and they forget about the sewer, all the while keeping the filth outside.

In all good conscience, I must make an exception for Feydeau. It is only through the lack of a little wit that he goes too far, but I would praise his latest novel, which, by way of a compliment, does have some excellent parts, if only the author did not have the habit of leaving nothing to the imagination of his readers (I will forget about *La Fille aux yeux d'or*). Be

*From *Le Figaro*, 28 January 1868. Translated for this volume by Barbara Gough.

that as it may, Mr. Feydeau, *observing the morals of his age*, has tried to write his own version of *Les Liaisons dangereuses*. He started from an austere point of view; he condemned in plain language the fancy behaviour of fashionable ladies; he painted his heroine with remarkably true colours; but he could not avoid the common fault. He is a kind of decadent Joseph Prudhomme. In two or three places he lays it on too thick, and one could apply to him the following point of comparison whereby the other *trivialist* novelists are condemned: it would be impossible for him to put his heroine on the stage.

That then is the touchstone. Balzac, the sublime dung-heap on which all these mushrooms are growing, concentrated all the corruptions and all the disgraces in one character, Mme Marneffe; and yet, since he never put Mme Marneffe in a position so visibly grotesque or trivial that her portrait could provoke laughter or disgust, Mme Marneffe was represented on the stage. I defy you to put Fanny on the stage: the principal scene would make her appear ridiculous. And I defy you to put the countess of Chalis there! I defy you to do the same with Germinie Lacerteux or Thérèse Raquin, those impossible phantoms which simply ooze death, having never breathed life, who are but nightmarish visions of reality.

The second reproach I shall address to this literature of violence is that it believes itself to be very malicious, whereas it is in reality very naïve: it is only an illusion.

It is easier to write a brutal novel, full of pus, crime, and prostitution than it is to write a restrained, moderate, watered-down novel, pointing out the sources of shame without uncovering them, moving the reader without nauseating him.

What a handy procedure it is to expose bruised flesh. Anyone can deal with decadent subjects and never miss making an effect. Even the most ñaïve of the Realists, while describing in a very unimaginative way old Montfaucon, would nauseate an entire generation.

To attract through disgust, to please by what is horrible is a strategy which unfortunately appeals to a very human instinct, but one which is at the same time the lowest and most disreputable instinct, the most universal and yet the most bestial instinct. The crowds which rush to the guillotine or hurry to the morgue, are they really the public that one should captivate, encourage and maintain in the cult of terror and purulence?

Chastity, candor, love in its heroic aspects, hate in all its hypocrisy, the truth of life, after all, cannot be represented without polish; they demand more work, more observation and are of more benefit to the reader. I am not claiming to restrict the domain of the writer. Everything, down to the flesh, is his territory, but tearing off skin is no longer simple observation, it is surgery, and if once, by chance, an écorché can be indispensable to a psychological demonstration, the écorché made into a system is no more than insanity and depravity.

I was saying that all these unhealthy imaginations were poor or lazy imaginations. I would only need to refer to their methods to prove it. They thrive on imitation. *Madame Bovary, Fanny* and *L' Affaire Clémenceau* bear the mark of an original and personal talent: so it is that these three superior works have remained models to be imitated, parodied and extended as if to make them grimace. To combine the judicial element with the pornographic element is the entire foundation of the art. Mystery with hysteria! that is the formula.

There is, however, a pitfall in these two words: the courts are a commonplace source of varied and facile episodes, and, in an age of nervous excesses, since one no longer has the keys to passion, passion gives way to nervous spasms. All this is just as effective and more convenient.

Having explained all this, I must own up to the special reason for my anger. My curiosity recently slipped into a pool of mud and blood called *Thérèse Raquin*, whose author, Mr. Zola, is reputed to be a young man of talent. At least, I know that he is ardently aspiring to fame. An enthusiast of crudeness, he published *La Confession de Claude*, the idyll of a student and a prostitute. He sees women as Mr. Manet paints them: the colour of mud with pink make-up. Intolerant of any criticism, he practises criticism himself with intolerance, and, at an age when most people are normally only capable of following their desires, Zola entitles his so-called literary studies: *Mes Haines* [*My Hates*]!

I do not know if Mr. Zola has the power to write a subtle, delicate, substantial and decent book. To renounce violence, one must have will, wit, ideas and style. But I can already point out one such conversion to the author of *Thérèse Raquin*.

Jules Claretie has also written a book full of erotic and fatal frenzy, but he quickly grew sick of the genre after his own success, and he went searching through history for more realistic tragedies, and for passions which were no less terrible but more heroic. A lot of people die in his *Derniers Montagnards*, but with a cry of hope and a love of freedom! No anger is spared, but with the effect that one is left in a kinder, more tolerant mood.

As for *Thérèse Raquin*, it is the residue of all the horrors which were published previous to it. All the blood and infamies of those works have been drained into it; it is Mother Bancal's bucket.

The subject matter, however, is quite simple: the physical remorse of two lovers who kill the husband in order to be freer to deceive him, but who find that, once the husband is dead (his name was Camille), they no longer dare embrace, for here, according to the author, is the subtle torture which awaits them: "They cried aloud and strained still closer so as not to leave any space between their bodies for the dead man. Yet they could still feel bits of Camille's flesh squashed disgustingly between them, freezing their bodies in places whilst the rest was on fire" [179].[1]

In the end, not managing to *crush* out the drowned man with their kisses, they bite each other, end up loathing each other and kill themselves in a double suicide brought about by their despair at not being able to murder each other.

If I told the author that his idea is immoral, he would be indignant, for the description of remorse is generally taken to be a moralizing spectacle; but if remorse was always limited to physical impressions and to carnal loathings, it would then be no more than a reaction of the temperament, and it would not be remorse. What constitutes the strength and the triumph of goodness is that, even with the flesh appeased and passions spent, goodness awakes and burns brightly in the mind. *A storm in the mind* is a sublime spectacle, whereas a storm in the loins is a very base sight.

The first time that Thérèse sees the man she will love, here is how the liking is presented: "The man's sanguine temperament, his loud voice, his fat laugh, the keen, powerful aroma given off by his whole person, threw the young woman off her balance and plunged her into a sort of nervous anguish" [57].

O Romeo! O Juliette! what prompt and subtle intuition did you have to fall in love so quickly? Thérèse is a woman in need of a lover. On the other hand, Laurent, her accomplice, decides to drown the husband after a walk during which he undergoes the following temptation: "He whistled and kicked the stones, but now and again there was a fierce glint in his eyes as he watched his mistress's swinging hips" [89].

After such stimulation, how could one resist assassinating poor old Camille, that sickly, tacky creature, whose name rhymes with ca-momil(l)e?

So they throw the husband into the water. From that moment on, Laurent frequents the morgue until such time as his drowned victim might be put on display. The author takes advantage of this occasion to describe for us the sensual pleasures of the morgue and its habitués.

Laurent takes particular delight in looking at the murdered women. One day he falls in love with the corpse of a girl who hanged herself; it is true that her "fresh, plump body took on most delicate hues with the pallor of death." Laurent "lingered over her for a long time, running his eyes up and down her body, lost in a sort of fearful desire" [109].

It appears that society women also go to the morgue; one of them lapses into a state of contemplation while looking at the robust body of a stonemason. "The lady — writes the author — went on studying him and, as it were, turning him over with her eyes, weighing him up. She raised the corner of her veil, took one last look, and went away" [111].

As for the street kids, "young louts have their first women in the Morgue" [111].

Since this article may be read just after lunch, I shall skip over the description of Camille's lovely rotting corpse. You can almost feel the worms crawling about.

Once the drowned man is properly buried, the lovers get married, and then their torment begins.

I am not being unfair in recognizing that certain parts of this analysis of the sensations of two murderers are well observed. Their horrible wedding-night is a very striking tableau. I am not systematically blaming the strident tones, the violent and violet brush-strokes; I am only complaining that they are isolated and unadulterated; what detracts most from this book could have been its strongest point.

But the monotony of the ignoble is the worst possible form of monotony. It is as if, to use a comparison appropriate to this book, the reader were lying under the tap of one of the tables in the morgue, and as if, right down to the last page, he could feel the slow, steady drip of the water used to wash down the dead bodies.

Man and wife, going from one fit of rage to another, from depravity to depravity, end up fighting, each one wanting to denounce the other. Thérèse turns to prostitution, and Laurent, "whose flesh is dead," regrets that he cannot do the same.

Finally, one day, these two slaves of the morgue fall exhausted, poisoned, on top of one another, in front of the chair of Camille Raquin's paralyzed old mother, who silently enjoys this punishment which avenges her son.

This book sums up too faithfully all the putridness of contemporary literature not to provoke a certain amount of anger. I would have said nothing about the work if it had been no more than an individual fantasy, but, the manner is contagious and whatever one reads one keeps coming across it. Let us force our novelists to prove their talent in other ways than by borrowing their subjects from the courts of law and the garbage dump.

At the sale of the pasha who has recently liquidated his gallery just like a European, Mr. Courbet depicted the last word in voluptuous pleasure in the arts by a painting that was put on display, and by another, hung in a toilet, that was shown only to indiscreet ladies and to connoisseurs. The entire shame of this school is in these two canvasses, as it is elsewhere in the novels: weary debauchery and crude anatomy. It is well painted, it is incontestably real, but it is horribly stupid.

When the literature of which I have been talking wants an emblem, it will have Courbet make a copy of these two canvasses. The possible painting will draw the customers to the door, and the other painting will be in the sanctuary, like the muse, the genie, the oracle.[2]

Notes

1. [Editor's note: For passages from *Thérèse Raquin*, the translation by Leonard Tancock (Harmondsworth: Penguin Books, 1962) has been used and page references have been included in the text.]

2. [Editor's note: Zola's reply to this article appeared in *Le Figaro* three days later (31

January 1868). The author of *Thérèse Raquin* scarcely mentions his own work, but prefers to defend *Germinie Lacerteux* against Ulbach's comments. He criticizes the indecency of the conventional and facile literature that Ferragus seems to prefer and argues that analytical novels, studies of the "fatalities of the flesh," are their own justification: "The truth, like fire, purifies everything."]

Note on a Question of the Hour   A. C. Swinburne*

There are two reasons, one personal and one general in its bearing, why I should trouble *The Athenæum* and myself with a word — that word shall be as brief as I can properly make it — on a subject of late so hotly and so loudly debated in the Parisian world of letters that some echoes of the wrangle have crossed over to the borderland of our own. And first let me set down the mere egoistic reason, and so have done with that minor part of the matter.

For six months together — from July 9th, 1876, to January 7th, 1877 — the pages of the magazine called *La République des Lettres* were distinguished or disfigured by the weekly instalments of a story or a study from life called *L'Assommoir*, and written by M. Emile Zola. During all those weeks my name continued to appear on the cover of the magazine among the names of its other contributors; a list on which I account it as no small honour to have seen that name enrolled. But during all those weeks not a line from my pen appeared on any one of the pages inside that cover.

Between the first week of them and the last, a single number of the magazine was made luminous and fragrant by the appearance of a poem on which I said my say some time since in these columns — or said at least some feeble and inadequate part of what I would fain have been as competent as I found myself incompetent to say. For that single week the publication of *L'Assommoir* was suspended. It can surely be no impertinent or unreasonable assumption if we infer — I know nothing personally on the subject — that for this momentary suspension there can be but one of two reasons assignable. Either Victor Hugo had distinctly stipulated that so it should be, as a peremptory condition of his contributing at all; or the conductors of the magazine felt by instinct that to act otherwise would be a gross hideous outrage on the simplest and deepest instincts of human decency. In the one case they knew, in the other case they felt, that on this matter the highest in station among their contributors was or must be of one mind with the humblest, and (probably in the one case, as assuredly in the other) would as soon have flung any poem of his in the fire as have permitted it to come before the world cheek by jowl with a chapter of *L'Assommoir*.

*From the *Athenaeum*, no. 2590 (16 June 1877):768.

This may seem a hard thing to say of a book which has found, I believe, its champions (however few and far between) among men of good repute; and which is, I know, the work of an author whose public character as a man of high ability is unquestionable, and whose private character — I am ready to take his own printed and published word for it — is such as cannot be refused to a man of simple and modest habits, of blameless and unambitious life. Such is M. Zola's plea, put forward on behalf of his book and of himself with the quiet force of unmistakable sincerity. But surely it needs not a tenth part of his intelligence to anticipate the instant rejoinder which inevitably must rise to any possible reader's lips. *Quid ad rem?* What in the name of common sense, of human reason, is it to us, whether the author's private life be or be not comparable only, for majestic or for infantile purity, to that of such men as Marcus Aurelius or St. Francis of Assisi, if his published work be what beyond all possible question it is — comparable only for physical and for moral abomination to such works as, by all men's admission, it is impossible to call into such a court as the present, and there bring them forward as the sole fit subjects of comparison; for the simple and sufficient reason, that the mention of their very names in print is generally, and not unnaturally, considered to be of itself an obscene outrage on all literary law and prescription of propriety?

To bring proof that I have said no harsh or unjustifiable word on this subject is — unluckily for myself, and obviously to my reader — a thing utterly out of the question. To transcribe the necessary extracts would for me — I speak seriously, and within bounds — would for me be physically impossible. For the editor of any known publication in England to print them would be morally impossible. But this much, I think, it is but proper and necessary to say of them. They are divisible into two equally horrible and loathsome classes. Under the one head I rank such passages as deal with physical matters which might almost have turned the stomach of Dean Swift. The other class consists of those which contain such details of brutality and atrocity practised on a little girl as would necessitate the interpolation of such a line as follows in the police report of any and every newspaper in London — "The further details given in support of the charge of cruelty were too revolting for publication in our columns."

One question remains to ask: Whether anything can justify, whether anything can excuse, the appearance of such a book as this against which I have said the least that is possible to say, in the mildest terms that are possible to use. To me it seems, on the whole, that nothing imaginable can. To others it may seem that one thing conceivable might. Considering the book, so to speak, as a medical drug of the purgative or emetic kind, they might hope or they might allege that it might remove, — that it might at least allay, — if duly administered or applied, the malady described in it as eating out the vitals of so many among the poorer class in Paris. And if we could know or if we could believe that one family might thus be saved from sinking into so horrible and foul a Malebolge as slowly or swiftly swallows up the several families whose history is here set down — if we could conceive of such a result as possible, I would not be slower than another to admit or to consider the force of this sole extenuating circumstance. But let us notice what is implied by such a plea. Nothing less is implied by it than this: — that such families as these are likely to take in such magazines as that which gave generous but incongruous shelter to the horrible homeless head of this wandering abomination — to a book which could find no other harbour, no port of refuge but this. The first chapters of *L'Assommoir* had appeared elsewhere — I know not in what other magazine. But no sooner did the conductors of that magazine become aware what manner of chapters lay behind or loomed ahead, than they refused to continue the publication — signified imperatively to M. Zola that he must take his unutterable wares elsewhither; that he must — was ever the phrase apter or more pertinent? — must drive his pigs to some other market. And this herd of worse than Gadarean swine, possessed by a devil whose name was not Legion but Sterquilinium, ran down into no Dead Sea, but through the unhappily open gate of a quiet little garden of letters, fashioned only to receive such guests as art and poetry and the brightest brood of fiction — and all these in the main of a somewhat strangely refined and delicately eclectic sort.

One word before I close — one last egoistic word of irrepressible even if damnable iteration. It is perhaps possible that to some reader the substance of this note may suggest some suspiciously suggestive reminiscence of "the Puff Oblique." I can desire no heavier punishment for any one whose mind could give entrance to such a shameful and insulting thought than that he should act on it, and read *L'Assommoir* from the first page to the last; a thing which I confess I most certainly have not done, and most assuredly could not do. If he does not find this perusal a most heavy and most loathsome form of judicial retribution, a chastisement comparable to none in Dante's Hell but that inflicted on the damned whose scalps were so densely overlaid with something I cannot here mention (as M. Zola would) by name — to borrow a bold phrase from Mr. Browning, so "immortally immerded" — that Dante could not see whether the crown were shorn or unshorn, — if he feels otherwise or less than this, he is not one for whose possible opinion or imputation I ever could greatly care. And herewith I thankfully wash my hands for ever of the subject, as I hopefully desire to cleanse my memory for ever from all recollection of the book; reiterating simply, on my own poor personal behalf, that whether it were or were not an accident which allowed not one line of this work to appear in that number of the magazine made sweet and splendid by the passing touch of Victor Hugo, it was by no manner of means an accident which during all the weeks and all the months of its long and loathsome progress kept out of the desecrated pages of *La République des Lettres* any line of verse, any message of prose, from the hand of

A.C. Swinburne.

The *Experimental Novel*   Ferdinand Brunetière*

"Here comes the buffalo! The greatest of all buffalo! The greatest of all bulls! He alone is a bull, next to him, all others are no more than bullocks! Make way for the buffalo, the greatest of all buffalo!" Thus it was long ago, in the heyday of Romanticism — so says Heinrich Heine — that a certain famous critic went about proclaiming the advent of a certain famous poet. For several years now Naturalism has vainly been seeking from all quarters just such a critic, or rather just such a kind of literary cornac. But from all sides there is nothing but silence and Naturalism, less fortunate than Romanticism, has not yet found its critic. Up until now, no one willing to tackle a didactic commentary on the beauties of *L'Assommoir* or *Le Ventre de Paris* has stepped forward, or, in other words, to put things bluntly, no one as naively infatuated with Mr. Zola as he is himself. Whereupon, only one thing remained for Mr. Zola to do; and this he has done: he has become his own critic. A weekly column was not enough for him. He has composed, primarily for exportation purposes, and generally for St. Petersburg, long studies on *Les Romanciers contemporains* (Contemporary novelists), or on *La République et la Littérature* (The republic and literature); now, for us, he has just finished writing a lengthy essay on *Le Roman expérimental (The Experimental Novel)*; the time has come to give him a taste of his own experiments, and to put, for once, this great judge of others on trial.

If some writers are inferior to the reputation they have by circumstance acquired, there are without fail others whose minds are superior to their works. In truth, I do not believe that this is quite Mr. Zola's case. However, even if he were the author of novels even worse than his own, it would still be possible for him to have some ideas about the novel that might be worth discussing. And even if the prose he uses in his columns or his studies were still colder and more clumsy than it is, this would not prevent him from having, in spite of all, a critical eye as accurate as his pen hand is hesitant, and thoughts as lofty or profound as his style is flat.

For his style is indeed flat; and I cannot even go along with the admirers of Mr. Zola who maintain that we must hail in him a "born writer," and even less "a master of the French language." We should not be

*From the *Revue des Deux Mondes*, 15 February 1880, 935–48. Translated for this volume by Janice Best.

34   Critical Essays on Emile Zola

deceived by a few pages of description. As a writer, Mr. Zola resembles that "King of the Markets" who was reputed to know every word of the French language, but not the proper way to use them. Mr. Zola also knows every word of the French language; he even knows some that do not belong to the French language, nor to any other language in the world; but whichever is the case, he is totally ignorant of the meaning, the function and the usage of these words. Let us take a closer look. "I sum up this first part by repeating that the naturalistic novelists observe and experiment, and that all their work is the offspring of the doubt which seizes them in the presence of truths little known and phenomena unexplained, until an experimental idea rudely awakens their genius some day, and urges them to make an experiment, to analyze facts, and to master them."[1] Please re-read this sentence carefully. It is obvious that Mr. Zola does not know what an experiment really is, and that he is talking about science here in much the same way as soon you will hear him start talking about metaphysics, with a placid ignorance that would make any scientist or any metaphysician burst out laughing. It is obvious that Mr. Zola does not weigh his words, because if he did, he would not call the idea of an experiment to be carried out an "experimental idea": if the association of these two words means anything at all, it can only mean an induction or a conclusion, an idea derived from the experiment; something subsequent to the experiment, not something prior to it; something acquired and not a conquest to be made. It is obvious that Mr. Zola does not know what the term "to experiment" means, because if the novelist, or the poet, carries out an experiment, he can only do so on himself, not on others. In order to carry out an experiment on Coupeau, one would have to get a Coupeau, obtain exclusive rights on him, get him drunk with a determined dosage of alcohol every day, prevent him from doing anything that might hinder or interrupt the course of the experiment, and open him up on the dissecting table as soon as he showed the first symptoms of a clear case of alcoholism. There is no other way, there can be no other way to carry out an experiment; there is nothing more than observation; and this is enough to destroy the very basis of Mr. Zola's theory of the *Experimental Novel.*

It seems pointless to cite any further examples. Take a look for yourself at this mixture of paradoxes and banalities that Mr. Zola has given to us under the title of the *Experimental Novel* and just try to find a sentence or even a word that stands out and seems worth remembering — you will have to search a long time just to find one clear, well-stated idea! If there is such a thing as an art of writing, and if this art has ever been defined as the correct use of words, as the harmonious construction of sentences and as the exact, carefully balanced and graduated development of ideas, then Mr. Zola has no conception of it. Yet it is in this regard, and no other, that someone worthy to be called a writer must prove himself. Descriptions and pictures do not prove that an author knows how to write: they only prove that he is a very sensitive individual. It is in the general ideas that he expresses that we look for and judge the quality of a writer. There is no doubt that Mr. Zola has succeeded in making himself heard, and this in itself is an accomplishment, but to call this man a "writer" is, in truth, just as inadmissible as calling him a "novelist."

Mr. Zola's greatest shortcoming, as a novelist, is that he is tiresome, wearying, and—to put it bluntly—boring. In answer to this, Mr. Zola triumphantly—or so he thinks—would point to the seventy-six or seventy-seven editions of *L'Assommoir*, not to mention the illustrated edition. Will it make him happy if we add that *Nana* will undoubtedly enjoy the same sort of commercial success? Granted! But what about *Une Page d'amour?* What about *Son Excellence Eugène Rougon?* What about *La Conquête de Plassans?* What about *La Faute de l'abbé Mouret?* How many editions have there been of these fragments of the interminable tale of the Rougons and the Macquarts . . .? This in itself should be enough to warn Mr. Zola that the success of *L'Assommoir*, like that of *Nana*, is simply the result of an external set of circumstances.

Recently the name of Restif de la Bretonne has been mentioned more than once in connection with Mr. Zola. This man, who was also in his day a fashionable and highly successful story-teller, used to reply, when it was pointed out to him that his works were only sold in proportion to the number of liberal passages they contained, that this was merely the opinion of a narrow-minded book-seller. But other points could be made in comparing the two of them. In fact, Restif was not only the chronicler of the seamier side of life, he was also, over a hundred years ago, as is well known, a sort of social reformer. "This is not," he stated, as an introduction to one of his works, "a pretty little piece of nonsense such as Marmontel or Louvet might write, this is a useful supplement to Buffon's *Natural History*." All you have to do is change the names: the author of *La Paysanne pervertie* carried on the work of Buffon. There is no doubt, people used to say to M. Nicolas, that your intentions are good and that you are preaching "the purest virtue", however are you not afraid of the risk involved in "exposing vice" in such a manner? What risk? "I defy the purists",[2] he would exclaim in tones of indignation, "in order to denounce vice and to enlighten parents." Mr. Zola, too, defies the purists, and he tells the tale of Nana, daughter of Coupeau, for the benefit of parents. And besides, how timid the author of *L'Assommoir* appears next to Restif, and how much more scrupulous a Naturalist was the eighteenth century story-teller than his rival! . . .[3]

It would not be entirely fair, however, totally to confound Mr. Zola with this comparison. As I have said, the Naturalists are at once very close and very far from the truth. It is a question of limits and nuances. Let us try to see if we can define the problem and shed a little light on it. First of all, is Mr. Zola, who so often complains that no one wants to understand him, so sure that he always understands others? Is it not just possible that sometimes he gets up on his high horse against a band of imaginary adversaries and that he wastes a lot of empty bravado battering down doors that are already open? Mr. Zola's great misfortune is that he is absolutely lacking in a literary education and in a philosophical background; and, in the vast ranks of literary men with no literary culture, he is, we might say, the first in line. He produces a great deal, now and again he thinks, but it is obvious that he has never done any reading. One cannot help thinking this way when one hears him calling out for someone to come and discuss with him the relationship between mind and matter, between free-will and moral responsibility, or yet again between environment and physiological heredity. How is it that some charitable adviser has not made him understand that there is a time and a place for everything, that such complex and difficult questions as these cannot be debated at the level of *Le Ventre de Paris* or *L'Assommoir*, and that, as far as the Rougon-Macquart or the Quenu-Gradelle are concerned, one cannot possibly expect people to choose between the system of physical premotion or the system of mean or conditioned science?

What does all this matter to us anyway? What does *indeterminism* or *determinism* have to do with the novel and the theatre? As far as we are concerned, we believe that each one of us creates his own destiny, that he is the creator of his own happiness, the clumsy or criminal author of his own misfortunes: this is one way of looking at life. Mr. Zola, on the contrary, believes, to borrow the celebrated expression, "that vice and virtue are products just like vitriol or sugar" and that we are composed of a soft sort of substance that circumstances fashion according to their chance combinations; that is another way of looking at life. But what does it matter one way or the other? In the first instance, if you are George Sand, you will write *Le Marquis de Villemer*; and, in the second instance, if you are Balzac, you will write *La Cousine Bette*. I have just one word of advice for Mr. Zola, that is to suggest that he not attempt to write for the theatre, because the theatre thrives on action, and action involves struggle, battling against people, or rebelling against the dominion of things in the world.

But what about the novel; the novel that Mr. Zola has never written, but that he aspires or thinks he aspires to write, the novel of *observation* and of *experimentation*, if we must stick to this ill-used word; the novel for which Balzac would have given us models, if only Balzac had known how to write in a language a little closer to French, the novel for which Mr. Flaubert would have established the laws, if only jealous gods had not refused Mr. Flaubert the good fortune of giving us a second *Madame Bovary*? Why will this novel never be? You choose a character, or, as you put it, a temperament; you want to "take apart its mechanism and put it back together again"; you claim to be seeking "what a certain passion, in a certain environment and in certain given circumstances, will produce from the point of view of the individual and of society?" All right. There is no doubt about it, if you insist, but allow me to point out just in passing that, if man is not free, he believes he is; that Western societies are founded on this belief — hypothesis, metaphysical prejudice or religious superstition, call it what you will; — and, as a result, you are eliminating from our *experimental novel* what is, perhaps, most interesting for man and most vital, in the full sense of the word, for him, that is to say: the tragedy of a will that thinks. But since one can certainly find amongst us people of weak will and people of no will at all, and since even the most energetic of men are almost always, in their daily lives, just as much slaves of their desires as masters of their will, you will have only had to sacrifice, by your own choosing, one of the many elements that make the novel interesting. The lute originally had seven strings; you have just eliminated one, that is all! You can still play a great many tunes all the same; and if your novel interests me, in one way or another — and, I repeat, there is no reason why it should not interest me — do not flatter yourself that I am going to resist my emotions and that "the pleasure of criticizing overrules the pleasure of being deeply touched by very beautiful things." Why do you not give me those beautiful things to start with, and we shall see about the rest later. But, in the meantime, let us not lose track of our subject. When someone talks to you about the novel, please do not answer by talking about metaphysics or physiology! If you have not attained your goal and if your work is a failure, all the brilliant theories in the world will not be able to do anything about it. Just try to be more skilful or more successful the next time. And do not be surprised that we refuse to be put off the scent by refusing to see you as the champion of a system: you are nothing more than its victim; and your talent is the dupe of your philosophy.

Mr. Zola is still further deceived by thinking that we reproach him for wanting to interest us in a love story involving Coupeau, the roofer, and Gervaise, the washer woman. And why not? It is up to him to know how to go about it. Who ever denied that there was something human to be found in every man, anyway? There was no need to call upon Claude Bernard and to repeat after him, "that we will never arrive at any truly fertile generalizations until we have carried out experiments for ourselves and turned over in the hospital, the amphitheatre and the laboratory, the rank and palpitating soil of life." We know this. What is it that makes Mr. Zola keep charging off to do battle with windmills? However low he may decide tomorrow to go searching for his heroes, can he possibly seek them any lower than Manon Lescaut and the chevalier des Grieux? Just because one likes to meet well-bred men and cultivated women in a novel (since reading, as the philosopher said, is like having a conversation with the most respectable people of all classes), does this necessarily mean that we would not be happy now and again to find a few folk who were not as well educated as diplomats, but decent all the same, or a few women, not dressed according to the latest fashions, but worthy nonetheless? It certainly is a strange way to discuss something to assume that one's adversaries have out of date prejudices! We simply wish to point out that whoever writes, writes first for those who think and, as a general hypothesis, that certain vulgar ways of thinking—which would be more appropriately called ways of not thinking—are no more suitable to be recorded by the novelist than certain modes of speech are worthy of being transcribed by the lexicographer. Now then, when a roofer or a washer-woman have been working at their trade for twelve or fifteen hours a day, they scarcely have the time, nor do they feel the need to think. They go to bed and start over again the next day. And this is why, if you wish to portray them true to life, you must show them to us if not with other characteristics, at least with more general characteristics than those of their social condition.

Do we mean by this that the novelist must never allow himself to depict social conditions? Of course not! But we maintain, on the basis of all great works of art, that the portrayal of characters is always and everywhere of universal human interest, whereas the portrayal of social conditions is not and can only be universally human in rigorously defined circumstances. Yes, you can take the king, as in Racine's tragedy; you can take the doctor, as in Molière's comedy; because in fact, the practise of certain functions, certain arts, certain trades, does modify the fundamentals of human nature in a specific way, and a specific way which it is possible, interesting and useful to determine. To act like a king, to speak like a doctor, these expressions have a meaning, a full and definite meaning. But hardware, for instance, or the art of making shoes, how can these activities possibly modify the loves or hates, the joys or sufferings which are the important part of life? And can you clearly conceive what it must be like for a woodworker to love, or for a fruit and vegetable merchant to suffer? This is only one of the thousand ways of repeating that one must make sacrifices, and how very right Voltaire was when he added: "that details are the vermin that gnaw away at great works." There is a prevailing view today that works of art will survive by the details they contain, whereas this is exactly what will cause them to perish. People say that details make a work true to life but, in little more than ten years from now, it will be the same details that will make it false. "Any document brought to light is beyond attack, fashion can do nothing to alter it." If we are talking about history, yes! If we are talking about literature, no! a thousand times no! On the contrary, it is precisely because of this, because of the document, the description of a costume and of furnishings, a restaurant owner's menu or an upholsterer's bill that, fifteen or twenty years from now, a work will be considered false.

In this regard, do we mean to say that one must, as our Naturalists pretend to believe, systematically leave one portion of reality in the shadows? There are grounds for supporting this idea, in fact, for some of our acts reveal the animal in us, and others distinguish us from it, and these are the acts that make us men. Certainly, our feelings are a part of us; I am only saying that they are an inferior part of us. Let us not be afraid of words: some acts are noble, such as devoting oneself to others or sacrificing oneself; other acts are indifferent, such as eating or drinking; and still others are base, such as, if you will allow La Bruyère a certain liberal choice of words, going to the privy. Therefore, I can conceive of a literature which would decide from the outset to subordinate physical sensations to feelings, and feelings to thoughts, and this literature will be legitimate, and this literature will be true. What am I saying? It will be naturalistic, for, after all, as someone who knew something about it once said: "Nature can only be improved by Nature's own methods."[4] But I can also very easily conceive that someone might be ambitious enough to want to depict the entire man. All we have left to do is to reach an agreement on this last word.

Now then, do you know why your descriptions, no matter how willing I, the reader, may be and however much talent you, the writer, put into them, sooner or later, but without fail, end up wearing me out? You show me a rug in a bedroom, a bed on this rug, a bedspread on this bed, a quilt on this bedspread. . . . What next? What makes this so tedious is, in part, the insignificance of these details, as in other places it is their baseness, but it is even more the fault of the endlessness of the description. There are some base details; there are especially a lot of useless details. Whether my bed is in the corner or the middle of the room, whether my curtains have valences or whether they are tied back in the Flemish style, I would be truly curious to know what all of this can tell you about my character. It can not be otherwise, if you intend to tell me all about a man's life, detail by detail. A man practises a trade, but he does not always behave, and in all the deeds of his life, like the typical man of this trade; a man is born into a certain social condition, and he dies in it, but he does not always behave, and in all the deeds of this life, like the typical man of his condition; a man has a certain type of character, and this character is very pronounced, but he does not always behave, and in all the deeds of his life, like the typical example of this character. Even the high-flown, stupid remarks of someone like Homais, the pharmacist, are intermittent; even someone like Baron Hulot has remissions of his lust. You speak of reality, you say that "it is the real that has made the world," and although this is not precisely the clearest of formulae, I nonetheless feel that I understand you, or rather, I am willing to proceed as if I understood you. But, you will have to agree with me that, in reality, Homais the pharmacist now and again utters a few words that are neither pretentious nor foolish, that are indifferent, that is to say, that tell us nothing about his character nor about his social status. And, in reality, Baron Hulot, like you, like me, like all of us, apparently performs certain deeds that reveal nothing of his passions nor of his appetite even to the most perceptive of observers. In *Madame Bovary*, however, Homais never opens his mouth without uttering a sentence worthy of his stately stupidity; and in *La Cousine Bette*, Baron Hulot never makes a single gesture, nor takes a single step which is not directed — so to speak — towards the satisfaction of his desires. Thus they are *true*, for Mr. Zola will grant me that they are just this, and they are true precisely in so far as they have ceased to be *real*. . . .[5]

There is only one area in which Mr. Zola's works resemble his doctrines: that is, in the wilful crudeness of their language and the deliberate vulgarity of their subjects. As for Mr. Zola himself, one is tempted to say that he, who is so "interested in foreign literatures," has meditated at length upon these words of advice from a great master (and this passage is not to be found in the *Histoire de la littérature anglaise*)[6]: "An author must accustom his imagination to the consideration of the vilest and basest things in nature, he will perfect himself by such a noble exercise: by so doing, he will succeed in giving birth to nothing but truly and totally base thoughts; by this exercise, he will lower himself far below reality."[7] And where have our novelists witnessed these morals that they depict for us, anyway? And have they ever actually witnessed them? I do not hesitate, as far as Mr. Zola is concerned, and I hope that after this little demonstration the reader will not hesitate any more than I have, to say: no! he has not witnessed them at all. But even if he had, what a strange sort of habit is this to look at humanity only at its worst. And to what purpose? We have not talked about the purpose yet! It is about time this bad joke came to an end! Whom does Mr. Zola expect to convince that Coupeau's *delirium tremens* is going to make one single drunkard give up his bottle; or that Nana's small-pox will ever outweigh, in the dreams of any unhappy, working-class girl, the temptations of freedom, pleasure and luxury which he has so amply described? There is no excuse for this sort of thing and we have had enough of it; decidedly, five hundred pages depicting nothing but low and stupid vices are just too many.

Open up your eyes, take a look around you: apparently this century is not so devoid of virtue that one cannot from time to time encounter a few good examples. From the Madeleine to the Bastille and from the Gare de l'Est to Montrouge, one can still find some fathers of families who save their money, some wives who are faithful to their husbands, and some mothers who darn their children's socks. Do not say that these people have no story! They have one of the most interesting and the truest of all, the story of the hard times that take up so great a part of all human lives, the hard times that we all must face and live through together; the story of happy times and of the smiles that fortune has brought as a reward for labour and effort; and — if you are talented — you can tell the story of the complex and subtle feelings which, day by day, delicately, yet ever more strongly, have linked together the lives of two or of several people, who have, each one of them, sacrificed to the others something of themselves, and have each one of them hidden some of their sorrows from the others, putting all their joys in together, relying each one of them upon all the others. Unfortunately, these are thoughts that will never occur to Mr.

Zola. He has his aesthetic principles and he has his system. Did he not write, in one of his most recent weekly columns, this astonishing sentence, which I quote verbatim: "Take a look at any drawing-room gathering, the most respectable one you can find; if you were to write down the sincere confessions of all the guests, you would leave behind a document which would scandalize thieves and assassins"? Any attempt at commentary would only detract from such a declaration of principles; any epithet would alter its lovely meaning; — and we must leave the reader with an impression such as this.

Notes

1. [Editor's note: *Emile Zola: The Naturalist Novel*, ed. with an introduction by Maxwell Greismar (n.p.: Harvest House, 1964), p. 7; selections from *The Experimental Novel*, tr. Belle M. Sherman (New York: Cassell, 1893).]

2. It should be noted that he used words with the same sense of their appropriateness as Mr. Zola himself and that everywhere that *purist* appears, one should read: *puritans*.

3. [Editor's note: In the omitted page Brunetière pursues the comparison between Zola and Restif, to the advantage of the latter.]

4. For the benefit of Mr. Zola, who prides himself on "being familiar with foreign literatures," this is Shakespeare: "Yet nature is mode better by nos mean, / But nature makes that mean" [*sic*].
[Editor's note: This bungled attempt to quote from *The Winter's Tale* (IV, iii, 89) in English somewhat deflates Brunetière's irony.]

5. [Editor's note: In the substantial section omitted here Brunetière gives his own recommendations on realism in literature and, after indicating the source of an episode of *Nana* in Thomas Otway's *Venice Preserved* (by way of Taine's *Histoire de la littérature anglaise*), argues that Zola's works are not realistic and that there is no common ground between his doctrines and his novels.]

6. [Translator's note: *A History of English Literature* by Hippolyte Taine, one of Zola's acclaimed masters. For the irony of the allusion, see the previous note.]

7. This quotation is taken from Swift's *Treatise on the Art of Grovelling in Poetry* [?]; the liberties which the author of *A Tale of a Tub* and *A Voyage to Laputa* allows himself when he deems them necessary to the expression of his thoughts are, moreover, well-known.

Concord Philosophy and Zola   Anonymous*

The Concord School has again assembled, meditated, and dispersed, and nothing remains of its speculative philosophizings save the echoes in the journalistic air, some of which are repeated on an inside page, and the

*From the *Literary World* (Boston) 17 (7 August 1886). 264.

intellectual impressions which have been produced in the few attentive minds. The discussions this year took a more practical turn than they have done sometimes, and were chiefly concerned with Dante and Plato and their respective places in literature. The remarks on Dante, as being the subject of perhaps the greater interest to most of our readers, are what we have selected from for reproduction, and the selections fairly represent the differing points of view and lines of criticism, as well as the various speakers.

The discussion of Plato and Socrates has been made the more conspicuous of the two in the public prints by reason of some feeling growing out of Professor Davidson's remarks on Zola. In the course of one of his papers Professor Davidson, as reported in the *Advertiser*, used the following language:

> I find in Socrates's irony of conversation one characteristic which distinguishes it from the irony of most other men. I can think of only four other men whose irony has the same characteristic — Aristotle, Jesus, Goethe and Zola. I know it will surprise most of you to hear me include Zola in this noble company; but I do so with knowledge of cause. Zola is much decried at present for an over devotion to truth, which he persists in telling in its entirety, yea, even when he uses irony. Let us then not join in the cry, remembering that Socrates, in his day, was put to death for atheism and for corrupting the youth of Athens, that Aristotle had to flee for similar reasons, that Jesus was crucified for blasphemy, that when Goethe's Wilhelm Meister was translated into English, it was saluted with a howl, as being immoral and corrupting. That howl is mostly hushed nowadays, and so will the present howl against Zola soon be. In the whole range of literature, I know of no more cool, calm, terrible irony than that of Zola. It is the very irony of truth itself — a new species of irony to add to our list.

Nobody can say anything in public like this without bringing some hearers to their feet. The *Advertiser*, editorially, interpreted Professor Davidson as predicting "the speedy coming of a cordial toleration of M. Zola's works," and asked: "Are we, then, drifting backward toward a condition of society and morals when the nastily truthful literature of the dramatists of the restoration will be again in vogue?" And an unnamed correspondent of the same journal, writing from Dublin, N.H., voiced the regret and pain which people would feel in hearing the Saviour put in a group with Zola, Goethe, and Aristotle. These and other outcries called forth from Professor Davidson an interesting rejoinder in a subsequent issue of the *Advertiser*, which we regret we have not space to insert in full, and in which he explains and justifies his meaning.

His opening remarks touching the sense in which "even God and the devil may be classed together" are hardly to the point, nor should we be disposed to enter into a discussion with him over the assertion that in the teachings of Jesus and Dante pride is "the blackest" and incontinence "the lightest" of mortal sins. When he comes to the actual quality and influence of Zola's novels he is, however, on ground where he treads intelligently if not wisely, and his views are certainly entitled to consideration. He reprobates most sincerely, he says, the publication of the details of vice, and would be glad to see all of Zola's social novels burned. But this we cannot afford to do, he claims, "for the simple reason that vice and its consequences, degradation and suffering, still exist, and, so long as they exist, it is highly desirable that they should be clearly understood by us, not only in their actuality, but in their causes, conditions, and ultimate effects." Continuing he says:

> Newspaper reports of vice and crime labor, for the most part, under this great defect, that they merely record disagreeable facts which repel the pure-minded and attract the impure-minded; in the former case doing no good, in the latter doing harm, in neither pointing the way to any remedy or arousing men's minds to apply any such. They are, therefore, deserving of entire reprobation. Zola's novels, on the contrary, while reporting the same facts, present them to us in their connection, show us their causes in existing social or other institutions, and their effects upon men's lives, and characters, and so at once suggest a remedy and rouse us to apply it. No one who has read Zola's novels understandingly will ever think of denying this; but I am quite aware that persons do read them, who see no earnest purpose in them, and who carry away from them only what some tourists carry away from Cologne — a sense of bad smells. Such persons, of course, ought not to read them, just as they ought not to read any book that depicts vice without suggesting to them the means of remedy. Among my audience in Concord I think I had a right to assume that no such persons were present.

To the remark that Zola might accomplish his purposes without use of disgusting details, Professor Davidson replies that one of the chief merits of that author's books he holds to be this very presentation of vice "in all its prosaic, dull, heartless, disgusting nakedness. No man," he affirms, "has ever made vice so unlovely, so sickening, as Zola has done. He puts his vicious people into a hell upon earth, compared with which Dante's Inferno is a land of old romance. If any can fall in love with vice from Zola's presentation of it, then there is no hope for him in this world or the next."

This certainly is the point on which the whole question turns. Are the writings of Zola, and of other novelists that might be named, in love with vice, or are they seriously intended to make us hate it, by realizations of its enormity and by pity over the miseries it entails? It is just here that opinions differ. Of Zola's writings Professor Davidson thinks the latter, and we are willing to concede that the view is one which may be defended with some force. Zola's novels, like Sam Jones's sermons, may be medicine for the vicious classes. The danger is that, like the bottle of carbolic acid whose contents got by mistake into a boy's stomach near Boston the other day, and killed him, such books will fall into the hands of readers to whom they will prove poison and death. If books could be prescribed by authority, and taken in doses under regulation like other powerful agents, the dangerous among them could be circulated with far greater safety.

Emile Zola   Jules Lemaître*

There are some writers and artists whose intimate, delicate, subtle charm is very difficult to seize upon and fix in a formula. There are also some whose talent is a very rich amalgam, a happy equilibrium of contrary qualities; and it is not very easy to seize upon these latter either, or to define them with precision. But there are others in whom some one faculty is strongly predominant, in a brutal and extravagant manner, some inclination, some mania; they are a species of powerful, simple, and clear monsters, whose prominent features it is pleasant to draw in bold outlines. In their case we can do something that may be called criticizing in fresco.

M. Emile Zola is one of these vigorous "extremists," especially since *L'Assommoir*. But as it seems that he has but little knowledge of himself, as he has done all that he can to give the public an absolutely false idea of his work and talent, it is perhaps well, before seeking what he is, to say what he is not.

I

M. Zola is not a man of critical feeling, although he has written *Le Roman Expérimental*, or rather because he has written it; and M. Zola is not a veracious novelist, although that is his great claim.

It is impossible to imagine a more surprising equivocation, or one sustained and developed at greater length, than that which forms the basis of his volume on the *Roman Expérimental*. But there has been enough ridicule of that assimilation of a novel with a chemical experiment to make it useless to dwell upon it. It remains that, for M. Zola, the novel *ought* to cling more closely to reality than is possible. If this be advice, it is good but commonplace. If it be a dogma, we rise up against it and claim the liberty of art. If M. Zola thinks that he preaches by example, he is mistaken.

We are quite ready to recognize with M. Zola that many things in romanticism have grown old and appear ridiculous; that the works which interest us most to-day are those that issue from the observation of men as

*From A. W. Evans, trans., *Literary Impressions* (London: Daniel O'Connor, 1921), 108–53. Originally published in *Les Contemporains. Etudes et portraits littéraires*. Première série: 1884 et 1885 (Paris, 1886), 249–84.

they are, dragging a body about with them, living in conditions and in an "environment" whose influence they undergo. But M. Zola also knows well that the artist, in order to bring his models into the novel or on to the stage, is *forced* to choose, to retain only the expressive features of reality, and to arrange them in such a manner as to bring into relief the dominant character either of an environment or of a person. And then that is everything. What models ought one to take? To what degree ought one to choose, and therefore to curtail? This is a matter of taste and temperament. There are no laws for it; he who proclaims them is a false prophet. Art, even naturalist art, is a transformation of reality; by what right do you fix limits which it must not pass? Tell me why must I be only moderately pleased by *Indiana* or even by *Julia de Trécoeur* and *Méta Holdenis*. And what is this strange and pedantic tyranny which busies itself with ruling over my pleasures? Let us enlarge our sympathies (M. Zola himself will gain by this), and let us allow everything to the artist, except to be mediocre and tiresome. I will even allow him, when he groups his recollections, to imagine characters of whom reality presents no models, provided that those characters have unity and imitate men of flesh and bone in the particular logic that presides over their actions. I admit it without shame, I still love Lélia, I adore Consuelo, and I even put up with George Sand's workmen; they have a sort of truth, and express a part of the ideas and passions of their time.

Thus M. Zola, under colour of literary criticism, has never done more than erect his own personal taste into a principle; and this is a mark neither of a free nor of a liberal mind. And, unhappily, he has done it without grace, with an air of imperturbability, in the form of commandments to the youth of France. In this way he has irritated a number of worthy people, and has supplied them with such good reasons for not understanding him that they are very much to be excused for having used them. For this is what has happened. On the one hand, these worthy people have treated M. Zola's theories as absurd; but at the same time they have affected to take them literally, and they have pleased themselves by showing that those theories have not been applied in his novels. They have, therefore, condemned the novels for not having observed rules which they themselves had just condemned. They have said, for example: "Nana is not much like the courtesans one knows; your middle-class people in *Pot-Bouille* are still less like ordinary middle-class folk; moreover, your books are full of filth, and the proportion of what is ignoble in them is certainly greater than it is in real life; therefore, they are not of the slightest value." In brief, they have employed against M. Zola arms with which he himself has supplied them, and they want to make him bear the penalty of the theories which he has dinned into our ears.

This is, perhaps, fair war; but it is not just criticism, for M. Zola's novels could run contrary to his doctrines and none the less be fine works. I should like, therefore, to defend him (without asking his permission to do so) both against his "detractors" and against his own illusions. "It is false," they shout at him, "and it is squalid into the bargain." I should like candidly to show that if M. Zola's pictures are far-fetched and conceived according to a system, it is through this that they are imposing, and that if they are often horrible, perhaps they are horrible with some force, some grandeur, and some poetry.

M. Zola is not a critic, and he is not a "naturalist" novelist in the sense in which he means. But M. Zola is an epic poet and a pessimist poet. And that is especially evident in his latest novels.

I mean by a poet a writer who, by virtue of an idea or in view of an ideal, notably transforms reality, and makes it live when it has thus been modified. By this reckoning many novelists and dramatic authors are poets; but what is interesting is that M. Zola denies it, though he is more of one than anybody else.

If you compare M. Daudet with M. Zola, you will see that M. Daudet is the naturalistic novelist, not M. Zola; that it is the author of *Nabab* who begins with the observation of reality, and is, as it were, possessed by it, while the author of *L'Assommoir* only consults it when his plan has been formed, and then summarily and with preconceived ideas. The one lays hold of real and almost always unusual personages, then looks for an action which binds them together and which is, at the same time, the natural development of the character or passions of his principal actors. The other wishes to paint a class, a group, which he knows in the mass, and which he represents to himself in a particular manner before making any special study; he afterwards imagines a very simple and very broad drama in which masses can be moved and very general types fully shown. Thus M. Zola invents far more than he observes; he is a true poet if we take the word in its etymological sense, which is a little crude — and an idealist poet if we give the word the reverse of its habitual meaning. Let us see then what sort of bold simplification this poet applies to the painting of men, things, and their surroundings, and we shall not be far from knowing him in his entirety.

II

When he was quite young, in his *Contes à Ninon*, M. Zola showed but a moderate fondness for the "real truth," and willingly indulged in some caprices of a rather insipid poetry. He had certainly nothing of the "experimenter" in him. But he already lacked wit and gaiety, and here and there he showed himself to be a vigorous describer of concrete things by means of an unwearied accumulation of details.

Now that he has found his way and his *material*, he appears to us, more and more, as the sad and brutal poet of blind instincts, coarse passions, carnal loves, and the base and repugnant sides of human nature. What interests him in man is above all the animal, and in each human type the particular animal which this type contains. It is this which he loves to show, and it is the remainder which he eliminates, in contradiction to properly idealist novelists. Eugène Delacroix used to say that every human face, by a bold simplification of the features, by the exaggeration of some and the reduction of others, can be reduced to the face of an animal. It is quite in this way that M. Zola simplifies souls.

Nana presents a striking example of this simplification. What is she but the most general, and consequently the least inviting, *a priori* conception of the courtesan? Nana is not a Manon Lescaut or a Marguerite Gautier, nor is she a Madame Marneffe nor an Olympe Taverny. Nana is a beautiful animal with a magnificent and unwholesome body, stupid, without grace and without heart, neither evil nor good, irresistible by the sole power of her sex. She is the "earthly Venus" with "coarse vulgar limbs." She is woman reduced to her simplest and crudest expression. And see how by this the author escapes the reproach of intentional obscenity. Having conceived of his heroine in this way, he was condemned by the logic of things to write the book he has written; being neither intellectual, nor evil, nor passionate, Nana could only be from head to heel — what she is. And to make her alive, to explain the sort of attraction which she exercises on men, the conscientious artist was obliged to plunge into the details which you know. Add that it was hardly possible for there to be any dramatic interest or progress in those crude adventures of the flesh. The caprices of her senses do not mark the phases of a development or of an internal toil. Nana is as obscene and unalterable as the stone image which the girls of Babylon worshipped on certain days. And, greater than nature, also like that image, there is in her, at moments, something abstract and symbolical; the author raises the ignominy of his conception by a certain sombre hypothesis which makes an impersonal Nana hover over the whole of Paris, and by depriving her of shame as well as conscience, he endows her with the grandeur of natural and fatal forces. When M. Zola succeeds in investing this idea with a concrete form, as in the great picture of the horse-races, when Paris, yelling around Nana, seems to salute in her the queen of lasciviousness, and no longer to be certain whether it acclaims the woman or the horse, that is indeed idealist art and pure poetry.

Do you want examples, at first sight less convincing, but still more significant, of this way of conceiving of and constructing a character? You will find them in the *Bonheur des Dames* and the *Joie de Vivre*. Notice that these are two "virtuous" novels, that is to say, novels in which virtue is depicted and in which it is finally triumphant. But what virtue? The story of Denise, of that poor and careful girl who ends by marrying her employer, is the theme for a Sunday-school tale. Now look at what this Sunday-school tale becomes. If Nana is vicious in the manner of an animal, it is also as an animal that Denise is virtuous, it is thanks to her perfectly balanced temperament, to her splendid physical health. The author is determined that we shall not be mistaken about this, that we shall not accidentally take her for a heroine, nor believe that she is intentionally careful, and he comes back to this point I know not how many times. One could not imagine a more immodest picture of a virgin. And it is in the same way that Pauline is good and devoted. If she has to struggle for a moment, it is against a physiological influence, and it is not her will which triumphs, but her health. All this is quite distinctly stated. Thus, by the suppression of free will, by the elimination of the old foundation of classic psychology which consisted essentially in the struggle between the will and the passions, M. Zola succeeds in constructing characters of coarse and imposing beauty, worn and grandiose images of elementary forces — evil and homicidal like the plague, or good and beneficent like the sun and like spring.

Only all approach to subtle psychology disappears. M. Zola's greatest effort does not go beyond painting the unopposed progress of a fixed idea, of a mania or a vice. Either motionless or always dragged along in the same direction, such are his characters. Even when he deals with a very special, very modern case which appears to be essentially psychological, like that of Lazare in the *Joie de Vivre*, he finds some means of applying to it also, in the same spirit, his simplifying methods. He soon effaces the over-subtle shades of feeling or thought, clears away the complexities of mental maladies, and in them also finds the animal beneath the man! Lazare must doubtless represent a whole section of modern youth, so interesting in its need for rare sensations, its distaste for action, its depravity and enervation of will, its pedantic and perhaps sincere pessimism: now all Lazare's pessimism finally reduces itself to the physical fear of death; and just as Pauline is as devoted as a little dog, so Lazare's pessimism is that of a cowardly dog.

III

M. Zola employs the same method of audacious simplification in his general compositions. Let us take *Pot-Bouille* as an example, not that it is the best of his novels, but it is one of those in which his manner is most frankly displayed. Exaggerations which by simplifying reality give excessive proportion to some of its characters, are repeated on every ten pages. — There are the domestic servants of the house gossiping from window to window, in the smelling inner courtyard, about the doings of their employers, tearing aside the veils with obscene banter. There is the ironical antithesis between the decent gravity of the great staircase and what takes place behind the fine mahogany doors — this is repeated after every particularly ignoble scene, like the refrain of a ballad. And, just as the house has its great staircase and its mahogany doors, so Uncle Bachelard always has his red nose, Duveyrier his pimples, Madame Josserand her huge breast, Auguste Vabre his left eye drawn by headache; and little old Josserand has his bands, and old Vabre has his hooks, and

Clotilde has her piano. M. Zola uses and abuses this device of "particular signs." And everywhere we see him choosing, abstracting, exaggerating. If out of all the magistracy he has been able to take a Duveyrier (who, moreover, is hardly more a magistrate than a notary or a pork-butcher), and out of all the middle-class women in Paris a Madame Josserand, it is surely by a selection as bold as that by which M. Octave Feuillet's women are taken from the Faubourg Saint-Germain. Add to this another application of the same method which has enabled M. Zola to unite so many contemptible characters in a single house, and to choose that particular house out of all the houses in Paris.

Thus conventions abound. Not a figure which is not *exaggerated* either in its ignominy or its dullness; their very grouping is an *exceptional* fact; the least details have been visibly *chosen* under the empire of a single tenacious idea, which is to humiliate humanity and to make it still more ugly with the ugliness of unconscious and base vices. So true is this that after a time the falseness of certain details no longer shocks one, no longer even appears in the general exaggeration. One has beneath one's eyes the hard and coarse picture, unnaturally large but harmonious and even monotonous, of middle-class squalor, lust, and stupidity; a picture more than ideal, sibylline and almost apocalyptic in its continuous violence. In it the middle classes are "the Beast." The house in the Rue de Choiseul becomes a "temple" where infamous mysteries are performed in secret. M. Gourd, the janitor, is its "beadle." The Abbé Maudit, melancholy and polished, is its "master of the ceremonies," having as his function "to cover with the mantle of religion the wounds of this decomposed world" and "to regulate the proper order of its stupidities and its vices." At one moment—the caprice of a coarse and mystical imagination—the image of the bleeding Christ rises above this cess-pool. The Vabre building becomes a sort of enormous and symbolical vision. The author ends by lending his own magnifying vision to his characters. The proprietor has let a garret to a pregnant girl, and this woman's belly becomes an obsession to M. Gourd. That belly "seems to him to throw its shadow over the cold propriety of the courtyard . . . and to fill the building with something shameful which gave an uncomfortable feeling to the walls." "At first," he explains, "this was hardly visible; that was possible; I did not say much about it. I hoped she would show some discretion. Well! I watched it, it grew visibly larger, it dismayed me by its rapid growth. And look, look, to-day! She does nothing to reduce it, she gives it full scope . . . A house like ours made a show of by such a belly!" These are unexpected images and grace-notes on the lips of a porter. A strange world in which janitors speak like poets, and all the other people like janitors!

Go through the *Rougon-Macquart* series. You will find in almost all of M. Zola's novels (and certainly in all the latter ones) something similar to that wonderful house in the Rue de Choiseul, some inanimate thing, a forest, a sea, a public-house, or a shop, which serves as the theatre or centre of the drama; which takes on a superhuman and terrible life; which personifies some natural or social force superior to individuals, and which at last assumes the aspect of a monstrous Beast, a devourer of souls and a devourer of men. The Beast in *Nana* is Nana herself. In *La Faute de L'Abbé Mouret* the Beast is the park of Paradou, that fantastic forest where everything blooms at the same time, where all odours are mingled, where are assembled all the amorous powers of Cybele, and which, like a divine and irresistible procuress, throws Serge and Albine into one another's arms, and then lulls the little fawness to sleep with its deadly perfumes. In *Le Ventre de Paris* it is the huge size of the Central Markets which causes a copious animal life to flourish about them, and terrifies and submerges the frail and dreamy Florent. In *L'Assommoir* it is old Colombe's public-house with its tin counter and its copper still, like the neck of some mysterious and malevolent animal, that pours over the workmen brutalizing drunkenness, idleness, anger, lust, and unconscious vice. In *Le Bonheur des Dames* it is Mouret's shop, a temple of modern commerce, where the employees deprave and infatuate the women purchasers, a formidable living machine which grinds the smaller shop-keepers in its cog-wheels and devours them. In *La Joie de Vivre* it is the Ocean, at first the accomplice of Lazare's loves and ambitions, then his enemy, whose victory completely ruins the weak head of that disciple of Schopenhauer. M. Zola excels in giving to things some quiverings, as it were, of that soul part of which he takes away from men, and, whilst he gives an almost human life to a forest, a market-place, a wine-seller's counter, or a shop, he reduces the sad and base creatures who move within them to an almost animal life.

But, whatever that life may be, though it be incomplete and truncated, he makes them live; he has this, the greatest of gifts. And not only the principal figures, but minor and subsidiary characters become animate under the large hands of this modeller of animals. Doubtless they live at little cost, most often by virtue of some coarse and energetic special sign; but they live, each apart and all together. For he also knows how to animate groups, how to put masses in movement. There is in almost all the novels, around the protagonists, a quantity of secondary characters, a *servum pecus* who often march in a band, who form the background of the scene; but who detach themselves and take part in the dialogue at intervals like a tragic chorus. There is the chorus of horrible peasants in *La Faute de l'Abbé Mouret*; the chorus of the friends and relations of Coupeau in *L'Assommoir*; the chorus of servants in *Pot-Bouille*; the chorus of employees and that of small shopkeepers in *Le Bonheur des Dames*; the chorus of fishermen and that of beggars in *La Joie de Vivre*. Through these the leading figures are mingled with a large portion of humanity; and since this humanity, as we have seen, is itself mingled with the life of things, there emerges from these vast combinations an impression of life, almost uniquely bestial and material, but swarming with living beings, profound, vast and unlimited.

IV

This impression is a sad one, and M. Zola wishes it thus. Never perhaps has a pessimistic determination been carried to such excesses. And the evil has only gone on increasing since his first novels. At least in the early stages of this miry epic poem, one still saw something like the intoxication of antique naturalism (exasperated, it is true, by the Christian notion of sin and by modern "nervousness"). In the exuberant pastoral of Miette and Silvère (*La Fortune des Rougon*), in the Paradisiacal nuptials of the Abbé Mouret and Albine, even in the bestial idyll of Cadine and Marjolin among the heaps of beans in the markets, M. Zola appeared at least to glorify physical love and its works. But he now seems to have a hatred and terror of all this flesh by which he is obsessed. He seeks to humiliate it; he lingers in the lower depths of human nature, amid all that is most insulting to human pride in the play of the forces of blood and nerves. He digs out and displays the secret deformities of the flesh and its secret vileness. He multiplies around adultery the circumstances that degrade it, that make it vulgar and disgusting (*Une Page d'Amour* and *Pot-Bouille*). He spurns love, reduces it to a tyrannical need and a squalid function (*Pot-Bouille*). The greater part of his novels is an impassioned commentary on the words *surgit amari aliquid*. Of woman he sees no more than the defiling mysteries of her sex (*Pot-Bouille* and *La Joie de Vivre*). With the sombre ardour of a fakir, he curses life at its source and man in his mother's womb. In man he sees the brute, in love copulation, in maternity obstetrics. Slowly and sadly he stirs up the secretions, the humours, all that is kept hidden in physical humanity. What a horrible and lamentable picture is that of the way "that slut Adèle" spends her nights! And what a pathological drama, how like the dream of some embittered medical student, is the atrocious confinement of Louise in *La Joie de Vivre!*

And neither clinical horrors nor moral putrefaction are enough for him, although there is a complete collection of them, going from the loves of Maxime to those of Léon Josserand, and passing through the fantasies of Baptiste, of Satin, of the little Angèle, and of the thin Lisa. He must have curious physiological states such as the case of Théophile Vabre or that of Madame Campardon. The mine is inexhaustible, and if he must now combine corporal infirmities with lusts and follies, the story of the Rougon-Macquarts will yet have fine chapters in it.

Thus bestiality and imbecility are in M. Zola's eyes man's very essence. His work presents to us so prodigious a mass of beings who are either idiots or a prey to the "sixth sense," that there exhales from it — like a miasma or the reek from a dung-heap — for most readers a feeling of profound disgust, for others one of black and heavy sadness. How shall we explain this strange determination of the author of *Pot-Bouille*? Shall we say that he likes force above all things, and that nothing is stronger than that which is blind, nothing is stronger than the instincts of animalism, nor than exhaustion and impotence (thus he has far more brutes than scoundrels), and nothing is more invariable, more formidable by its eternity, its universality, and its unconsciousness than stupidity? Or rather, does not M. Zola, in truth, see the world as he paints it? Yes, there is in him the pessimism of a tempted ascetic, and, before the flesh and its adventures, a morose intoxication which invades his whole being, and which he could not shake off even if he would. If it is true that the men of the present day reproduce, with more complication, the types of past ages, M. Zola has been, in the early Middle Ages, a very chaste and very serious monk, but with too healthy and too vigorous an imagination, who saw the devil in everything, and who cursed the corruption of his time in obscene and hyperbolical language.

It is therefore a great injustice to accuse M. Zola of immorality, or to believe that he speculates on the bad instincts of readers. In the midst of low obscenities, among visions of places of ill-fame or of clinical studies, he remains grave. If he accumulates certain details, be sure that with him it is a matter of conscience. As he claims to paint reality, and as he is persuaded that it is ignoble, he shows it to us thus, with the scruples of a soul which is delicate in its own way, which does not want to deceive us, and which gives us good measure. Sometimes he forgets himself, he brushes in vast pictures from which the ignominy of the flesh is absent; but suddenly a remorse seizes him; he remembers that the Beast is everywhere, and, in order not to fail in his duty, at the moment when this is least expected he slips in a lewd detail and as it were a *memento* of the universal filth. These species of *repentances* are especially remarkable in the development of the characters of Denise and Pauline (*Au Bonheur des Dames* and *La Joie de Vivre*). And, as I have said, a frightful melancholy exhales from all this physiological movement.

V

If the impression is sad, it is powerful. I compliment those subtle and delicate spirits for whom measure, decency, and correction are so essentially all a writer requires, that, even after *La Conquête de Plassans*, *La Faute de l'Abbé Mouret*, *L'Assommoir*, and *La Joie de Vivre*, they hold M. Zola in slight literary esteem, and tell him to go back to school because his classical studies have not been thorough, and perhaps he does not always write perfectly well. I could not rise to so distinguished a judgment. If one refuses everything else to M. Zola, is it possible to deny him creative power, restricted if you will, but prodigious in the domain in which it is exercised? Struggle against it as I may, even those brutalities impress me, I do not know how, by their number, and those obscenities by their mass. With the regular efforts of a grime-stained Hercules, M. Zola arranges in heaps the dung of the Augean stables (it has even been said that he has added to it).

One is amazed and alarmed by its size, and by the labour that has been needed to make so fine a heap. One of M. Zola's virtues is indefatigable and patient vigour. He has an excellent vision of concrete things, of all the external side of life, and he possesses a special faculty for representing what he sees — the power of retaining and accumulating greater quantity of details than any other describer of the same school, and of doing this coldly and calmly, without lassitude or disgust, and of giving to all things the same clear and crude prominence. So that the unity of each picture no longer consists, as is the case with the classics, in the subordination of details (which in their case were not numerous) to the whole, but, if I may so express myself, in their interminable monochrome. Yes, this artist has a marvellous power of piling things up so as to produce a single effect. I am quite ready to believe what is told of him, that he always writes at the same rate and fills the same number of pages every day. He constructs a book as a mason builds a wall, by putting unhewn stones one on top of the other, without hurrying, indefinitely. That is certainly fine in its own way, and it is perhaps one of the forms of that prolonged patience of which Buffon speaks, which is genius. This gift, joined to the others, at all events, gives him a robust originality.

Nevertheless, many people persist in refusing him the quality which, it is said, preserves works — style. But here it is first of all necessary to distinguish between his critical or polemical works and his novels. The books in which he had to give expression to abstract ideas are, in truth, not always well written, whether it be that the embarrassment and ambiguity of thought communicate themselves to the style, or that M. Zola is naturally incapable of rendering ideas with complete exactness. The form of his novels is much more defensible. But even in these it is necessary to distinguish. M. Zola has never been an impeccable writer nor very sure with his pen; but in his early novels (up to *Nana*, it seems to me) he took more trouble with his writing; his style was more wrought and richer. There are, even if we consider nothing but the form, some truly fine pages, of great brilliancy and quite pure enough, in *La Fortune des Rougon* and in *La Faute de l'Abbé Mouret*. Since *Nana*, at the same time as under the pretext of truth he more and more forgets decency, one can say that under colour of simplicity and out of hatred of romanticism (which is at once his father and his pet aversion) he has set himself to despise style a little, to write much more quickly, in a manner that is "more fine and large," without bothering much about the details of his phrasing. In both of these two manners, but especially in the second, it is not difficult to find faults that are offensive enough and that are particularly cruel to those who are accustomed to converse with the classics, to those who have had a good university education, to old professors who know their own speech well — improprieties of language, strange incongruities, a surprising mixture of far-fetched expressions, "poetic" expressions as they used to be called, and low or trivial phrases, certain bad

habits of style, sometimes inaccuracies, and above all, a continual straining; never any of the more delicate shades or any refinement. Yes, all this
is true, and I am very sorry for it. But, in the first place, it is not true
everywhere, far from it. And then as everything in the novels is constructed on a large scale, intended to be comprehended at once and
without close examination, we must not cavil over phrases, but take them
as they have been written, in blocks and in large sections, and judge the
worth of the style by the total effect of the picture. You will admit that,
upon the whole, such a heap of phrases, though all of them are not
irreproachable, yet end by giving us a vast and impressive vision of the
objects, and that this magnifying style, without any of the finer shades,
and sometimes without precision, is eminently suitable, by its monotonous
exaggerations and its multiplied insistences, for rendering with grandeur
the great and general effect of concrete things.

VI

Germinal, the last novel that has appeared, marvellously confirms
the description of M. Zola's work which I have attempted. Everything
which I thought I saw in the former novels abounds in *Germinal*, and one
can say that never have either M. Zola's moroseness and his epic faculty, or
the methods which they imply and whose use they demand, been more
powerfully employed than in that imposing and sombre book.

The subject is very simple — it is the story of a strike, or rather it is the
poem of *the* strike. Some miners, as a result of a measure that seems to
them to be unjust, refuse to go down into the pits. Hunger exasperates
them to pillage and murder. Order is restored by the troops. On the day
that the workers go down again, the mine is flooded and some of the
leading characters are drowned. This last catastrophe, the deed of an
anarchist workman, is the only feature which distinguishes this strike from
so many others.

It is thus the story, not of a man or of some men, but of a multitude. I
do not know any novel in which such masses are made to live and move, at
one moment it crawls and swarms, at another it is carried along in a dizzy
movement by the urge of blind instincts. The poet, with his robust
patience, with his gloomy brutality, with his power of evocation, unrolls a
series of vast and lamentable pictures, composed of monochrome details
which pile up, pile up, ascend and spread out like a tide — a day in the
mine, a day in the workmen's dwellings, a meeting of the strikers in a
clearing of the woods, the furious rush of three thousand unhappy souls
over the flat country, the impact of this mass against the soldiers, ten days
of lingering death in the flooded mine. . . .

M. Zola has given a magnificent rendering of all that is fatal, blind,
impersonal, irresistible in a drama of this sort, the contagion of assembled
anger, the violent and easily enraged collective soul of the crowd. He often

collects the scattered heads into one formidable mass, and this is the sort of breath he pours forth:

> The women appeared, nearly a thousand women, with dishevelled hair, loosened by the journey, in rags showing their bare skin, the nakedness of women weary of giving birth to starvelings. Some of them held their little one in their arms, lifting it up and moving it like a flag of mourning and of vengeance. Others, younger, with the inflated throats of female warriors, brandished sticks, while the old women howled so loudly that the tendons of their fleshless necks seemed to break. And the men sprung out afterwards, two thousand furious men, haulers, hewers, menders, a compact mass which advanced in a single block, crowded together and so mixed up that one could not see either their faded breeches or their tattered woollen vests which were effaced in the same dirty uniformity. Their eyes burned; one only saw the holes of dark mouths singing the *Marseillaise*, the verses of which were lost in confused bellowings accompanied by the rattle of clogs on the hard ground. Above their heads, amid bristling bars of iron, an axe was carried along, borne upright, and this single axe, which was as it were the standard of the band, looked in the clear sky like the profile of the blade of a guillotine.

> Anger, hunger, those two months of suffering, and this wild, helter-skelter rush over the fields had lengthened the placid faces of the Montsou colliers into the jaws of wild beasts. At this moment the sun was setting; its last rays, of a sombre purple, stained the plain with the colour of blood. Then the journey seemed to be a drift of blood; the women and men continued to run on, bleeding like butchers in a slaughter-yard.

However, the drama had to be concentrated on some individuals. Accordingly, the poet has shown us, on the side of the workers, the Maheu family and their "lodger," Etienne, and on the side of the Company, the Hennebeau family, and about forty secondary figures in both camps; but always there is the swarming and growling multitude around those figures. Etienne himself, the leader of the strike, is himself dragged onward more than he drags on others.

The heads which emerge for a moment and which can be distinguished from the crowd are those of Maheu, a worthy fellow, a thoughtful, resigned, and reasonable man who little by little becomes a fanatic; the woman Maheus [*sic*], with Estelle, her latest born, *always* hanging at her pale breast, the woman whose man and whose children are killed by hunger, by the soldiers' guns, and by the mine, and who appears at the end like a *Mater Dolorosa*, a stupid and terrible Niobe; Catherine, who plays the part of young girl in this dark epic, always wearing the trousers of a labourer, who has the sort of beauty, modesty, and charm that she can have; Chaval, the traitor, who is *always* "mouthing"; Etienne, the Socialist workman, of rather more refined a nature than his companions, with his sudden outbursts of anger, and the alcoholism which he has inherited from Gervaise Coupeau; Alzire, the little hunchback, so gentle, and *always* acting the part of a little woman; old Mouque, who only speaks once, and old Bonnemort, who is *always* spitting out tobacco juice, Rasseneur, the old workman who has become a publican, a fat, unctuous, and prudent revolutionist; Pluchart, the itinerant Socialist lecturer, *always* hoarse and hurried; Maigrat, the grocer, a sort of Pasha who pays himself out of the miners' wives and daughters; Mouquette, the good girl, and simple-minded prostitute; the sly Pierrone, who has the regular character- istics of a prostitute; Jeanlin, the wretched marauder with his broken paws and freckles, his projecting ears and his green eyes, who treacherously kills a young soldier, for nothing, instinctively, and for the sake of pleasure; Lydie and Bébert, *always* terrorized by Jeanlin; Brulé, the old woman whose husband has been killed by the mine, *always* moaning and shaking her witch-like arms; Hennebeau, the manager, a cold and exact official, with a wound in his heart, a husband tormented by a Messalina who refuses herself to nobody but him; Négrel, the brown little engineer, brave and sceptical and his aunt's lover; Deneulin, the energetic and adventur- ous man of business; the Grégoires, comfortable and easy shareholders, and Cécile, and Jeanne, and Lucie, and Levaque, and Bouteloup, and old Quandieu, and Jules, the little soldier; and the old horse, Bataille, "fat and shining with an air of good-nature," and the young horse, Trompette, haunted in the depth of the mine by a vision of meadows and sunshine (for M. Zola loves animals and endows them with at least as much soul as men — remember the dog, Mathieu, and the cat, Minouche, in *La Joie de Vivre*); and apart from all this world, the Russian Souvarine, fair and with a girl's features, *always* silent, contemptuous, and gentle — all figures strongly marked by a "particular sign" the mention of which returns regularly, who stand upright and come to life in some way that I do not know, almost by the sole virtue of that repeated sign.

Their life is above all an external life; but the drama which M. Zola has conceived does not require more psychology than he can give to it. The soul of such a mass consists of very simple instincts. The inferior beings who hold a subordinate position in the book, are moved, as they ought to be, by physical necessities, and by very crude ideas which become *images*, and which at length fascinate them and make them act. "All misfortune disappeared as if driven away by a great flash of sunlight, and, as if by fairy enchantment, justice descended from Heaven. . . . A new society sprang up as in dreams in a day, an immense city as splendid as a mirage, in which each citizen lived by his own toil and took his share in the common joys." The inner life even of Etienne ought to be reduced to a very simple matter, for he is hardly superior to his companions — aspirations towards absolute justice, confused ideas as to the means of achieving it; sometimes the pride of thinking more than the rest, and sometimes an almost avowed feeling of his own incapacity; the pedantry of the workman who has read, and the discouragement that follows enthusiasm; middle-class tastes and intellectual feelings mingling with his apostle's fervour. This is all, and it is enough. As for Souvarine, it is with deliberate intention that M. Zola leaves him enigmatical, and only shows us the external side of him — his anarchism is only there in order to form a striking contrast with the uncertain and sentimental Socialism of the French workman, and in order to prepare for the final catastrophe. It is said, perhaps with truth, that M. Zola does not possess to a high degree the gift of entering into souls, of analysing them, of noting the origin and progress of ideas and feelings within them, or the way in which they echo a thousand external influences: so he has here desired not to write the story of a soul, but that of a crowd.

And it is not a drama of feelings either, that he has wished to write, but a drama of sensations, an entirely material drama. The feelings are reduced to instincts or something close to them, and the sufferings are especially physical sufferings, as when Jeanlin has his legs broken, when little Alzire dies of hunger, when Catherine climbs two thousand feet of stairs, or when she dies in the pit in Etienne's arms, close by Chaval's corpse. It will be said that it is easy to stir the heart or to jangle the nerves at such a cost, and that this is the crudest melodrama. Do you think so? But these deaths and these tortures are drama itself, for M. Zola had no intention of composing a psychological tragedy. And there is more than the description of atrocious spectacles; there are the novelist's gloomy pity and compassion which a determination based on the philosophy of pessimism turns into an impassibility that is cruel for us as well as for him. He is not one of those to whom moral pain is nobler than physical suffering. In what is it more noble, since our feelings are as involuntary as our sensations? And then, let us be sincere, and is it not the suffering of the body that is the most terrible? And is it not above all this suffering that makes the world so miserable?

And for those holocausts of flesh there are the executioner and the god, both of them 'Beasts." The executioner is the mine, the beast that devours men. The god is that mysterious being to whom the mine belongs and who grows fat on the hunger of the miners; he is a monstrous and invisible idol, crouching somewhere, one knows not where, like the God Mithra in his sanctuary. And the two beasts are regularly evoked in turn, the beast that kills, and the other, the beast that causes her to kill. And at intervals we hear the "heavy and long respiration" of the beast that kills (it is the noise of the exhaust pump). She lives, she is so much alive that at last she dies:

> And then a frightful thing was seen; one saw the machine, dismembered in its whole body, its limbs torn to pieces, struggling against death. It moved, it stretched out its connecting-rod, its giant's knee, as if to stand up; but it expired, broken and engulfed. Its chimney alone, ninety feet high, remained upright though shaken, like a mast in a hurricane. One thought that it was going to crumble and fly into dust,

when suddenly it subsided in a single block, swallowed up by the earth, melted like a colossal candle, and nothing remained on top, not even the point of the lightning-conductor. It was ended; the evil beast, crouching in those hollows, gorged with human flesh, no longer drew her long and heavy breath. The entire Voreux had just fallen into the pit.

And how many other symbolical evocations there are! The bloody rag torn away by the women from Maigrat, is also an evil beast that is finally crushed and trampled and spat upon. Old Bonnemort, idiotic, deformed, and hideous, strangling the plump, fair, and gentle Cécile Grégoire, is ancient and irresponsible Hunger hurling herself with fatal spring upon irresponsible Idleness. And every moment, by methods that are frankly and ingenuously displayed, but that hold us nevertheless, the poet, in a sinister manner, mingles nature with his pictures in order to heighten them and make them the more horrible. The miners' meeting is held before a background of pale moonlight, and the journey of the three thousand desperate men and women is performed in the blood-stained light of the setting sun. And it is with a symbol that the book ends. Etienne leaves the mine on a spring morning, one of those mornings when the "buds are bursting into green leaves" and when the fields are "trembling with the growth of the grass." At the same time he hears deep blows underneath his feet, the blows of his comrades tapping in the mine: "Still, still, more and more distinctly, as if they were drawing closer to the soil, his comrades kept on tapping. Under the kindled stars, on this morning of youth, it was with this murmur that the countryside was big. Men were growing; a black, avenging army was sprouting in the furrows, growing for the harvest of a future age whose germination was soon to burst through the earth." And hence the title of the book.

What does this enigmatic end mean? What is this future revolution? Is it the pacific accession of the disinherited or the destruction of the old world? Is it the reign of justice or the long-delayed feast of the greatest number? This is mystery, or is it merely rhetoric? For the rest of the novel does not contain an atom of hope or of illusion. I recognize, moreover, M. Zola's lofty impartiality. The great exploiters are not seen and do not see. We only perceive the Grégoires, small shareholders, worthy people whose daughter is killed by the exploited. And as for Hennebeau, the manager, he is as much to be pitied as the starving workmen. "Beneath the window groans burst forth with redoubled violence: 'Bread! Bread! Bread!' – 'You fools,' said M. Hennebeau from between his clenched teeth; 'am I happy?' "

Suffering and despair from top to bottom! But at least these wretches have the animal Venus to console them. They "love" like dogs, pell-mell, everywhere, at every hour. There is a chapter in which one cannot take a single step without walking upon couples. And this is astonishing enough in the case of dull-blooded men, broken down by toil, in a cold and rainy district. They "love" in the depths of the flooded mine, and it is after six days of agony in it that Etienne becomes Catherine's lover. And I would prefer that he had not become her lover, the instinctive modesty which they felt in one another's presence being almost the sole vestige of higher humanity which the writer has allowed to exist in his bestial poem.

Here and there in this epic of pain, hunger, lust, and death, there breaks forth the lamentation of Hennebeau, which gives the moral of the story and obviously expresses M. Zola's thought. "A terrible bitterness poisoned his mouth . . . *the uselessness of everything, the eternal pain of existence.*"

> Who was the fool who said that the happiness of this world lay in the division of wealth? If those revolutionary visionaries could demolish society and build up another, they would not add a joy to humanity, they would not take away a pain from it, by each of them cutting off his own slice of cake. They would even extend the earth's misery, they would one day make the very dogs howl with despair, when they had left the tranquil satisfaction of the instincts and risen to the unsatiated suffering of the passions. No, the only good was not to exist, and if one did exist, to be a tree, to be a stone, to be still less, to be the grain of sand which did not bleed under the heel of those who passed over it.

A band of wretches, roused by hunger and instinct, attracted by a crude dream, moved by fatal forces, and advancing in whirls and eddies to break themselves against a superior force — that is the drama. Men appearing like waves on a sea of darkness and unconsciousness — that is the very simple philosophical vision into which the drama resolves itself. M. Zola leaves it to the psychologists to write the monograph of each of those waves and to make of them a centre, and as it were a microcosm. He has only an imagination for vast material wholes, and infinite external details. But I ask myself whether anybody has ever had this in the same degree,

VII

I repeat in conclusion, and with greater confidence after having read *Germinal*, was I not right to call M. Zola an epic poet? And are not the dominant characters in these long narratives precisely those of epic poetry? With a little good-will, and by straining words a little, one could maintain and carry further this comparison, and there would be a great basis of truth beneath the artifice of this rhetorical game.

The subject of the epic is a national subject, interesting to a whole people, intelligible to a whole race. The subjects chosen by M. Zola are always very general, can be understood by everybody, have nothing special, exceptional, "curious" — the story of a family of workmen who sink into drunkenness, of a courtesan who fascinates and ruins men, of a prudent girl who ends by marrying her employer, a strike of miners, etc., and all these narratives together have at least the pretension of forming the typical history of a single family. The *Rougon-Macquart* history is thus, as in an epic poem, the collective history of an epoch.

The characters in epic poetry are not less general than the subject, and, as they represent vast groups, they appear to be larger than in nature. It is the same with M. Zola's characters, although this is reached by a contrary method. Whilst the old poets endeavour to deify their figures, we have seen that he animalizes his. But this even adds to the epic appearance; for he manages, through the falsehood of this reduction, to give to modern figures the simplicity of primitive types. He sets masses in motion, as in epic poetry. And the *Rougon-Macquart* series has also its marvels. In epic poetry the gods were originally the personifications of natural forces. M. Zola lends to those forces, either freely let loose or disciplined by human industry, a terrifying life, the beginnings of a soul, an obscure and monstrous will. The marvels in the *Rougon-Macquart* series are Paradou, old Colombe's dram-shop, Octave Mouret's shop, the mine in *Germinal*.

There is an artless and rudimentary philosophy in epic poetry. It is the same with the *Rougon-Macquart* series. The only difference is that the wisdom of the old poets is generally optimistic, and consoles and ennobles man as much as it can, whilst that of M. Zola is black and desperate. But in both there is the same simplicity, the same artlessness of conception. Finally and especially, the procedure of M. Zola's novels is, I know not how, that of the ancient epics, by the slow power, the broad sweep, the tranquil accumulation of details, the absolute frankness of the narrator's methods. He no more hurries than Homer does. He is as much interested (in another spirit) in Gervaise's kitchen as the old singer is in that of Achilles. He is not afraid of repetitions; the same phrases return in the same words, and from time to time we hear the "snoring" of the shop in *Le Bonheur des Dames*, the "heavy and prolonged breathing" of the machine in *Germinal* as in the *Iliad* we hear the moaning of the sea, πολυφλοσβοῖο θαλάσσης.

If then we gather up all that we have said, it will not appear too absurd to define the *Rougon-Macquart* series as a pessimist epic of human animalism.

La Terre: To Emile Zola

Paul Bonnetain,
J.-H. Rosny, Lucien Descaves,
Paul Margueritte, Gustave Guiches*

Not so long ago it was still possible for Zola to write, without raising serious recriminations, that literary youth was on his side. Too few years

*From *Documents of Modern Literary Realism* (Princeton, N.J.: Princeton University Press, 1963), 345–49. Translated by George J. Becker. The article originally appeared in *Le Figaro*, 18 August 1887. Reprinted by permission of Princeton University Press.

had passed since the appearance of *L'Assommoir*, since the vigorous polemics which consolidated the basis of Naturalism, for the rising generation to think of revolt. Even those of them who were particularly weary of the irritating repetition of clichés remembered too well the impetuous breach made by the great writer and his routing of the romantics.

We had seen him so strong, so superbly stubborn, so audacious that our generation, nearly all of us caught in a sickness of the will, revered him if only for that strength, that perseverance, that audacity. Even his peers, even his predecessors, the original masters who had long prepared the way for the battle, were patient in recognition of past services.

However, even on the morrow of *L'Assommoir*, serious errors were committed. It seemed to the young that the master, after giving things a push, was losing ground in the manner of those revolutionary generals whose bellies make demands which their brains encourage. They had hoped for better than to sleep on the field of battle; they awaited the results of this outburst of energy; they hoped for a fine infusion of life into books and into the theatre and a stop to the decay of art.

He, however, went on deepening his furrow; he went on tirelessly, and youth followed him, accompanying him with the applause and sympathy which are so sweet even to the most stoical beings; he went on and the oldest and wisest henceforth closed their eyes, wishing to deceive themselves and avoid seeing the master's plow mired in ordure.

Certainly it was a painful surprise to see Zola desert and migrate to Médan, turning his energies — though minimally at that time — which could have been used in works to advance and consolidate the battle to satisfactions of an infinitely less aesthetic order. No matter; youth was willing to pardon the physical desertion of the man! But a more terrible kind of desertion was already becoming evident: the treason of the writer to his work.

Zola in fact every day more deeply betrayed his program. Incredibly lazy in carrying out *personal experiment*, armed with trumpery documentation gathered at second hand, full of Hugoesque turgidity — which was all the more irritating in that he was sharply preaching simplicity — collapsing into repetitions and endless clichés, he disconcerted even the most enthusiastic of his disciples.

Moreover, even the least perspicacious had finally come to see the ridiculousness of that so-called *Natural and Social History of a Family under the Second Empire*, the tenuous nature of the thread of heredity, the childishness of the famous genealogical tree, and the profound ignorance of the Master in things medical and scientific.

No matter; they refused, even among themselves, to make an outright statement of their disappointment. There were some "Perhaps he should have . . .", "Don't you think a little less . . .", and all the timid observations of disappointed Levites who did not wish to push to the very bottom of their disillusionment. It was hard to give up the banner! And even the most daring went no further than to whisper that after all Zola was not Naturalism and that study of real life *had not been invented* after Balzac, Stendhal, Flaubert, and the Goncourts; but nobody dared to write down this heresy.

However, this disheartened feeling obdurately increased, especially as a result of the growing exaggeration of indecency in the use of dirty words in the *Rougon-Macquart*. It was vain to excuse everything on the basis of the principle set forth in the preface to *Thérèse Raquin*: "I do not know if my novel is moral or immoral; I admit that I never concerned myself about making it more or less chaste. What I know is that I never thought for a moment about putting in it the dirtiness that moral people find there; this is because I wrote every scene, even the most heightened ones, with pure scientific curiosity."

They asked only to believe this, and indeed some of the young writers had, out of a need to exasperate the middle class, exaggerated the *curiosity of the scientist*. But it was becoming impossible to be satisfied with such arguments: the sharp, irrestible *feeling* of everyone before certain pages of the *Rougon-Macquart* was no longer one of the brutality of a document but of a violent penchant for obscenity.

Then while some attributed this to an illness of the writer's lower organs, to the manias of the solitary monk, others preferred to see it as an *unconscious* development of an insatiable appetite for sales, as *instinctive* canniness on the part of the novelist in perceiving that his big success in repeated printings depended on the fact that "the imbeciles buy the *Rougon-Macquart*, caught not so much by their literary quality as by the reputation for pornography which the popular voice has given them."

Now it is very true that Zola seems excessively concerned with sales (and those of us who have heard him talk are well aware of this); but it is also well-known that he early lived a life of isolation and exaggerated continency, first by necessity, later by principle. As a young man he was very poor and very timid with women, whom he did not experience at the age when he should have and who haunted him with a vision that was evidently false. The difficulty in maintaining balance which comes from the illness of his loins no doubt contributes to his being excessively concerned with certain functions and impels him to magnify their importance. Perhaps Charcot, Moreau (of Tours), and the doctors of the Salpêtrière Hospital who have given us studies of coprolaliacs might be able to hit upon the symptoms of his illness. And to these sickly causes should we not add the anxiety so frequently observed among misogynists, as well as among very young men, as to their competence in matters of love-making?

However that may be, until very recently people have shown themselves to be indulgent; fearful whisperings were quieted with a promise: *La Terre*. They gladly waited on the struggle of the great writer with some high subject in the expectation that he would decide to abandon a worn-out soil. They liked to imagine Zola living among the peasants, heaping up *personal documents*, intimate documents, patiently analyzing the rural temperament, in short, beginning once again the superb work of *L'Assommoir*. Hope of a masterpiece stilled all tongues. Certainly the subject, simple and broad, gave promise of interesting revelations.

La Terre appeared. The disappointment has been profound and painful. Not only is the observation superficial, the devices outmoded, the narration ordinary and flat, but dirtiness is carried still further, going so low as at times to make you think you are reading a collection of scatology: the Master has gone down to the very depths of uncleanness.

Very well, that is the end of the adventure! We vigorously repudiate this imposture of true literature, this effort toward the spicy and salacious concocted by a brain sick for success. We repudiate those good fellows decked out in Zolaesque rhetoric, those enormous, superhuman, and misshapen silhouettes which, divested of complication, are thrown brutally in heavy masses into a setting casually glimpsed through the window of an express train. Resolutely, though not without sadness, we turn away from this latest work of the great mind which gave *L'Assommoir* to the world, from this bastard *La Terre*. It pains us to push away the man whom we have too warmly loved.

Our protest is the outcry of probity, the dictate of conscience on the part of young men anxious to defend their works — good or bad — against possible identification with the aberrations of the Master. We would willingly have waited longer, but we have no more time; tomorrow it will be too late. We are convinced that *La Terre* is not the ephemeral falling-off of a great man but the last stage in a series of descents, the irremediable morbid depravity of a chaste man. We can expect nothing from the *Rougon-Macquart* hereafter; we are all too able to foresee what the novels on the Railroads and on the Army will be like: the famous genealogical tree spreads out its sickly arms and will henceforth bear no fruit.

Now let it be clearly stated once again that no hostility brings us to make this protest. We should have found it pleasant to watch the great man pursue his career in peace. Even the decline of his talent is not the motive that animates us; it is the compromising anomaly of that decline. There are surrenders of principle which cannot be borne: we can no longer stand for the spontaneous labeling as realistic of every book which is drawn from reality. We would bravely face any persecution in defense of a just cause: we refuse to have any part in a shameful degeneration.

It is the misfortune of men who stand for a doctrine that it becomes impossible to spare them when they compromise that doctrine. Then what is to be said to Zola, who has provided so many examples of a frankness that was often brutal? Did he not celebrate the *struggle for life, struggle* in its simple form, incompatible with the instincts of a developed race, *struggle* authorizing violent attacks? "I am a force," he shouted, crushing both friends and enemies, closing to those who came after him the breach in the wall which he himself had opened.

For our part, full of admiration for the immense talent which the man has often displayed, we deny any idea of disrespect. But is it our fault if the celebrated formula: "A corner of nature seen through a temperament," has been transformed with respect to Zola into "a corner of nature seen through a *morbid sensory apparatus*," and if it is our duty to take the hatchet to his works? It is imperative that the judgment of the public aim straight at *La Terre* lest the sincere books of tomorrow be peppered by a general discharge of lead.

It is necessary that with all the strength of our hard-working youth, with all the loyalty of our artistic consciences, we adopt a proper demeanor and dignity toward literature without nobility, that in the name of healthy and manly ambition, in the name of our dedication, we protest our profound love, our supreme respect for art.

Zola: The Man and His Work   Havelock Ellis*

Zola's name—a barbarous, explosive name, like an anarchist's bomb—has been tossed about amid hoots and yells for a quarter of a century. In every civilised country we have heard of the man who has dragged literature into the gutter, who has gone down to pick up the filth of the streets, and has put it into books for the filthy to read. And in every civilised country his books have been read, by the hundred thousand.

To-day, his great life-work is completed. At the same time, the uproar that it aroused has, to a large extent, fallen silent. Not that there is any general agreement as to the rank of the author of the Rougon-Macquart series; but the storms that greeted it have worn themselves out, and it is recognised that there are at least two sides to this as to any other question. Such a time is favourable to the calm discussion of Zola's precise position.

The fundamental assertion of those who, in their irreconcilable opposition to Zola, have rightly felt that abuse is not argument, has always been that Zola is no artist. The matter has usually presented itself to them as a question of Idealism *versus* Realism. Idealism, as used by the literary critic, seems to mean a careful selection of the facts of life for artistic treatment, certain facts being suited for treatment in the novel, certain other facts being not so suited; while the realist, from the literary critic's point of view, is one who flings all facts indiscriminately into his pages. I think that is a fair statement of the matter, for the literary critic does not define very clearly; still less does he ask himself how far the idealism he

*From *Affirmations* (London: Constable, 1898), 131–57. First published in the *Savoy* 1 (January 1896):67–80.

advocates is merely traditional, nor, usually, to what extent the manner of presentation should influence us. He does not ask himself these questions, nor need we ask him, for in the case of Zola (or, indeed, of any other so-called "realist") there is no such distinction. There is no absolute realism, merely a variety of idealisms; the only absolute realism would be a phonographic record, illustrated photographically, after the manner of the cinematograph. Zola is just as much an idealist as George Sand. It is true that he selects very largely from material things, and that he selects very profusely. But the selection remains, and where there is deliberate selection there is art. We need not trouble ourselves here — and I doubt whether we are ever called upon to trouble ourselves — about "Realism" and "Idealism." The questions are: Has the artist selected the right materials? Has he selected them with due restraint?

The first question is a large one, and, in Zola's case at all events, it cannot, I think, be answered on purely æsthetic grounds; the second may be answered without difficulty. Zola has himself answered it; he admits that he has been carried away by his enthusiasm, and perhaps, also, by his extraordinary memory for recently-acquired facts (a memory like a sponge, as he has put it, quickly swollen and quickly emptied); he has sown details across his page with too profuse a hand. It is the same kind of error as Whitman made, impelled by the same kind of enthusiasm. Zola expends immense trouble to get his facts; he has told how he ransacked the theologians to obtain body and colour for *La Faute de l'Abbé Mouret*, perhaps the best of his earlier books. But he certainly spent no more preliminary labour on it than Flaubert spent on *Madame Bovary*, very far less than Flaubert spent on the study of Carthage for *Salammbô*. But the results are different; the one artist gets his effects by profusion and multiplicity of touches, the other by the deliberate self-restraint with which he selects and emphasises solely the salient and significant touches. The latter method seems to strike more swiftly and deeply the ends of art. Three strokes with the brush of Frans Hals are worth a thousand of Denner's. Rich and minute detail may impress us, but it irritates and wearies in the end. If a man takes his two children on to his knees, it matters little whether he places Lénore on his right knee and Henri on his left, or the other way about; the man himself may fail to know or to realise, and the more intense his feelings the less likely is he to know. When we are living deeply, the facts of our external life do not present themselves to us in elaborate detail; a very few points are — as it has been termed — focal in consciousness, while the rest are marginal in subconsciousness. A few things stand out vividly at each moment of life; the rest are dim. The supreme artist is shown by the insight and boldness with which he seizes and illuminates these bright points at each stage, leaving the marginal elements in due subordination. Dramatists so unlike as Ford and Ibsen, novelists so unlike as Flaubert and Tolstoi, yet alike impress us by the simple vividness of their artistic effects. The methods adopted by Zola render such effects extremely difficult of attainment. Perhaps the best proof of Zola's remarkable art is the skill with which he has neutralised the evil results of his ponderous method. In his most characteristic novels, as *L'Assommoir, Nana, Germinal*, his efforts to attain salient perspective in the mass of trivial or technical things—to build a single elaborate effect out of manifold details—are often admirably conducted. Take, for instance, the Voreux, the coal-pit which may almost be said to be the hero of *Germinal* rather than any of the persons in the book. The details are not interesting, but they are carefully elaborated, and the Voreux is finally symbolised as a stupendous idol, sated with human blood, crouching in its mysterious sanctuary. Whenever Zola wishes to bring the Voreux before us, this formula is repeated. And it is the same, in a slighter degree, with the other material personalities of the book. Sometimes, in the case of a crowd, this formula is simply a cry. It is so with the Parisian mob who yell "A Berlin!" in the highly-wrought conclusion to *Nana*; it is so with the crowd of strikers in *Germinal* who shout for bread. It is more than the tricky repetition of a word or a gesture, overdone by Dickens and others; it is the artful manipulation of a carefully-elaborated, significant phrase. Zola seems to have been the first who has, deliberately and systematically, introduced this sort of *leit-motiv* into literature, as a method of summarising a complex mass of details, and bringing the total impression of them before the reader. In this way he contrives to minimise the defects of his method, and to render his complex detail focal. He sometimes attains poignantly simple effects by the mere repetition of a *leit-motiv* at the right moment. And he is able at times, also, to throw aside his detailed method altogether, and to reach effects of tragic intensity. The mutilation of Maigrat's corpse is a scene which can scarcely have been described in a novel before. Given the subject, Zola's treatment of it has the strength, brevity, and certainty of touch which only belong to great masters of art. That Zola is a great master of his art, *L'Assommoir* and *Germinal*—which, so far as I have read Zola, seem his two finest works—are enough to prove. Such works are related to the ordinary novel much as Wagner's music-dramas are related to the ordinary Italian opera. Wagner reaches a loftier height of art than Zola; he had a more complete grasp of all the elements he took in hand to unite. Zola has not seen with sufficient clearness the point of view of science and the limits of its capacity for harmonising with fiction; nor has he with perfect sureness of vision always realised the ends of art. He has left far too much of the scaffolding standing amid his huge literary structures; there is too much mere brute fact which has not been wrought into art. But, if Zola is not among the world's greatest artists, I do not think we can finally deny that he is a great artist.

To look at Zola from the purely artistic standpoint, however, is scarcely to see him at all. His significance for the world generally, and even for literature, lies less in a certain method of using his material—as it may be said to lie, for example, in the case of the Goncourts—than in the material itself, and the impulses and ideas that prompted his selection of that material. These growing piles of large books are the volcanic ejecta of an original and exuberant temperament. To understand them we must investigate this temperament.

A considerable and confused amount of racial energy was stored up in Zola. At once French, Italian, and Greek — with a mother from the central Beauce country of France, more fruitful in corn than in intellect, and a father of mixed Italian and Greek race, a mechanical genius in his way, with enthusiastic energies and large schemes — he presents a curious combination of potential forces, perhaps not altogether a very promising combination. One notes that the mechanical engineer in the father seems to have persisted in the son, not necessarily by heredity, but perhaps by early familiarity and association. Young Zola was a delicate child and by no means a brilliant schoolboy, though he once won a prize for memory; such ability as he showed was in the direction of science; he had no literary aptitudes. He seems to have adopted literature chiefly because pen and ink come handiest to the eager energies of a poor clerk. It is scarcely fanciful to detect the mechanical aptitudes still. Just as all Huxley's natural instincts were towards mechanics, and in physiology he always sought for the "go" of the organism, so Zola, however imperfect his scientific equipment may be, has always sought for the "go" of the social organism. The history of the Rougon-Macquart family is a study in social mathematics: given certain family strains, what is the dynamic hereditary outcome of their contact?

To the making of Zola there went, therefore, this curious racial blend, as a soil ready to be fertilised by any new seed, and a certain almost instinctive tendency to look at things from the mechanical and material point of view. To these, in very early life, a third factor was added of the first importance. During long years after his father's death, Zola, as a child and youth, suffered from poverty, poverty almost amounting to actual starvation, the terrible poverty of respectability. The whole temper of his work and his outlook on the world are clearly conditioned by this prolonged starvation of adolescence. The timid and reserved youth — for such, it is said, has been Zola's character both in youth and manhood — was shut up with his fresh energies in a garret while the panorama of the Paris world was unfolded below him. Forced both by circumstances and by temperament to practise the strictest chastity and sobriety, there was but one indulgence left open to him, an orgy of vision. Of this, as we read his books, we cannot doubt that he fully availed himself, for each volume of the Rougon-Macquart series is an orgy of material vision.[1]

Zola remained chaste, and, it is said, he is still sober — though we are told that his melancholy morose face lights up like a gourmet's at the hour of his abstemious dinner — but this early eagerness to absorb the sights as well as the sounds, and one may add the smells, of the external world, has at length become moulded into a routine method. To take some corner of life, and to catalogue every detail of it, to place a living person there, and to describe every sight and smell and sound around him, although he himself may be quite unconscious of them — that, in the simplest form, is the recipe for making a *roman expérimental*. The method, I wish to insist, was rooted in the author's experience of the world. Life only came to him as the sights, sounds, smells, that reached his garret window. His soul seems to have been starved at the centre, and to have encamped at the sensory periphery. He never tasted deep of life, he stored up none of those wells of purely personal emotion from which great artists have hoisted up the precious fluid which makes the bright living blood of their creations. How different he is in this respect from the other great novelist of our day, who has also been a volcanic force of world-wide significance! Tolstoi comes before us as a man who has himself lived deeply, a man who has had an intense thirst for life, and who has satisfied that thirst. He has craved to know life, to know women, the joy of wine, the fury of battle, the taste of the ploughman's sweat in the field. He has known all these things, not as material to make books, but as the slaking of instinctive personal passions. And in knowing them he has stored up a wealth of experiences from which he drew as he came to make books, and which bear about them that peculiar haunting fragrance only yielded by the things which have been lived through, personally, in the far past. Zola's method has been quite otherwise: when he wished to describe a great house he sat outside the palatial residence of M. Menier, the chocolate manufacturer, and imagined for himself the luxurious fittings inside, discovering in after years that his description had come far short of the reality; before writing *Nana*, he obtained an introduction to a courtesan, with whom he was privileged to lunch; his laborious preparation for the wonderful account of the war of 1870, in *La Débâcle*, was purely one of books, documents, and second-hand experiences; when he wished to write of labour he went to the mines and to the fields, but never appears to have done a day's manual work. Zola's literary methods are those of the *parvenu* who has tried to thrust himself in from outside, who has never been seated at the table of life, who has never really lived. That is their weakness. It is also their virtue. There is no sense of satiety in Zola's work as there is in Tolstoi's. One can understand how it is that, although their methods are so unlike, Tolstoi himself regards Zola as the one French novelist of the day who is really alive. The starved lad, whose eyes were concentrated with longing on the visible world, has reaped a certain reward from his intellectual chastity; he has preserved his clearness of vision for material things, an eager, insatiable, impartial vision. He is a zealot in his devotion to life, to the smallest details of life. He has fought like the doughtiest knight of old-world romance for his lady's honour, and has suffered more contumely than they all. "On barde de fer nos urinoirs!" he shouts in a fury of indignation in one of his essays; it is a curious instance of the fanatic's austere determination that no barrier shall be set up to shut out the sights and smells of the external world. The virgin freshness of his thirst for life gives its swelling, youthful vigour to his work, its irrepressible energy.

It has, indeed, happened with this unsatisfied energy as it will happen with such energies; it has retained its robustness at the sacrifice of the sweetness it might otherwise have gained. There is a certain bitterness in Zola's fury of vision, as there is also in his gospel of "Work! work! work!" One is conscious of a savage assault on a citadel which, the assailant now well knows, can never be scaled. Life cannot be reached by the senses alone; there is always something that cannot be caught by the utmost tension of eyes and ears and nose; a well-balanced soul is built up, not alone on sensory memories, but also on the harmonious satisfaction of the motor and emotional energies. That cardinal fact must be faced even when we are attempting to define the fruitful and positive element in Zola's activity.

The chief service which Zola has rendered to his fellow-artists and successors, the reason of the immense stimulus he supplies, seems to lie in the proofs he has brought of the latent artistic uses of the rough, neglected details of life. The Rougon-Macquart series has been to his weaker brethren like that great sheet knit at the four corners, let down from Heaven full of four-footed beasts and creeping things and fowls of the air, and bearing in it the demonstration that to the artist as to the moralist nothing can be called common or unclean. It has henceforth become possible for other novelists to find inspiration where before they could never have turned, to touch life with a vigour and audacity of phrase which, without Zola's example, they would have trembled to use, while they still remain free to bring to their work the simplicity, precision, and inner experience which he has never possessed. Zola has enlarged the field of the novel. He has brought the modern material world into fiction in a more definite and thorough manner than it has ever been brought before, just as Richardson brought the modern emotional world into fiction; such an achievement necessarily marks an epoch. In spite of all his blunders, Zola has given the novel new power and directness, a vigour of fibre which was hard indeed to attain, but which, once attained, we may chasten as we will. And in doing this he has put out of court, perhaps for ever, those unwholesome devotees of the novelist's art who work out of their vacuity, having neither inner nor outer world to tell of.

Zola's delight in exuberant detail, it is true, is open to severe criticism. When, however, we look at his work, not as great art but as an important moment in the evolution of the novel, this exuberance is amply justified. Such furious energy in hammering home this demonstration of the artistic utility of the whole visible modern world may detract from the demonstrator's reputation for skill; it has certainly added to the force of the demonstration. Zola's luxuriance of detail — the heritage of that romantic movement of which he was the child — has extended impartially to every aspect of life he has investigated, to the working of a mine, to the vegetation of the Paradou, to the ritual of the Catholic Church. But it is not on the details of inanimate life, or the elaborate description of the industrial and religious functions of men, that the rage of Zola's adversaries has chiefly been spent. It is rather on his use of the language of the common people and on his descriptions of the sexual and digestive functions of humanity. Zola has used slang — the *argot* of the populace — copiously, chiefly indeed in *L'Assommoir*, which is professedly a study of low life, but to a less extent in his other books. A considerable part of the power of *L'Assommoir*, in many respects Zola's most perfect work, lies in the skill with which he uses the language of the people he is dealing with; the reader is bathed throughout in an atmosphere of picturesque, vigorous, often coarse *argot*. There is, no doubt, a lack of critical sobriety in the profusion and reiteration of vulgarisms, of coarse oaths, of the varied common synonyms for common things. But they achieve the end that Zola sought, and so justify themselves.

They are of even greater interest as a protest against the exaggerated purism which has ruled the French language for nearly three centuries, and while rendering it a more delicate and precise instrument for scientific purposes, has caused it to become rather bloodless and colourless for the artist's purposes, as compared with the speech used by Rabelais, Montaigne, and even Molière, the great classics who have chiefly influenced Zola. The romantic movement of the present century, it is true, added colour to the language, but scarcely blood; it was an exotic, feverish colour which has not permanently enriched French speech. A language rendered anæmic by over-clarification cannot be fed by exotic luxuries but by an increase in the vigorous staples of speech, and Zola was on the right track when he went to the people's common speech, which is often classic in the true sense and always robust. Doubtless he has been indiscriminate and even inaccurate in his use of *argot*, sometimes giving undue place to what is of merely temporary growth. But the main thing was to give literary place and prestige to words and phrases which had fallen so low in general esteem, in spite of their admirable expressiveness, that only a writer of the first rank and of unequalled audacity could venture to lift them from the mire. This Zola has done; and those who follow him may easily exercise the judgment and discretion in which he has been lacking.

Zola's treatment of the sexual and the digestive functions, as I pointed out, has chiefly aroused his critics. If you think of it, these two functions are precisely the central functions of life, the two poles of hunger and love around which the world revolves. It is natural that it should be precisely these fundamental aspects of life which in the superficial contact of ordinary social intercourse we are for ever trying more and more to refine away and ignore. They are subjected to an ever-encroaching process of attenuation and circumlocution, and as a social tendency this influence is possibly harmless or even beneficial. But it is constantly extending to literature also, and here it is disastrous. It is true that a few great authors — classics of the first rank — have gone to extremes in their resistance to this tendency. These extremes are of two kinds: the first issuing in a sort of coprolalia, or inclination to dwell on excrement, which we find to a slight extent in Rabelais and to a marked extent in the half-mad Swift; in its fully-developed shape this coprolalia is an uncontrollable instinct found in some forms of insanity. The other extreme is that of pruriency, or the perpetual itch to circle round sexual matters, accompanied by a timidity which makes it impossible to come right up to them; this sort of impotent fumbling in women's placket-holes finds its supreme literary exponent in Sterne. Like coprolalia, when uncontrolled, prurience is a well-recognised characteristic of the insane, leading them to find a vague eroticism everywhere. But both these extreme tendencies have not been found incompatible with the highest literary art. Moreover, their most pronounced exponents have been clerics, the conventional representatives of the Almighty. However far Zola might go in these directions, he would still be in what is universally recognised as very good company. He has in these respects by no means come up with Father Rabelais and Dean Swift and the Rev. Laurence Sterne; but there can be little doubt that, along both lines, he has missed the restraint of well-balanced art. On the one hand he over-emphasises what is repulsive in the nutritive side of life, and on the other hand, with the timid obsession of chastity, he over-emphasises the nakedness of flesh. In so doing, he has revealed a certain flabbiness in his art, although he has by no means diminished his service in widening the horizon of literary speech and subject. Bearing in mind that many crowned kings of literature have approached these subjects quite as closely as Zola, and far less seriously, it does not seem necessary to enter any severer judgment here.

To enlarge the sphere of language is an unthankful task, but in the long run literature owes an immense debt to the writers who courageously add to the stock of strong and simple words. Our own literature for two centuries has been hampered by the social tendency of life to slur expression, and to paraphrase or suppress all forceful and poignant words. If we go back to Chaucer, or even to Shakespeare, we realise what power of expression we have lost. It is enough, indeed, to turn to our English Bible. The literary power of the English Bible is largely due to the unconscious instinct for style which happened to be in the air when it was chiefly moulded, to the simple, direct, unashamed vigour of its speech. Certainly, if the discovery of the Bible had been left for us to make, any English translation would have to be issued at a high price by some esoteric society, for fear lest it should fall into the hands of the British matron. It is our British love of compromise, we say, that makes it possible for a spade to be called a spade on one day of the week, but on no other; our neighbours, whose minds are more logically constituted, call it *le cant Britannique*. But our mental compartments remain very water-tight, and on the whole we are even worse off than the French who have no Bible. For instance, we have almost lost the indispensable words "belly" and "bowels," both used so often and with such admirable effect in the Psalms; we talk of the "stomach," a word which is not only an incorrect equivalent, but at best totally inapt for serious or poetic uses. Any one who is acquainted with our old literature, or with the familiar speech of the common folk, will recall similar instances of simple, powerful expressions which are lost or vanishing from literary language, leaving no available substitute behind. In modern literary language, indeed, man scarcely exists save in his extremities. For we take the pubes as a centre, and we thence describe a circle with a radius of some eighteen inches — in America the radius is rather longer — and we forbid any reference to any organ within the circle, save that maid-of-all-work the "stomach"; in other words, we make it impossible to say anything to the point concerning the central functions of life.

It is a question how far real literature can be produced under such conditions, not merely because literature is thus shut out from close contact with the vital facts of life, but because the writer who is willing to be so shut out, who finds himself most at home within the social limits of speech, will probably not be made of the heroic stuff that goes to the moulding of a great writer. The social limits of speech are useful enough, for we are all members of society, and it is well that we should have some protection against the assaults of unbridled vulgarity. But in literature we may choose to read what we will, or to read nothing, and the man who enters the world of literature timidly equipped with the topics and language of the drawing-room is not likely to go far. I once saw it stated depreciatingly in a grave literary review that a certain novel by a woman writer dealt with topics that are not even discussed by men at their clubs. I had never read it, but it seemed to me then that there might be hope for that novel. No doubt it is even possible in literature to fall below the club standard, but unless you can rise above the club standard, better stay at the club, tell stories there, or sweep the crossing outside.

All our great poets and novelists from Chaucer to Fielding wrote sincerely and heroically concerning the great facts of life. That is why they are great, robustly sane, radiantly immortal. It is a mistake to suppose that no heroism was involved in their case; for though no doubt they had a freer general speech on their side they went beyond their time in daring to mould that speech to the ends of art, in bringing literature closer to life. It was so even with Chaucer; compare him with his contemporaries and successors; observe how he seeks to soothe the susceptibilities of his readers and to deprecate the protests of the "precious folk." There is no great art at any epoch without heroism, though one epoch may be more favourable than another to the exercise of such heroism in literature. In our own age and country daring has passed out the channels of art into those of commerce, to find exercise, foolish enough sometimes, in the remotest corners of the earth. It is because our literature is not heroic, but has been confined within the stifling atmosphere of the drawing-room, that English poets and novelists have ceased to be a power in the world and are almost unknown outside the parlours and nurseries of our own country. It is because in France there have never ceased to be writers here and there who have dared to face life heroically and weld it into art that the literature of France is a power in the world wherever there are men intelligent enough to recognise its achievements. When literature that is not only fine but also great appears in England we shall know it as such by its heroism, if by no other mark.

Language has its immense significance because it is the final incarnation of a man's most intimate ideals. Zola's style and method are monotonous — with a monotony which makes his books unreadable when we have once mastered his secret — and the burden they express is ever the same: the energy of natural life. Whatever is robust, whatever is wholesomely exuberant, whatever, wholesomely or not, is possessed by the devouring fury of life — of such things Zola can never have enough. The admirable opening of *La Terre*, in which a young girl drives the cow, wild for the male, to the farm where the stock-bull is kept, then leading the appeased animal home again, symbolises Zola's whole view of the world. All the forces of Nature, it seems to him, are raging in the fury of generative desire or reposing in the fulness of swelling maturity. The very earth itself, in the impressive pages with which *Germinal* closes, is impregnated with men, germinating beneath the soil, one day to burst through the furrows and renew the old world's failing life. In this conception of the natural energies of the world — as manifested in men and animals, in machines in every form of matter — perpetually conceiving and generating, Zola reaches his most impressive effects, though these effects are woven together of elements that are separately of no very exquisite beauty, or subtle insight, or radical novelty.

In considering Zola, we are indeed constantly brought back to the fact that most of the things that he has tried to do have been better done by more accomplished artists. The Goncourts have extended the sphere of language, even in the direction of slang, and have faced many of the matters that Zola has faced, and with far more delicate, though usually more shadowy, art; Balzac has created as large and vivid a world of people, though drawing more of it from his own imagination; Huysmans has greater skill in stamping the vision of strange or sordid things on the brain; Tolstoi gives a deeper realisation of life; Flaubert is as audaciously naturalistic, and has, as well, that perfect self-control which should always accompany audacity. And in Flaubert, too, we find something of the same irony as in Zola.

This irony, however, is a personal and characteristic feature of Zola's work. It is irony alone which gives it distinction and poignant incisiveness. Irony may be called the soul of Zola's work, the embodiment of his moral attitude towards life. It has its source, doubtless, like so much else that is characteristic, in his early days of poverty and aloofness from the experiences of life. There is a fierce impartiality — the impartiality of one who is outside and shut off — in this manner of presenting the brutalities and egoisms and pettinesses of men. The fury of his irony is here equalled by his self-restraint. He concentrates it into a word, a smile, a gesture. Zola believes, undoubtedly, in a reformed, even perhaps a revolutionised, future of society, but he has no illusions. He sets down things as he sees them. He has no tendernesses for the working-classes, no pictures of rough diamonds. We may see this very clearly in *Germinal*. Here every side of the problem of modern capitalism is presented: the gentle-natured shareholding class unable to realise a state of society in which people should not live on dividends and give charity; the official class with their correct authoritative views, very sure that they will always be needed to control labour and maintain social order; and the workers, some brutalised, some suffering like dumb beasts, some cringing to the bosses, some rebelling madly, a few striving blindly for justice.

There is no loophole in Zola's impartiality; the gradual development of the seeming hero of *Germinal*, Etienne Lantier, the agitator, honest in his revolt against oppression, but with an unconscious bourgeois ideal at his heart, seems unerringly right. All are the victims of an evil social system, as Zola sees the world, the enslaved workers as much as the overfed masters; the only logical outcome is a clean sweep — the burning up of the chaff and straw, the fresh furrowing of the earth, the new spring of a sweet and vigorous race. That is the logical outcome of Zola's attitude, the attitude of one who regards our present society as a thoroughly vicious circle. His pity for men and women is boundless; his disdain is equally boundless. It is only towards animals that his tenderness is untouched by contempt; some of his most memorable passages are concerned with the sufferings of animals. The New Jerusalem may be fitted up, but the Montsou miners will never reach it; they will fight for the first small, stuffy, middle-class villa they meet on the way. And Zola pours out the stream of his pitiful, pitiless irony on the weak, helpless, erring children of men. It is this moral energy, combined with his volcanic exuberance, which lifts him to a position of influence above the greater artists with whom we may compare him.

It is by no means probable that the world will continue to read Zola much longer. His work is already done; but when the nineteenth century is well past it may be that he will still have his interest. There will be plenty of material, especially in the newspapers, for the future historian to reconstruct the social life of the latter half of the nineteenth century. But the material is so vast that these historians will possibly be even more biassed and one-sided than our own. For a vivid, impartial picture — on the whole a faithful picture — of certain of the most characteristic aspects of this period, seen indeed from the outside, but drawn by a contemporary in all its intimate and even repulsive details, the reader of a future age can best go to Zola. What would we not give for a thirteenth century Zola! We should read with painful, absorbed interest a narrative of the Black Death as exact as that of nineteenth century alcoholism in *L'Assommoir*. The story of how the serf lived, as fully told as in *La Terre*, would be of incomparable value. The early merchant and usurer would be a less dim figure if *L'Argent* had been written about him. The abbeys and churches of those days have in part come down to us, but no *Germinal* remains to tell of the lives and thoughts of the men who hewed those stones, and piled them, and carved them. How precious such record would have been we may realise when we recall the incomparable charm of Chaucer's prologue to *The Canterbury Tales*. But our children's children, with the same passions alive at their hearts under incalculably different circumstances, will in the pages of the Rougon-Macquart series find themselves back again among all the strange remote details of a vanished world. What a fantastic and terrible page of old-world romance!

Note

1. "My memories," he told a psychological interviewer, "have an extraordinary power and vividness; I have a remarkable, prodigious memory, that troubles me; when I recall objects that I have seen, I visualize them again as they really are, with their contours, forms, colours, smells, sounds; *it is an extreme form of materialization*; the sun that shines on them almost dazzles me; the smell suffocates me, details crowd in on me and prevent me from seeing the whole. To recapture it I must therefore wait a while. This power of recall does not last very long; the vividness of the image has an unprecedented exactness, intensity, then the image fades, disappears, and it all goes away." This description suggests myopia, and it is a fact that Zola has been short-sighted from youth; he first realised it at sixteen. His other senses, especially smell, are very keen—largely, however, as an outcome of attention or practice. Thus while his tactile sensibility and sensibility to pain are acute, his olfactory keenness is rather qualitative than quantitative, that is to say that it mainly consists in a marked memory for odours, a tendency to be emotionally impressed by them, and an ability to distinguish them in which he resembles professional perfumers. All these and many other facts have been very precisely ascertained by means of the full psychological and anthropological study of M. Zola which has been carried out by experts under the superintendence of Dr. Toulouse. [Editor's note: Zola's words, quoted by Ellis in French, have been translated.]

Poem of the Earth   Heinrich Mann*

Homeric landscapes with a Greek idyll, much passion at the market place, high innocence and great craftiness, heroic goals, but pitiful and tragic results all the same: so begins the twenty-volume poem. *La Fortune*

*From "Zola," *Die Weisser Blätter* 2 (1915):1312–82. Translated for this volume by Dolorès A. Signori and reprinted with the permission of Aufbau-Verlag Berlin und Weimar.

des Rougon starts out with a canticle to the people, to a people from the south, for Plassans lies where Aix is located — a canticle to their warmth, their instinctive strength, their loving humanity, their willingness to revolt against masters and oppressors. This region is vast and free like these souls, with its moonlight as distant as the slopes of the hills, and near the farthest slope, behind the last cloud of grey foliage of the olive trees, rolls the sea. A glance from above! Through a gap, lost in the distance, there appears a swarm of struggling creatures, human creatures, souls with a common urge. Their number increases; they rush from side-roads in hordes, weapons glisten, rustic implements which are supposed to be weapons. The stench of poverty accompanies them; over their heads, carried by a girl in a red coat, their red flag sways, and their song rises up, the Hymn of the Revolution. Yet these are no longer revolutionaries, as they were but three years earlier, in 1848; now they are known only as insurgents. Time passes them by, puts a new complexion on events; resolute desires triumph over their uncertain enthusiasm. After a brief upsurge of moral will, a sense of reality has asserted itself once again in the population, and the most austere of military rules is announced. Victors just a short time ago and in unison with the heart of the country, they now represent an obsolete, stray rebellion, which passes through a sleeping countryside in the moonlight, a noble, unsuspecting Ideal destined to die even before it fights. But in the shadow of the city lie in wait those who are on good terms with ordinary life, treat it like a brother, and do business with it. They are the *Bourgeois*. Their very nature tells them: an idealistic republic cannot live; they are expected to come to the aid of the forces that destroy it. The new imperialism will have power and pleasures to distribute; they cannot wait to prove themselves useful to it: underhandedly, that goes without saying, and with restraint, in case events take a different course. The Rougon family, hitherto a ragtag crew despite their lack of scruples, incited by every possible desire, becomes a Bonapartist agent, channels petit bourgeois hate and fear of the common people, and works in a hundred devious ways for the one great moment when blood will flow. For only blood captures the imagination and ensures the irrevocable. Only on sites slippery with blood are strong empires founded. The victory of order is most assuredly guaranteed through a crime. The Bonapartes operate this way in Paris, the Rougons in Plassans. What is history in Paris and is called a coup d'état, is shabby villainy in the small town; the Tuileries which have to be conquered here are the tax-collector's house. But the rise of the Rougon family has the same origin as the ascent of that other family; they too have betrayed; and even during their victory celebration there lies forgotten under the bed a shoe with a blood-stained heel. They have fat, flabby bodies, shapeless from activities which constitute neither intellectual nor physical work. It seems that they have no right to be feared. Moreover they only become terrifying for the sake of a small, insignificant gain. We would like not to have to fear them as we fear the great butchers of mankind. But when the time comes, they will be just like them. Here too it is fear which leads to their crime: "Necessity knows no law," they also say before they commit it; and in their sleep, where the event becomes the symbol, it does not matter that it is only the petits bourgeois who are dreaming. Pale and sweating between their sheets they see blood raining down and every drop turn into a gold coin on the ground. An imperial dream indeed! Who is to say that even when they are awake they cannot achieve great thoughts? Some dream of power, incomparably greater than the wretched desires of which they make use. Such is Félicité, Rougon's wife: the will to power of a generation become woman. Such too are their sons, the minister and the speculator. But the third son, Doctor Pascal Rougon, speaks: "I shall be accused of being a Republican. Good, that does not bother me. I really am one, if what is meant by that is a person who wishes to bring about happiness for all." For this family and this humanity is divided into those who believe in power and those who wish for happiness. The latter constitute the common people, the others the bourgeoisie. It is not only the intellectuals who are opposed to the bourgeois as in Flaubert's works. Here the intellectuals also oppose the bourgeoisie, but together with the common people. The enemies of the bourgeois have grown, for the bourgeoisie itself has grown. The most shameless and unrestrained of all empires that it has created until then has opened its doors. The talent, the only one through which it can rise above itself, the talent for speculation, becomes inexhaustible. Already in the first volume of this history of a bourgeois empire we can sense the approach of a Witches' Sabbath without equal; and sense too that the hour will come when everything will be swept away and purer forces will have to come into play. This was written when that time was approaching; suffering impatience helped. When will the empire topple? The people whose day approaches are here transfigured as only a deep longing can transfigure. In opposition to the bourgeois, who are crafty, criminal and unsuccessful in their limited ability to think, the people rise up in a single unit, like the gathering storm of the single idea that urges them on. The children of the common people genuinely love one another, with the purity of lovers in antiquity. The dirt and smell of their work have vanished, as if they were back from past millenia. For Zola there is always poetry only in the rough classes, among people who do not seek it. His aspirations are with them. And his memories. For Zola still recollects and will always recollect how free, good and inspired by the purest natural nobility the people were, the Mediterranean people, to which he belonged before he went to live in the city. An ideal picture of the people, of true humanity, will secretly accompany him throughout his entire opus, even in the most hopeless depictions of reality. In his old age it will finally eclipse everything, all knowledge, all bitterness, and alone will remain. Thus it happened, because he was Hellenic. Greek—such an eye is accustomed to looking into the pure distance and is capable of embracing earthly spaces at a glance. He will plunge into the abysses of society, aspire to passions which both the world and God have forgotten — and will always know that everything human is embraced by the vast sky and destined to fade away — human destinies, families, empires — and return to the eternal earth. He writes his poems from on high; and in all he sees life pulsating before him in but a little corner of land. His poem speaks to the Earth.

And for this reason he notices symbols, creates in symbols. The novel about the Parisian market becomes the parable of the Fat and the Thin, of a triumphant humanity and a conquered humanity. The story of a minister unfolds just as eternally on earth the destiny of power unfolds, typical to the point of being intangible, and rendered concrete once again through the power of the idea. Such is the man of strength, the master incarnate, but quite useless if he is not the master. The pointless power of those heavy shoulders! — in the case of a fallen ruler who awaits his return and only waits, with no spiritual interests, without an occupation beyond power itself, ready for anything, so that he may exercise it, ready to deny his entire past, or even, if it came to it, ready to play with the life of his prince — for he was never anything but a pretext for the lust for power of his most faithful servant. . . . What is Nana? In the first instance she is the "poem of male desires." In the end it only requires a little imagination for her poxed flesh to represent France of the Second Empire struggling against death. And it requires but a little imagination for her to mean more, a "force of nature," unaware of the evil that she does. The city; the daughter of the down-trodden people wreaks vengeance over the rich by means of her poisoned beauty. The gutter splashes up in their faces and they perish. A cycle of vice, a cycle of death; human agitation, magnificent like nature; poetry of the extremes; in the dankest corner Pan still breathes: the city still, but stone is part of the earth. The youth who dreamt about depicting humanity in all its ages, in every century, not in the one, has here made his contribution. He has always made a contribution; "the sublime of which my cursed skull cannot cease from dreaming"; and suddenly on the most commanding heights to which the mature man has risen, the youth that he was has come closer to fulfilling his dream than other men may hope for themselves and their dreams. This miracle is called La Terre — a work of the utmost truth, as severe as the gospels, and no less powerful. What could remain to be transfigured or achieved by struggles after this work in which the earth itself is the main protagonist, the earth which gives birth and devours its creatures, the earth which allows them no margin of freedom from its law, no desires, no thoughts that are not of the earth; the earth, mother and instigator of every good deed and every crime. The closer man is to her, the more ruthless he is. Only one idea inhabits these peasants: to possess the earth — even if parents have to be killed for it. Even when they are in love, the earth holds her children firmly in her filth; they are betrothed in a stream of liquid manure; and man only becomes pathetic because of his inseparability from her, his surrender to this voracious and thankless earth. For what does she give in return, for so much work, so much passion? How does she appease hopes for a better life, for happiness, progress, refinement? She only just appeases hunger and only just provides bread. She allows herself to be made fertile and for all eternity her fruit is the same. A fruitfulness, which is a useless prostitution: thus she lives, so too her children. When a poor human beast of burden collapses dead on the vast furrowed earth that does not see it, a few haystacks further on another woman has her first experience with a man. Animal destinies! — and a cow and a woman give birth together on either side of a wall, in the most penetrating smell of the earth that descriptive pages have ever exhaled. Then there is a donkey that gets drunk as do men. Life on the land is grotesque, idyllic or frightful, but always unfeeling, this is the truth. The earth has the insensitivity of a giant's back on which insects swarm. In its colossal width the miseries and desires of the insects disappear. What remains is space. What remains is eternity. *La Terre* moves along as if outside of time, an epic without limits. Its chapters are breaths of eternity, chapters of storms, sun, celebrations, crimes, the chapter of winter and of death. *La Terre* goes on playing for ever and never ends.

Nevertheless this too is a novel of the age, the age in which the empire is judged as well. It is feared and hated like the two vicious dogs called "Emperor" and "Massacre." The agrarian crisis which shakes up the country is the work of this empire of speculators. The worst of all conceivable régimes, capitalistic militarism, drives this people towards a catastrophe, and if it is not war, it will be revolution. The threat of revolution accompanies the action, heightens it and is furthered by it. The peasants, at first merely amusing and worthy of pity in their greed for land, receive the first warning only when they are drunk and seem to listen senselessly to one of their own kind who has gone to the dogs, and who does not care a straw about the earth, which he drinks away, because the earth is bad business, a trap, a vampire. Then things grow dark, the mistakes of their greed for land seem inextricable. An itinerant speaker talks of expropriation, of this brutal act that will deliver them from their needs. Finally a man rises who has witnessed all that has occurred among men and who has always cautiously kept silent; he rises up in an outburst of fanaticism and cries for blood; but there is already murder there, murder out of greed for the earth. What do you want, you who are caught up in your destinies, and destined to become more and more ensnared right to the end which will be yours alone? For your children will be ensnared like you, and, like you, with no chance to look backwards or forwards. Again and again the old peasant, a victim of his children, staggers across the land which he has loved too much. He yielded it to them only when his strength failed him, and now he is pursued by them for the sake of a few savings, the proceeds from an entire lifetime of struggle with the land. Yet what does it offer its worn out lover? Hiding

places, nothing more, hiding places, when he flees with the shame of one
who has been discovered, with the anger of one who is powerless. The pity
of even the humblest turns into laughter. And he who cannot die, is
savagely, horribly killed by his own children. Look at him, this eternal
human form, and say what remains for you to hope for. What rebellion,
what upheaval could save you from this greed for the earth, from your
earthly desire! The peasants sit together in the evenings, all of them
around the same candle, and read their history aloud to one another from
the almanac, the history of their past sorrows and their long struggle. All
of the facts that they hear justify the revolution, which then came, but
their profound feeling of incurable misery deprives it of all value in their
eyes. Our fight is necessary and vain. The almanac which the peasants
read is a propaganda pamphlet for the empire. The empire is to bring
happiness. But no empire brings happiness, and each empire and each
new wave of generations is only worth a crumb of earth that you can pick
up, crush and let fall. The land is too big for you, its insensitivity
confounds your zeal, your haste is thwarted by its slowness. It devours a
thousand of your generations, and still nothing has occurred. Yet you must
weep and bleed for it, as hail and frost descend on your harvests. Yet you
must work and produce like the earth. Who knows? One day, the
Immortal Power which goes on creating life out of our crimes and
miseries, will reveal its obscure goal.

The Zola Centenary   Georg Lukács*

Emile Zola the novelist is the "historian of private life" under the
Second Empire in France in the same way as Balzac was the historian of
private life under the restoration and the July monarchy. Zola himself
never disclaimed this heritage. He always protested against the assumption
that he had invented a new art form and always regarded himself as the
heir and follower of Balzac and Stendhal, the two great realists of the
beginning of the nineteenth century. Of the two, he regarded Stendhal as
the connecting link with the literature of the eighteenth century. Of course
so remarkable and original a writer as Zola could not regard his literary
predecessors as mere models to copy; he admired Balzac and Stendhal but
vigorously criticized them none the less; he tried to eliminate what he
considered dead and antiquated in them and to work out the principles of
a creative method which could have a fertilizing influence on the further

*From Edith Bone, trans., *Studies in European Realism* (London: Hillway Publishing
Co., 1950), 85–96. Originally published in Hungarian in *Balzac, Stendhal, Zola* (Buda-
pest: Hungária, 1949), 139–56. Reprinted by permission of The Merlin Press Ltd., London, England.

evolution of realism. (It should be said here that Zola never speaks of realism, but always of naturalism.)

But the further development of realism in Zola's hands took a far more intricate course than Zola himself imagined. Between Balzac and Zola lies the year 1848 and the bloody days of June, the first independent action of the working class, which left so indelible an impression on the ideology of the French *bourgeoisie*, that after it *bourgeois* ideology ceased to play a progressive part in France for a long time. Ideology grew adaptable and developed into mere apologetics on behalf of the *bourgeoisie*.

Zola himself, however, never stooped to be an apologist of the *bourgeois* social order. On the contrary, he fought a courageous battle against the reactionary evolution of French capitalism, first in the literary sphere and later openly in the political. In the course of his life he gradually came ever closer to socialism, although he never got beyond a paler version of Fourier's Utopianism, a version lacking, however, Fourier's brilliantly dialectical social criticism. But the ideology of his own class was too deeply ingrained in his thinking, his principles and his creative method, although the conscious sharpness of his criticism of society was never dulled; on the contrary, it was much more vigorous and progressive than that of the Catholic Royalist Balzac.

Balzac and Stendhal, who had described the ghastly transformation of bourgeois France from the heroic period of the revolution and Napoleon to the romantically hypocritical corruption of the restoration and the no longer even hypocritical philistine filth of the July monarchy, had lived in a society in which the antagonism of bourgeoisie and working-class was not as yet the plainly visible hub around which social evolution moved forward. Hence Balzac and Stendhal could dig down to the very roots of the sharpest contradictions inherent in bourgeois society while the writers who lived after 1848 could not do so: such merciless candour, such sharp criticism would have necessarily driven them to break the link with their own class.

Even the sincerely progressive Zola was incapable of such a rupture.

It is this attitude which is reflected in his methodological conception, in his rejection, as romantic and "unscientific," of Balzac's bred-in-the-bone dialectic and prophetic fervour in the exposure of the contradictions of capitalism, for which he, Zola, substitutes a "scientific" method in which society is conceived as a harmonious entity and the criticism applied to society formulated as a struggle against the diseases attacking its organic unity, a struggle against the "undesirable features" of capitalism.

Zola says: "The social cycle is identical with the life-cycle: in society as in the human body, there is a solidarity linking the various organs with each other in such a way that if one organ putrefies, the rot spreads to the other organs and results in a very complicated disease."

This "scientific" conception led Zola to identify mechanically the human body and human society, and he is quite consistent when he criticizes Balzac's great preface to *The Human Comedy* from this angle. In this preface Balzac, as a true dialectician, raises the same question: he asks to what extent the dialectic of race evolution as developed by Geoffroy de Saint Hilaire applies to human society; but at the same time he sharply stresses the new categories created by the specific dialectic of society. Zola thinks that such a conception destroys the "scientific unity" of the method and that the conception itself is due to the "romantic confusion" of Balzac's mind. What he then puts in the place of Balzac's ideas, as a "scientific" result, is the undialectic conception of the organic unity of nature and society; the elimination of antagonisms is regarded as the motive power of social movement and the principle of "harmony" as the essence of social being. Thus Zola's subjectively most sincere and courageous criticism of society is locked into the magic circle of progressive *bourgeois* narrow-mindedness. On this basis of principle, Zola carries on the tradition established by the creative methods of Balzac and Stendhal with great consistence. It is not by accident nor a result of some personal bias in favour of his older friend and comrade-in-arms Flaubert that Zola found in the latter the true realization of all that in Balzac was merely a beginning or an intent.

Zola wrote about *Madame Bovary*: "It seems that the formula of the modern novel, scattered all over Balzac's colossal *œuvre*, is here clearly worked out in a book of 400 pages. And with it the code of the modern novel has now been written."

Zola stresses as the elements of Flaubert's greatness: above all the elimination of romantic traits. "The composition of the novel lies only in the way in which incidents are chosen and made to follow each other in a certain harmonic order of evolution. The incidents themselves are absolutely average. . . . All out-of-the-ordinary inventions have been excluded. . . . The story is unfolded by relating all that happens from day to day without ever springing any surprises." According to Zola, Balzac, too, had in his greatest works sometimes achieved this realistic presentation of everyday life. "But before he could reach the point of concerning himself only with accurate description, he revelled for a long time in inventions and lost himself in the search for false thrills and false magnificence."

He continues: "The novelist, if he accepts the basic principle of showing the ordinary course of average lives, must kill the 'hero.' By 'hero' I mean inordinately magnified characters, puppets inflated into giants. Inflated 'heroes' of this sort drag down Balzac's novels, because he always believes that he has not made them gigantic enough." In the naturalist method "this exaggeration by the artist and this whimsicality of composition are done away with" and "all heads are brought down to the same level, for the opportunities permitting us to depict a truly superior human being are very rare."

Here we already see quite clearly the principles on the basis of which

Zola criticizes the heritage left by the great realists. Zola repeatedly discusses the great realists, particularly Balzac and Stendhal and constantly reiterates the same basic idea that Balzac and Stendhal were great because, in many details and episodes of their works, they described human passions faithfully and contributed very interesting documents to our knowledge of human passions. But according to Zola both of them, and particularly Stendhal, suffered from a mistaken romanticism. He writes, about the end of *Le Rouge et le Noir* and Julien Sorel: "This goes absolutely beyond everyday truth, the truth we strive for; the psychologist Stendhal, no less than the story-teller Alexander Dumas, plunges us up to our necks in the unusual and extraordinary. Seen from the viewpoint of exact truth, Julien Sorel provides me with as many surprises as d'Artagnan." Zola applies the same criticism to Mathilde de la Mole, all the characters in *The Monastery of Parma*, Balzac's Vautrin and many other Balzac characters.

Zola regards the whole relationship between Julien and Mathilde as mere brain-gymnastics and hair-splitting and both characters as unusual and artificial. He entirely fails to realize that Stendhal could not raise to the highest level of typicality the great conflict which he wanted to depict unless he invented these two absolutely above-average and quite extraordinary characters; only thus could he bring in his criticism of the hypocrisy, duplicity and baseness of the restoration period, and show up the infamously greedy and mean capitalist essence of its feudal-romantic ideology. Only by creating the figure of Mathilde, in whom the romantic ideology of reaction 'grows into a genuine passion, even though in heroically exaggerated form, could Stendhal raise the plot and the concrete situations to a level on which the contrast between these ideologies and their social basis on the one hand, and the plebeian Jacobinism of the Napoleon-admirer Julien Sorel on the other, could be fully developed. Similarly, Zola failed to realize that Balzac could not possibly dispense with Vautrin's larger-than-life figure if he wanted the otherwise merely personal and individual catastrophe of Lucien de Rubempré's ambitions to become the tragedy of the whole ruling class of the restoration period; it was only by this device that Balzac was enabled to weave into this tragicomedy the entire tissue of the moribund society of the restoration, from the king meditating a *coup d'état* to the bureaucrat carving a career for himself.

But Zola could not see this. He says of Balzac: "His imagination, that unruly imagination which drove him to exaggeration and with which he wanted to re-create the world in his own image, irritates me more than it attracts me. If the great novelist had had nothing but this his imagination, he would now be merely a pathological case, a curiosity of our literature."

According to Zola, Balzac's greatness and his claim to immortality lay in the fact that he was one of the first who "possessed a sense of reality." But Zola arrived at this "sense of reality" by first cutting out of Balzac's life-work the great contradictions of capitalist society and accepting only the presentation of everyday life which was for Balzac merely a means of throwing the contradictions into bolder relief and giving a total picture of society in motion, complete with all its determinants and antagonisms.

It is most characteristic that Zola (and with him Hippolyte Taine) should speak with the greatest admiration of General Hulot, a character in the novel *La Cousine Bette*. But both of them see in him only a masterly portrait of an oversexed man. Neither Zola nor Taine say a word about the artistry with which Balzac traces Hulot's passions to the conditions of life in the Napoleonic era; and yet it would not have been difficult to notice this, for Balzac uses Crevel — a character also painted with no less consummate mastery — as a counterfoil to show up the difference between the eroticism of the Napoleonic era and that of the reign of Louis Philippe. Neither Zola, nor Taine mention the doubtful operations with which Hulot tries to make money, although in describing them, Balzac gives an admirable picture of the infamies and horrors of incipient French colonial policy.

In other words both Zola and Taine insulate Hulot's erotic passion from its social basis and thus turn a socially pathological figure into a psychopathological one. It is natural that looking at it from this angle he could see only "exaggeration" (i.e. romanticism) in the great, socially typical characters created by Balzac and Stendhal.

"Life is simpler than that" Zola says at the end of one of his criticisms of Stendhal. He thus completes the transition from the old realism to the new, from realism proper to naturalism. The decisive social basis of this change is to be found in the fact that the social evolution of the *bourgeoisie* has changed the way of life of writers. The writer no longer participates in the great struggles of his time, but is reduced to a mere spectator and chronicler of public life. Zola understood clearly enough that Balzac himself had to go bankrupt in order to be able to depict César Birotteau; that he had to know from his own experience the whole underworld of Paris in order to create such characters as Rastignac and old Goriot.

In contrast, Zola — and to an even greater extent Flaubert, the true founder of the new realism, — were solitary observers and critical commentators of the social life of their own day. (The courageous public fight put up by Zola in connection with the Dreyfus affair came too late and was too much a mere episode in Zola's life to effect any radical change in his creative method.) Zola's naturalist "experimental" novels were therefore merely attempts to find a method by which the writer, now reduced to a mere spectator, could again realistically master reality. Naturally Zola never became conscious of this social degradation of the writer; his theory and practice grew out of this social existence without his ever becoming aware of it. On the contrary, inasmuch as he had some inkling of the change in the writer's position in capitalist society, he, as the liberal positivist that he was, regarded it as an advantage, as a step forward, and therefore praised Flaubert's impartiality (which in reality did not exist) as a new trait in the writer's make-up. Lafargue who, in accordance with the traditions of Marx and Engels, severely criticized Zola's creative method and contrasted it with that of Balzac, saw very clearly that Zola was isolated from the social life of his time. Lafargue described Zola's attitude to reality as similar to that of a newspaper reporter and this is perfectly in accordance with Zola's own programmatic statements about the correct creative method in literature.

Of these statements we quote only one, in which he gives his opinion on the proper conception of a good novel: "A naturalist writer wants to write a novel about the stage. Starting from this point without characters or data, his first concern will be to collect material, to find out what he can about this world he wishes to describe. He may have known a few actors and seen a few performances . . . Then he will talk to the people best informed on the subject, will collect statements, anecdotes, portraits. But this is not all. He will also read the written documents available. *Finally* he will visit the locations, *spend a few days* in a theatre in order to acquaint himself with the smallest details, pass an evening in an actress' dressing-room and absorb the atmosphere as much as possible. When all this material has been gathered, the novel will take shape of its own accord. All the novelist has to do is group the facts in a logical sequence . . . *Interest will no longer be focussed on the* peculiarities of the story — on the contrary, the more general and commonplace the story is, the more typical it will be."

Here we have the new realism, *recte* naturalism, in concentrated essence and in sharp opposition to the traditions of the old realism; a mechanical average takes the place of the dialectic unity of type and individual; description and analysis is substituted for epic situations and epic plots. The tension of the old-type story, the co-operation and clashing of human beings who are both individuals and at the same time represent- atives of important class tendencies — all these are eliminated and their place is taken by "average" characters whose individual traits are accidents from the artistic point of view (or in other words have no decisive influence on what happens in the story) and these "average" characters act without a pattern, either merely side by side or else in completely chaotic fashion.

It was only because he could not always consistently adhere to his own programme that Zola could ever come to be a great writer.

But we must not assume that Zola represents the same "triumph of realism" of which Engels speaks in connection with Balzac. The analogy is merely formal and the assumption would therefore be wrong. Balzac boldly exposed the contradictions of nascent capitalist society and hence his observation of reality constantly clashed with his political prejudices. But as an honest artist he always depicted only what he himself saw, learned and underwent, concerning himself not at all whether his true-to-life description of the things he saw contradicted his pet ideas. It was out of this conflict that the "triumph of reality" was born, but then Balzac's *artistic* objectives did not preclude the extensive and penetrating presentation of social reality.

Zola's position was totally different. There is no such wide gap between Zola's social and political views and the social-critical tendencies of his work as there is in Balzac's. True, his observation of facts and of historical evolution did slowly radicalize Zola and bring him closer to Utopian socialism, but this did not amount to a clash between the writer's prejudices and reality.

The contrast in the sphere of art is all the sharper. Zola's method, which hampered not only Zola himself but his whole generation, because it was the result of the writer's position as solitary observer, prevents any profoundly realistic representation of life. Zola's "scientific" method always seeks the average, and this grey statistical mean, the point at which all internal contradictions are blunted, where the great and the petty, the noble and the base, the beautiful and the ugly are all mediocre "products" together, spells the doom of great literature.

Zola was a far too naive liberal all his life, far too ardent a believer in *bourgeois* progress, ever to harbour any doubts regarding his own very questionable, positivist "scientific" method.

Nevertheless the artistic implementation of his method was not achieved without a struggle. Zola the writer was far too conscious of the greatness of modern life (even though the greatness was inhuman) for him to resign himself without a struggle to the grey tedium which would have been the result of a method such as his, if consistently carried through. Zola hated and despised far too much the evil, base, reactionary forces which permeate capitalist society, for him to remain a cold, unsympathetic "experimenter" such as the positivist-naturalist doctrine required him to be.

As we have seen, the struggle resulting from this was fought out within the framework of Zola's own creative method. In Balzac it was reality and political bias that were at war with each other, in Zola it was the creative method and the "material" presented. Hence in Zola there is no such universal break-through as the "triumph of realism" in Balzac, there are only isolated moments, details, in which the author breaks the chain of his own positivist, "scientific," naturalist dogmas in order to give free scope to his temperament in truly realist fashion.

We can find such a break-through in almost every one of Zola's novels and hence there are admirably life-like *single episodes* in every one of his major books. But they can not permeate the entire work, for the doctrine still triumphs in the general lay-out of each of them. Thus the strange situation is created that Zola, although his life-work is very extensive, has never created a single character who grew to be a type, a by-word, almost a living being, such as for instance the Bovary couple or Homais the apothecary in Flaubert, not to mention the immortal figures given us by such creators of men as Balzac or Dickens.

But there was an urge in Zola, to go beyond the grey average of naturalism in his composition. Thus it is that he created many extraordinarily effective pictures. No reader can fail to be deeply impressed by his admirable descriptions of pits and markets, the stock exchange, a racecourse, a battlefield or a theatre. Perhaps no one has painted more colourfully and suggestively the outer trappings of modern life.

But only the *outer* trappings.

They form a gigantic backdrop in front of which tiny, haphazard people move to and fro and live their haphazard lives. Zola could never achieve what the truly great realists Balzac, Tolstoy or Dickens accomplished: to present social institutions as human relationships and social objects as the vehicles of such relationships. Man and his surroundings are always sharply divided in all Zola's works.

Hence, as soon as he departs from the monotony of naturalism, he is immediately transmuted into a decorative picturesque romanticist, who treads in the footsteps of Victor Hugo with his bombastic monumentalism.

There is a strange element of tragedy here.

Zola, who as we have seen, criticized Balzac and Stendhal so vehemently for their alleged romanticism, was compelled to have recourse to a romanticism of the Victor Hugo stamp in order to escape, in part at least, from the counter-artistic consequences of his own naturalism.

Sometimes Zola himself seemed to realise this discrepancy. The romantic, rhetorical and picturesque artificiality of style produced by the triumph of French naturalism, was at variance with Zola's sincere love of truth. As a decent man and honest writer he felt that he himself was much to blame for this. "I am too much a son of my time, I am too deeply immersed in romanticism for me to dream of emancipating myself from certain rhetoric prejudices. . . . Less artificiality and more solidity — I should like us to be less brilliant and to have more real content. . . ."

But he could find no way out of this dilemma in the sphere of art. On the contrary, the more vigorously he participated in the struggle of opinions, the more rhetorical his style became.

For there are only two roads leading out of the monotonous commonplace of naturalism, which results from the direct, mechanical mirroring of the humdrum reality of capitalism. Either the writer succeeds in revealing the human and social significance of the struggle for life and lifting it to a higher plane by artistic means (as Balzac did) — or else he has to overstress the mere outward scenery of life, rhetorically and picturesquely, and quite independently of the human import of the events depicted (like Victor Hugo).

Such was the romantic dilemma which faced French naturalism. Zola (as before him Flaubert) took the second road because he was in sincere opposition to the ideology of the post-revolutionary *bourgeoisie*; because he hated and despised that glorification of false ideals and false "great men" which was the fashion of his time and because he was quite determined to expose all this without mercy. But the most honest and sincere determination to fight for such things could not make up for the artistic falsity of the method and the inorganic nature of the presentation resulting from it.

Goethe in his old age had already seen this parting of the ways, the "romantic" dilemma of the nascent new literature. In the last years of his life he read almost simultaneously Balzac's *The Asses' Skin* and Victor Hugo's *Notre-Dame of Paris*. About Balzac's novel he wrote in his diary: "I have continued reading 'The Asses' Skin.' . . . it is an excellent work of the latest literary method and excels among other things by moving to and fro between the impossible and the intolerable with vigour and good taste and succeeds in most consistently making use as a medium of the miraculous and of the strangest states of mind and events, to the details of which one could give much more praise."

In other words, Goethe saw quite clearly that Balzac used the romantic element, the grotesque, the fantastic, the bizarre, the ugly, the ironically or sententiously exaggerated only in order to show up essential human and social relationships. All this was for Balzac merely a means, if a roundabout one, to the creation of a realism which, while absorbing the new aspects of life, would yet preserve the qualities of the older great literature.

Goethe's opinion of Victor Hugo was the exact opposite of his attitude to Balzac. He wrote to Zelter: "Victor Hugo's 'Notre Dame' captivates the reader by diligent study of the old scenes, customs and events, but the characters show no trace of natural animation. They are lifeless lay figures pulled about by wires; they are cleverly put together, but the wood and steel skeletons support mere stuffed puppets with whom the author deals most cruelly, jerking them into the strangest poses, contorting them, tormenting and whipping them, cutting up their bodies and souls, — but because they have no flesh and blood, all he can do is tear up the rags out of which they are made: all this is done with considerable historical and rhetorical talent and a vivid imagination; without these qualities he could not have produced these abominations. . . ."

Of course Zola cannot simply be identified with Victor Hugo, although Hugo, too, had gone a little way in the direction of realism. *Les Misérables* and *"1793"* doubtless show a higher level of characterization than *Notre-Dame of Paris* although of *Les Misérables* Flaubert angrily remarked that such a characterization of social conditions and human beings was impermissible in an age in which Balzac had already written his works.

But Hugo was never able to get away from his basic mistake, which was that he portrayed human beings independently of their social environment — and from the resulting puppet-like nature of his characters. The aged Goethe's judgment of Hugo is valid, with some mitigation, in respect of all Hugo's novels. Zola, who followed this tradition, is equally incapable of penetrating and convincing characterization.

Zola depicts with naturalist fidelity the biological and "psychological" entity of the average human being and this preserves him from treating his characters as arbitrarily as Victor Hugo. But on the one hand this method sets his characterization very narrow limits and on the other hand the combination of two contradictory principles, i.e. of naturalism and romantically rhetorical monumentality again produce a Hugoan discrepancy between characters and environment which he cannot overcome.

Hence Zola's fate is one of the literary tragedies of the nineteenth century. Zola is one of those outstanding personalities whose talents and human qualities destined them for the greatest things, but who have been prevented by capitalism from accomplishing their destiny and finding themselves in a truly realistic art.

This tragic conflict is obvious in Zola's life-work, all the more as capitalism was unable to conquer Zola the man. He trod his path to the end, honourably, indomitably, uncompromisingly. In his youth he fought with courage for the new literature and art (he was a supporter of Manet and the impressionists) and in his riper years he again played the man in the battle against the conspiracy of the French clericals and the French general staff in the Dreyfus affair.

Zola's resolute struggle for the cause of progress will survive many of his one-time fashionable novels, and will place his name in history side by side with that of Voltaire who defended Calas as Zola defended Dreyfus. Surrounded by the fake democracy and corruption of the Third Republic, by the false so-called democrats who let no day pass without betraying the traditions of the great French revolution, Zola stands head and shoulders above them as the model of the courageous and high-principled *bourgeois* who — even if he failed to understand the essence of socialism — did not abandon democracy even when behind it the Socialist demands of the working class were already being voiced.

We should remember this to-day when the Republic has become a mere cover for a conquest-hungry colonial imperialism and a brutal oppression of the metropolitan working class.

The mere memory of Zola's courageous and upright figure is an indictment of the so-called "democracy" represented by the men who rule France to-day.

The Man-Eater   Roland Barthes*

Nana is the daughter of Coupeau, the alcoholic worker of *L'Assommoir*. A bad actress but a good courtesan, Nana gathers around her a whole society of men: bankers, journalists, officers, aristocrats, high officials in Napoleon III's government. She lives sumptuously off them, squanders fortunes, drives some into ruin, others to stealing, and those that are left to suicide. When she has destroyed everything around her, Nana simply departs, disappears into some mythical Russia for a time; then she comes back to Paris to die of smallpox on the very day that war is declared (1870).

The symbolic movement of this work is clear: Nana, the working-class girl, corrupts the bourgeoisie, destroys it — and destroys herself in the process. Corresponding to the military debacle of 1871 is the more fundamental disintegration of imperial France, both physical and moral: corrupted by Nana, the whole society of the Second Empire crumbles. Thus the People have their revenge. But alienated by the bourgeoisie, they are dragged into the collapse that they cause: the whole of France succumbs in the wake of imperial fascism.

Nana is truly an epic book; not only because of the admirable excess of the descriptions, but also because of the very tempo of the work, the familiar tempo of catastrophes. Zola wishes to describe a degradation, a collapse, and the whole movement of his narrative bows to that intention. For example, at the beginning the pace is slow, meticulous, sluggish, as we are presented with the happiness of an inflation of pleasures and the author dwells at length upon the events of a single evening. Then, as the rot sets in, as the men are more and more tenaciously held in Nana's sway, the narrative gains speed and months at the end of the story are like minutes at the beginning: the disintegration is swept along in a progressive movement which conveys its implacable nature in such a fascinating manner.

Another epic trait is the way in which Nana herself is the victim of the havoc that she wreaks, without any kind of compensation or even any kind of lesson. We know that the essential movement of tragedy is one of decline, of progressive loss — Oedipus, for example, led into solitude and exile by the carefully measured discovery of his identity, or the Shakespearian kings, dethroned by some solar successor, so many individuals gradually lost in the night. Why, therefore, is *Nana* an epic work, rather than a tragic work? It is because tragic heroes have a double fate: in the very movement that plunges them into misfortune, they acquire a more acute awareness of their humanity, they discover their own worth, and the very

*From the *Bulletin Mensuel* of the Guilde du Livre (Lausanne), June 1955, 226–28. Translated for this volume by David Baguley. Reprinted by permission of Les Editions Claire-fontaine.

excess of their suffering comes in the end to comprise an ultimate form of wisdom and knowledge that is precisely their victory over destiny (Oedipus is happy at Colonus, Richard II becomes his true self in prison). Now, none of this applies to Nana: she has no tragic power, because she has no power of understanding; she remains to the very end an instrument, an explosive or corrosive mechanism (as the case may be), mercilessly placed in the society of the Second Empire, fulfilling her task of destruction without any possible redemption. Thus *Nana* is truly an epic, the narrative account of a development about which there is never any awareness situated within the work itself, a work in which there is never that kind of self-reflexion among the characters that we see in tragedy. Zola's remains the only consciousness of the catastrophe precisely because he wished the catastrophe to have no other consciousness than that of history itself; he is the bard, human, yet all the more terrifying for the manner in which he always maintains, a little ahead of us so that we can see it better and avoid being engulfed by it, this agonizing fresco of the swallowing up of a whole society.

We should also attribute to the epic nature of *Nana* a common procedure of Zola's works (though procedure is not really the proper term, for in reality it is a question of the fundamental principle of his art), which involves reducing the world to a few sensations, which become in the process like palpable essences (what is called, in Classical epic, the characteristic epithet: Athene's sea-green eyes). Zola's depiction is always obsessional: for example, love is never described other than as overheating, and Zola never alludes to a desire without immediately coupling it with the same thematic trait, heat. It is a wonderful procedure for effecting useful distortions, and we can see yet again how much genius is above all a matter of persistency.

This means that Zola arrives at the truth, whatever academic classifications say, by other means than Naturalism. Zola is an epic writer, a distorter: he distorts in the direction of an illustrative truth, not a natural truth; he does not copy reality, he ex-presses it (just as one expresses the flesh of fruit to squeeze out the juice); that is to say that far from reconstituting hundreds of details and nuances by using the very proportions of the original, he digs deeply, makes a choice, looks for the essential theme and turns it into a kind of nail which he hammers powerfully from one end of the book to the other. What Zola produces this way are types, but types that are palpable, endowed less with the algebraic psychology of the Classical moralists than with flesh, with a humour, with blood by which their condition, their weakness, their vulgarity or their hereditary trait is revealed. This thematics of the flesh is not gratuitous, however; it attempts to provide evidence of understanding, contribute to a reading of History that is more profound than the pleasures of the novel.

This inspired distortion has allowed Zola, in *Nana*, to depict the society of the Second Empire with the kind of terrible detached stance of an ethnologist studying a Kwakiutl tribe. As I have just indicated, with Zola it is not a question of scientific objectivity, but, on the contrary, of a distorting objectivity which involves taking the samples of humanity in question as real objects to which two or three adjectives are joined whenever they are mentioned. Now, Zola's capacity for objectifying (and not his objectivity) is enormous, especially when it is applied to the men and women of the Second Empire; to our great amazement we find ourselves faced with a piece of anthropology as strange as the life of the Papuans; we even have the impression that these human beings, some of whom however might quite simply have been our grandparents (not a very flattering prospect), did not have the same morphology as ourselves, that they had different humours, different sensations, gestures, smells, appetites, and that, in general, they lived in a different physical world from our own. This is so much so that we find it difficult sometimes to understand the wholesale devastation that Nana brings about; affectively, it seems to us almost as improbable as the seductive power of the Venus of the Hottentots. (Yet this is not at all important: *Nana* remains a fascinating book, for its beauty, its power of persuasion, lies in the materiality of its demonstration, not in the verisimilitude of its scheme.)

That is not to say, however, that Zola's distorting genius is alone responsible for this sense of remoteness. In fact — and it is not an insignificant fact — we are ordinarily far more familiar with earlier periods of our past: our adventure stories, our historical dramas (think how many plays there are on Magellan, Christopher Columbus, Savonarola, the Sun King, etc.), our cinema, all our imaginative arts assimilate much more easily Classical or pre-Classical man, the grandee of Spain, the musketeer, or the marquis, than they do the frock-coated individual of the Second Empire. It is an age that is out of favour with us now; it does not even have the caricatural charm of 1900. It is for us an improbable age, one without attractions, bizarre, and both baroque and vulgar. From the point of view of human history, it was however, fundamentally, a fascinating age, though politically sinister: its daring commercial adventures, the fabulous construction of modern types of business, all this should pique our curiosity far more than a Louis III cavalcade or a Romantic interior.

Nana will do nothing, in our estimation, to lessen the remoteness of the mental habits of that age. Indeed it will have the opposite effect. But for that very reason, by lending an excess of colour to that world, Zola forces us even today to direct at that spectacle the eyes of History itself. Far from boring us, as many novelists do, by describing a kind of episode in the barely historicized life of the Eternal Woman, eternally the man-eater, Zola presents us with this supposedly universal phenomenon in all its historical particularity. And we stop sighing and start judging. Then we have a better understanding of this epic art: by restoring the human dimension to History, the artist invites us to take actively full cognizance of it. Nana, the woman of perdition, ceases to be a character of all ages to recapture an individuality whose very strangeness calls upon a sense of judgement and not a feeling of identification. This is why *Nana*, despite the terrible bitterness of its portrayal, is a very fine book, a very great book, and, when all is said and done, I would even suggest, if the word had not acquired tedious traditional associations, that are thoroughly contradicted by its powerful interest, a civic book.

Emile Zola

F. W. J. Hemmings*

Shortly after the conclusion of the Franco-Prussian war a young English reporter on the staff of the *Illustrated London News* found himself at Versailles, with an assignment to cover the deliberations of the National Assembly. One day a French colleague pointed out to him a pale, shabby, worried-looking individual, and said with a snigger: "Look, there's Zola. You know — the man who believes in Manet!"

At that time Zola had published six novels, besides a volume of short stories and a collection of critical essays. But he was still remembered mainly for the frightful scandal he had caused before the war by his campaign in favour of Manet. He was still thought of by the public at large as the man who insisted there was talent in "Le Déjeuner sur l'herbe" and the rest of the extraordinary daubs perpetrated by this crude barbarian, this practical joker whom no respectable art critic could take seriously.

Zola's defence of Manet had been published as a pamphlet under the title *Une nouvelle manière en peinture,* which could be reasonably translated "innovations in painting." This was in 1867, and later the same year Zola had brought out his novel *Thérèse Raquin* which might have been (though it was not) reviewed under the heading "innovations in fiction." *Thérèse Raquin* may not be a great work of literature, but nothing quite like it had been written before.

At first it did not sell too well; then someone on the staff of *Le Figaro* focused attention on it by publishing a violently hostile article entitled "Putrid Literature." Reviewers were a good deal more uninhibited in those days. Zola's novel was referred to as "a puddle of mud and blood," and he was accused of "seeing woman as M. Manet paints her, mud-coloured and daubed with pink lipstick" — a side-swipe, no doubt, at Manet's notorious "Olympia." Thanks to this calculated rudeness, people started to buy *Thérèse Raquin* and it went rapidly into a second edition. Zola added a preface in which he alluded to the diatribe in *Le Figaro* and professed

*Reprinted, by permission of the author, from the *Listener* 75 (21 April 1966):574–80. This study was originally a B.B.C. talk in the series "The Novelist as Innovator."

himself amazed that his book should be judged sordid. He was not aware, he said, that he was being any more improper than painters who set out to render a nude model on canvas. In deliberately drawing the analogy — a dubious one, I would say — between the novelist's work and the painter's, and in implicitly accepting his reviewer's comparison between *Thérèse Raquin* and "Olympia," Zola shows at least what his ambition was: to innovate in the same kind of way as Manet had innovated. And the proof that he was doing this would be that public reaction to *Thérèse Raquin* would be as violently hostile as it had been to "Olympia" when that picture was exhibited in 1865, three years before.

If we read *Thérèse Raquin* today, almost a century after its publication, few of us are going to be shocked. This is natural enough, since any literary innovation, if it is at all fruitful, is bound in time to lose its power to shock, though if it is at all significant it should retain its power to impress. Zola thought that his principal innovation had been to invent characters without souls, as he put it. What he meant was that his characters are governed entirely by their animal appetites and are therefore incapable of making moral choices. But it is obvious that his characters do make moral choices — bad ones — and suffer the consequences, just as they would if they had been created by a novelist convinced of the spiritual nature of man. Zola prefers to talk about nervous breakdowns and avoids talking about pangs of conscience, and this has its significance, no doubt, but makes little difference to the situation. Thérèse and her lover Laurent conspire to murder Thérèse's husband Camille. The crime escapes detection, but the two murderers end by punishing themselves and each other; both finally commit suicide. The moral law, then, exists, and though it may be temporarily upset, it will in the end reassert itself. This is not a particularly disturbing thesis, nor a particularly materialistic one.

Yet *Thérèse Raquin* remains a disturbing work; not by reason of its emphatic materialism, which hardly matters, but because of the quality of imagination that Zola manifests here for the first time. *Thérèse Raquin* is a masterpiece of the macabre, sufficiently related to day-to-day reality to avoid the absurdities of the run-of-the-mill horror story. If one is looking for parallels one will turn, perhaps, to Poe or Hawthorne or think of certain scenes in Dickens. With Zola, as with these others, the potency of the effect on the reader derives most probably from the coincidence between some deep-seated private obsession or neurosis in the writer and certain rudimentary psychic fears present, if buried, in most people's minds. In the case of *Thérèse Raquin* the personal origin of some of Zola's more dreadful inventions is demonstrable, as far as such things are demonstrable.

Towards the end of the novel there is a particularly revolting scene where Thérèse and Laurent, having got married after Camille has met his end in what passes as a boating accident, find themselves simultaneously suffering from the hallucination that Camille's drowned corpse is lying between them in bed, preventing them from embracing. They imagine they can feel the clammy wetness and the sponginess of the rotting flesh. They suppose that, even after death, Camille continues to show himself jealous; they have gone to the trouble of killing him, and all to no purpose. In *Germinal*, a novel written many years later, there is a scene in which the hero and heroine, Etienne and Catherine, are trapped below ground when the coal-mine they are working in is flooded. Catherine's man Chaval, a brutal bully, has been killed by Etienne, and his body is floating in the flood-water. Being in the dark, Catherine and Etienne cannot see the corpse, but as they sit on a ledge of rock just above the level of the water, a current keeps washing it against their feet. Zola's comment here was this: "Chaval would not go away, he wanted to be with them, against them . . . There was no point in having smashed his head in, if they were to have him come back between them, obstinately jealous. To the very end he would be there, even dead, to prevent them coming together."

It is difficult to believe that this is a deliberate echo in *Germinal* of the episode in *Thérèse Raquin*. Both passages are, or bear every sign of being, compulsive representations of the same private neurosis. This is where we touch on what is so individual in Zola's art, so difficult to tease out, and at the same time so fascinating and necessary to study: the irresistible intrusion of personal fantasies in works which Zola did his deliberate utmost to construct as impartial, objective studies.

But even on the level of explicit intention Zola was a portentous innovator: not in *Thérèse Raquin*, and not in fact until ten years later when he started writing the series of masterpieces of which the first was *L'Assommoir*. When *Thérèse Raquin* was published Zola, who knew all the tricks of the trade, having been publicity manager in the firm of Hachette for some years, wrote to Hippolyte Taine suggesting he should review the book in the *Journal des Débats*; no doubt he would have liked Taine to champion him as he had championed Manet. Taine was too cautious to rise to the bait, though he did send Zola a long letter of encouragement and advice. Zola had been reading Taine with admiration for some time; what had struck him most was Taine's bold positing of analogies between the physical sciences and what were then called the moral sciences. Everything can be accounted for, according to Taine; a man does not run a temperature for no reason, similarly he does not turn to crime for no reason. The scientist's job—the moral scientist's job—is to analyse the circumstances and to arrive at the causes by deduction.

Taine was, in a sense, tracing the programme of the still embryonic sciences of psychology and sociology. As a strictly academic discipline, sociology came into being within Zola's lifetime, but as far as I know he never read the seminal works of Durkheim and Gabriel Tarde, though Durkheim's *Règles de la méthode sociologique* came out in 1895 and Tarde's *Études de psychologie sociale* in 1898. Nevertheless, in his most important and influential books, which were published in the eighteen-seventies and eighties, Zola proceeded much as a sociologist might; it could be said that he raised sociology to the dignity of art before sociology had acquired the status of a science.

All through the century novelists had been observing and commenting on the social scene, depicting the conflict between old rank and new wealth, the cleavage between the provinces and the capital, the impact of the industrial revolution, the occult power of the Church. But earlier writers had never considered giving these particular aspects of the social scene precedence over the drama of the individual, which remained their central preoccupation. When we read the second part of *Illusions perdues* we are given a lively and horrifying picture of the underworld of journalism in the early days of newspapers; but it is clear that Balzac's real interest, in composing this work, lay in charting the swift rise to fame and sudden fall into ignominy of Lucien de Rubempré, who exists as a highly specific individual, charming, gifted, ambitious, but a snob, weak-willed, sensual, and lacking in moral fibre; we feel that, if a journalistic career had not happened to offer the right framework, Balzac would have cheerfully substituted some other field of activity in which to display Lucien with the good and evil in him. The social problem of an irresponsible and corrupt press manipulated by unscrupulous financiers and shady politicians was comparatively marginal. The difference is one of approach rather than emphasis, as can be realized when one compares this novel of Balzac's with, say, Evelyn Waugh's *Scoop.*

Similarly, Julien Sorel may have been to some extent typical of the young plebeian of the post-Napoleonic period, educated beyond his station and discontented with his lot; but Stendhal's hero is so much more than this—he is both typical and exceptional, as will be, in her turn, Emma Bovary. Flaubert said of her: "My poor Emma suffers and weeps in twenty villages in France at this very time." He did not say "in twenty hundred villages." In other words, though you could find unhappy wives like Emma, you could not generalize from Emma's predicament and reach valid conclusions about the working of marriage among the bourgeoisie in rural France in the middle of the nineteenth century.

VICTIMS OF SOCIAL PHENOMENA

Zola, on the other hand, means us to generalize. He never created a Lucien de Rubempré, a Julien Sorel, or an Emma Bovary. Since he shared the interests of the social scientist, it was to the social problem that he addressed himself first; the characters were to function within the terms of the problem. He kept, of the old-fashioned novel, at any rate the formula of the central character who however was not meant to be regarded as significant in himself; he was intended to be no more than a witness, or perhaps a victim, of the particular social phenomenon that the novel was really about.

We can regard *L'Assommoir*, if we like, as conforming to the type of the time-honoured "fictional biography," like *Le Rouge et le Noir* or *Madame Bovary*, or like George Moore's *Esther Waters*, written later and to some extent in imitation of *L'Assommoir*. Indeed, Zola's first idea for a title was *The Simple Life of Gervaise Macquart*. The book describes Gervaise's career, tells us what she hoped to get out of life, and how grievously disappointed she was in the end.

But is that the subject of the book? Gervaise emerges as a figure for whom one can feel some compassion, some admiration; but her freedom of action is too circumscribed, the choices open to her are too limited, for her to bear by herself the weight of the structure of the book. The point has been made with some force in one of the chapters of Ian Gregor and Brian Nicholas's study, *The Moral and the Story*. Gervaise, it is said here, "is illustrative not so much of a human or cosmic as of a social truth. She is not a tragic victim, but a casualty, in a particular milieu where the casualty rate is high." The writers go on to observe, plausibly enough, that the misfortunes that overtake Gervaise could have befallen any other person in that particular milieu: "The point being made is a general sociological one: Gervaise is chosen to give it undogmatic illustration." If one agrees that a novel has value chiefly as it provides opportunity for the discussion and elucidation of personal issues of behaviour — as do all novels that fit into what has been called the "great tradition" — then one will conclude, with Gregor and Nicholas,[1] that *L'Assommoir* belongs to an aesthetic of "strictly limited potentialities"

The mistake these critics have made is to suppose that the novel is about Gervaise and that discussion of the novel should centre on her. But Zola rejected the title *La Simple Vie de Gervaise Macquart*. He substituted the name of the gin-shop that plays a certain part in bringing about Gervaise's downfall, but even this can be misleading: *L'Assommoir* is not really about the ravages of drink in the lower classes, though the Victorians supposed it was and for that reason accorded it qualified approval. Drink is a social problem, but not a sociological one. *L'Assommoir* really deals with the immovability of class barriers. Gervaise has ambitions to rise out of the proletariat into the class immediately above and, for a while, she succeeds; she opens a laundry business and becomes a small-scale employer of labour. Then the business folds up and she is back where she started.

HISTORICAL THEMES

All Zola's important novels after *L'Assommoir* similarly treat of big social issues, like the difficulty of moving from one class to the next one up.

I say "big" because there is a difference between the problems Zola interested himself in and the relatively circumscribed ones that Dickens, for instance, occasionally dealt with. The social scandals exposed by Dickens — unsupervised private schools, bureaucratic red tape, the cumbrous slowness of the law — were susceptible to treatment by reform; Zola was not a reformer — not, at least, when he was writing novels. His themes were, more than anything, historical: the transformation of retail trade with the emergence of the big emporiums; the fatal conservatism of the small farmer at a time of revolutionary changes in food production; the prevalence of belief in faith-healing at the end of a century which had seen more rapid strides in medicine than had any previous century. These gave him the subjects of *Au Bonheur des Dames*, *La Terre*, *Lourdes*, three novels unlike anything anyone had written before. (Balzac, who was not a sociologist, ran into endless trouble trying to write his novel on the rural classes in France, and finally abandoned *Les Paysans* without finishing it.) And what was the subject of *Germinal?* Zola spelled it out for himself at the beginning of his plan: the novel was to deal with "the struggle between capital and labour"; this would turn out to be "the most important question of the twentieth century."

The innovation was a striking one, not well understood at the time, though Henry James did at least see that the question to be asked about Zola was why he wrote novels at all, instead of devoting himself, as he put it with a touch of irony, "to an equal task in physics, mathematics, politics, or economics." It has proved a fruitful innovation. We have only to think of the number of novels currently being written about, for instance, the problem of racial intolerance, whether set in South Africa, the United States, or parts of England. Their authors may never have read a line of Zola but they are nevertheless exploring the country he opened up. Truly, an aesthetic "of strictly *un*limited potentialities."

All the same, it is doubtful whether Zola would be as significant a writer as he is if all he had done was to annex sociology to the novel. Many writers, since 1885, have attempted to dramatize "the struggle between capital and labour," but not even out of Russia has come a second *Germinal*. The impact of *Germinal* depends in the last resort not on the subject but on the way Zola treated his subject. The relative weakness of some of his other novels, like *L'Argent* or *La Débâcle*, is traceable to the fact that their interest depends on little else but the subject.

NANA

Take one I have not so far mentioned: *Nana*. In *Nana* the sociological fact that Zola started from was the well-known one that the large armies of prostitutes which used to patrol the streets of big cities in his day were recruited from the lower classes. And so Nana, the daughter of Gervaise Macquart, born and bred, in the slums, exists as a social reality, the "brutal *fille*," as Henry James unfeelingly described her, "without a conscience or a soul, with nothing but devouring appetites and impudences." But if she were totally describable in such terms, would *Nana* still be read? There were any number of novels written in France in the eighteen-seventies and eighties about the lives of prostitutes, before and after *Nana*; well-written books, some of them, but all of them works of pornography in the original meaning of the word, that is, as the dictionary defines it: "descriptions of the lives and manners of prostitutes and their patrons." Though their authors—Edmond de Goncourt, Huysmans, Charles-Louis Philippe—were men of talent, these books are seldom opened today.

Nana, on the other hand, still has its readers by the thousand, the reason being that it is something more than the fictional biography of a prostitute, because its heroine is something more than a prostitute. At the end of the last-but-one chapter, immediately after Zola has described her breaking out in a fit of tearful repentance when it is borne in on her how many domestic tragedies she has unwittingly caused, he shows her, having recovered her spirits, standing in the hall of her luxurious mansion, buttoning on her gloves. Nana, he wrote, "was standing alone in the midst of the heaped-up treasures of her house, with a nation of men at her feet. Like those monsters of ancient fable whose fearful lair was strewn with bones, she set her feet on skulls."

If Manet had chosen to paint this scene, instead of the "realistic" Nana that he actually did paint, he would have produced something more like a Gustave Moreau than a Manet. Nana, here, transcends the sociological facts. She is a mythical figure belonging to epic poetry, a symbol of the destructiveness of sexual passion, just as the very different figure of Penelope is the mythical embodiment of wifely fidelity in the proto-novel *The Odyssey*. One is at liberty, of course, to postulate some latent dread of sex in Zola, manifesting itself in *Nana*; the creation is personal, but its origins all the same are as diffuse as the origins of the religions of man. Hesiod speaks of Eros as "him who loosens the limbs and damages the mind," and early Greek vase-paintings show the god of love as no playful putto, but as a formidable figure wielding an axe or a whip. As Thomas Mann asked in his essay on Wagner: "Is not that Astarte of the Second Empire, called Nana, a symbol and a myth? How does she come by her name? It is a primitive sound, one of the early, sensual lispings of mankind; Nana was a cognomen of the Babylonian Ishtar. Did Zola know this? All the more remarkable and significant if he did not know it."

Not only in *Nana*, but in all Zola's major works, beginning with *L'Assommoir*, we are aware of this extra dimension, of the fact that beneath the sociological superstructure flow fierce, primitive undercurrents, like an age-old torrent thundering below a solidly constructed, utilitarian modern bridge. Why did he choose to dramatize the "struggle between capital and labour," in *Germinal*, by showing us a community of miners instead of, for instance, factory workers, who were just as subject to wage-cuts, just as apt to go on strike? He chose the mine because it was important to him that the action of *Germinal* should take place in the bowels of the earth, representing the deep underground tunnels of the subconscious, that "cellarage" where Hamlet's father's ghost moves around, the hell of Christian and pagan mythologies.

Why, in *La Bête humaine*, is there so much furtiveness, deception, spying, and fear of exposure, so that there is scarcely a character who has not some secret to hide from the others? What has all this to do with railways, or even with the growing gap between technological advance and moral progress, Zola's ostensible themes in *La Bête humaine*? We know today that at the time he was writing the book, Zola had just embarked on a love-affair — his first infidelity in eighteen years of married life. This fact, taken in conjunction with the qualities of *La Bête humaine* just mentioned, helps us to realize the extent to which Zola, this allegedly objective reporter on the social scene, used his novels for disguised confession of his own anxieties, which are also our anxieties, unless our private lives have always been so blameless that we have never had anything to hide.

Did he know what he was doing? One comes back to Thomas Mann's words: "All the more remarkable and significant if he did not know it." If he had understood himself better, he might have understood better what he was doing, though that would not have helped him and might have inhibited him. He supposed that what he was doing was to show that psychology is only a special branch of physiology; he imagined that he was indicating to legislators and administrators the pressing tasks awaiting their attention; he flattered himself that scientists and economists would look more closely at the unsolved problems to which he drew attention in his books. And all the time what he was chiefly doing was to add his quota to the gods and monsters of that legendary era, the nineteenth century.

Note

1. *The Moral and the Story.* Faber, 1962.

Zola's Blue Flame

Michel Butor*

The transfer of an unchanged characteristic from person to person down a family line, its presence within a family, is one of the basic characteristics of the Ancien Régime. Furthermore, it is one of the roots of the notion of nobility. The hereditary characteristic is contained in the blood, the same blood being present in all members of one family. In truth this red fluid, which flows from wounds, is an intimate manifestation of that special character trait which so deeply affects each descendant of the founding hero.

Zola's physiological imagination is of untold wealth; one would welcome a study of him comparable to that of Michelet by Roland Barthes. Fluids, especially those called class "humours" are very important.

For the *Rougon-Macquart*, *Le Docteur Pascal* plays almost the same role as the *Etudes philosophiques* in relation to *la Comédie Humaine*. There all the themes are brought together and echoed in a near-fantastic key. If its relation to the whole is examined, it emerges as an admirable, metaphoric commentary containing some of the most highly poetic scenes of our author.

Blood inexhaustibly transmits the distinctive characteristic among the nobility. In Zola's works, the distinctive characteristic embodied by Adélaïde Fouque, though doubtless previously apparent, will only be passed on the length of time required for the fictional experiment. In *Le Docteur Pascal* only one member of the fifth generation prominently displays this characteristic, the others, it would seem, have not inherited it. In this sense, Adélaïde Fouque's "blood" runs out with the death of young Charles.

Charles is the son of Maxime Saccard and a domestic, Justine Megot, a native of the countryside around Plassans, to which she returns with a pension to raise him. She has married and has two other children.

> Charles at the age of fifteen hardly seemed twelve years old, and he still had the stammering intelligence of a five-year-old. He bore a striking resemblance to his great-great-grandmother, tante Dide, . . . he was of a slender, delicate gracefulness similar to one of those small anemic kings crowned with long pale hair, light as milk, who are the last of their line.

Every time he speaks of Charles, Zola refers to this "royal" appearance.

*This article is an extract from a lecture at the Collège de France published (in full) in *Critique* (April 1967) and in *Répertoire IV* (1974), and (as here) in *Les Cahiers naturalistes* (1967). The translation by Michael Saklad appeared in *Yale French Studies*, 1969, 9–25, and is reproduced by permission of the author, *Yale French Studies*, and Les Editions de Minuit.

> Whenever Charles was not at his mother's house . . . he was to be found
> at the home of Félicité or another relative, coquettishly dressed, buried
> in toys and living like the small effeminate dauphin of an extinct race.
>   Nevertheless, this illegitimate child with royal blond hair caused
> much pain to old Mme. Rougon. . . .

His hemophilia is another indication of royalty. He bleeds freely from
the smallest scratch and especially from the nose.

The ancestress Adélaïde Fouque, nicknamed tante Dide, goes mad
after seeing her grandson Silvère Mouret murdered when Pierre Rougon
takes power in Plassans. She is locked away in the Tulettes asylum. Charles
is then taken to see her, and with the permission of the authorities, he
spends afternoons with her, cutting out drawings of soldiers, captains and
especially kings dressed in purple and gold. Usually the watchwoman stays
in the room, but one hot August day, once again noticing the extraordinary
resemblance, she thinks them both so well-behaved that she takes advantage of this to take a break. At first all goes well. The old woman gazes
fixedly at the boy, but then he starts to fall asleep: "His lily white head
seemed to bend under his overly heavy mane of regal hair; he let it fall
gently amongst the drawings and fell asleep with one cheek against the
gold and purple kings."

A glimmer appears in the eyes of the ancestress.

> An event had just occurred; a red drop was flowing along the edge of the
> child's left nostril. This drop fell, then another formed and followed it.
> It was the blood, the dew of the blood which was forming, with no
> bruise or contusion this time, emerging all alone and flowing away in
> the flaccid erosion of degeneracy. The drops became a fine trickle
> flowing over the gold of the drawings. A small pool covered them and
> made its way to a corner of the table; then, new drops formed, falling
> heavy and thick, one by one, on the floor of the room.

Charles awakes, finds himself covered with blood and calls out, but
his voice is already weakening.

Adélaïde then regains all her lucidity; she makes a superhuman effort
to cry out, but she cannot make a sound. She is almost paralyzed by the
shock and looks on, as her own blood runs out. Her royal descendant, her
own likeness, gradually weakens before her eyes: "Charles, now seemingly
asleep and silent, was losing his last blood. It was flowing from his veins
endlessly, almost noiselessly. His lily-white skin turned deathly pale. His
lips lost their color, faded into a wan pink, and finally turned white."

He opens his eyes for the last time. With her own eyes Adélaïde can
see his becoming blank. "Suddenly, they became blank, their light went
out. It was the end, the death of the eyes, and Charles had died without a
quiver, emptied like a spring, whose water has flowed away."

He lies there "divinely handsome, his head resting in the blood,
amongst his tousled royal-blond hair like one of those small, anemic

dauphins" breathing his last breath until the arrival of Pascal. The doctor comes in, accompanied by his mother Félicité Rougon and his niece Clotilde, and discovers his death, the running out of Adélaïde's blood.

The presence of these witnesses momentarily restores her speech. Several times she shouts, "the gendarme!" Three bloody deaths are superimposed in her mind: the death of her lover Macquart, the poacher killed by a gendarme foreign to her "race"; the death of her favorite grandson Silvère, indirectly murdered during the capture of Plassans by his two uncles who are her own sons, the legitimate Pierre Rougon and the illegitimate Antoine Macquart; lastly, the death of this great-great-grandson who died "by his own hand." Of course this will lead to her own death several hours later.

The shock of recognition and the lucidity and speech regained after many years of absence have already been suggested by the heavy gaze of the old woman during the last pages of *Thérèse Raquin*. We will encounter them again in the second of the four *Evangiles*, *Travail*, when old Jérôme Qurignon, standing in front of the smoky ruin of his factory, gathers a few people together to tell them his entire life, although for thirty years he had not said a word: "What a frightful story stored in the head of this eighty-seven-year-old man, and what a series of horrible facts to summarize an entire century of struggle, illuminating the past, present and future of a family! And what a frightening thing was this mind where the story seemed to sleep, this mind which slowly awakened threatening that soon everything would be divulged in a wave of overflowing truth if the already stammering lips were to shout distinct words."

Jérôme Qurignon's long speech seems to grow out of Adélaïde's two words. It is punctuated by the refrain "We must give back . . . we must give back. . . ." In the scene in *Le Docteur Pascal*, Zola explains to us that the "gendarme" represents the law of atonement. This sudden awareness is the awareness of guilt. Of Jérôme Qurignon, Zola says: "He seemed to have survived so many disasters and an entire family of blessed and cursed persons only to understand the most important point. On the day of awakening, before going to his death, he unfolded the long agony of a man who, having believed in his race rooted deep in the empire he founded, survived long enough to see the race and empire blown away by the winds of the future. And he said why he was passing judgment and why he was making amends."

If Jérôme Qurignon suffers from individual guilt as the founder of an industrial empire, how could poor Adélaïde suffer from the same feelings? Of course, little Charles has "execrable ancestors," but this adjective cannot apply to her who is the ancestor par excellence. In the Rougon-Macquart as in the Qurignon family, there is a hereditary unity; the same "personality" is shared by different individuals. The gaze of the fore-fathers, Adélaïde or Jérôme, with its long periods of staring and silence, during which it records everything said and done by its execrable descendants, is the first incarnation of the original distinctive characteristic (first in terms of those persons being studied; there may have been previous incarnations such as the first Qurignon or Adélaïde's father). Conspicuous guilt, which can suddenly restore speech, is present in all individuals in whose bodies flows this "different" blood.

It is not Adélaïde the person who is guilty, but rather her "blood"; Corneille did not say it any differently. The last drops of guilty blood coincide with the first words of speech. If the other individuals are actively guilty, the gaze of the forefathers is guilty on account of its silence. What Charles rids himself of is everything that kept Adélaïde from speaking.

In *Travail*, Jérôme Qurignon delivers himself of all his knowledge and of the complete history of his guilty family.

Thus, the bloody stain, — *"ce lac de sang hanté par de mauvais anges"* — into which not only young Charles is drained and then drowned but also the hereditary difference of the Rougon-Macquart, represents the reports, the evidence about the entire family so scrupulously accumulated by Doctor Pascal Rougon in his large closet. His mother, Félicité, who does not share the blood she has so closely espoused, insists on washing this stain and making it disappear.

There is no doubt that Zola himself felt stained by just such a difference which in various circumstances and settings could become vice, revolt, crime or genius. How could it be channeled into genius?

It would certainly be fascinating to study all the many reflections and characters in the *Rougon-Macquart* representative of the author in relation to the others. But, let us only discuss those for whom he uses the word "genius." There is Claude Lantier, the painter in many ways inspired by Cézanne, but more by Zola than by Cézanne, more deeply Zola than his other representation in *l'OEuvre*, his childhood friend, the author Pierre Sandoz, an unsuccessful yet gifted Lantier, a genius in new form, "when neurosis is under control, Claude shows authentic genius." There is also Doctor Pascal, last figuration of the author, the one who has succeeded in writing books.

Zola is known to have taken the name Monsieur Pascal during the exile in London following the "Dreyfus affair."

Nevertheless, if there is some genius in Doctor Pascal, he considers himself a perfect example of "innateness" which, in the language of Doctor Lucas as adopted by Zola, means the signs of heredity are no longer recognizable in him and that with him there is a return, at least in appearance, to a more general type. Then there is Pascal, symbolizing redemption and resurrection. No longer is there any sign of his membership in the execrable and sometimes gifted family; nothing separates him from those of another blood. The difference, with all its advantages for some of those having it, becomes very ordinary in him. It is not because of his hereditary genius that Doctor Pascal collects his documentation and writes the history of the Rougon-Macquart, but it is rather because he writes the history that the hereditary difference becomes completely unrecognizable in him and turns into pure genius.

This is an execrable family, certainly, but one carrying its genius within it. It is an irreplaceable family, though, since all Second Empire France confesses and empties its guilty blood in it and through it; indeed, this is the reason for which on Charles' death, the family suddenly appears so royal, something quite unexpected at first glance.

However, a rereading of *La Faute de l'abbé Mouret* demonstrates how sensitive Zola was to the medieval idea of man as master of creation.

> However, at this hour the entire park was theirs. They had sovereignly taken possession of it. . . . On the meadows, the grass and waters were theirs. The grass enlarged their kingdom by continually unrolling silver rugs before them; the waters were the greatest of their pleasures. . . . They ruled everywhere, even over the rocks, the streams and this terrible earth which, with its monstrous plants, had quivered under the weight of their bodies. . . .
> Only the plants had not surrendered. Albine and Serge walked regally through the crowd of animals obedient to them.

The emergence of a positive difference allows an individual to be the sole possessor of this royalty. A certain permanence in that difference, which supports the notion of nobility, contributes to consolidating this variation to the advantage of a family line. However, as soon as some usurp royalty, the dispossessed are relegated to the rank of mere animals. Here, the Catholic Church plays an essential role by masking the loss of a kingdom on earth with the promise of a kingdom in heaven. Furthermore those who under other circumstances would have gained by usurpation find themselves in far worse condition. The same hereditary stain, instead of having a positive value, can lead to crime, vice and madness; for instance, it is only necessary that the blood no longer be legitimate or that a person be a Macquart rather than a Rougon. The fate of Jacques Lantier, the "human animal," so human and filled with such admirable qualities, is worse than that of an animal.

And if the permanence of blood, considered by nobility as absolute, is in reality extremely temporary, and if after several generations the positive hereditary difference disappears from the reigning line, any remarkable individual appearing outside this line, even a genius, can only present a danger to those in power and is thus seen to be remarkably bad. The deposed king becomes a monster, and most of the time the man replacing him on the throne is totally unworthy.

The entire history of the Rougon-Macquart unfolds against a background of usurpation. To Zola, as to all nineteenth century writers, Napoleon was obviously a genius. To their mind this explained and almost excused his seizure of power. In his spurious successor Napoleon III, on the other hand, the original distinctive trait, if indeed it remained recognizable, manifested itself entirely differently. The *coup d'état* of the second of December was an absolute usurpation which of necessity resulted in the dehumanization of millions of people.

Old Qurignon repeats, "We must give back, we must give back," and in the context of *Travail* we know this means, "We must give back the fortune we have usurped," especially that represented by the "Abyss" (the name of his factory) in which, as in the "Voreux" (the mine shaft in *Germinal*), the very humanity of the workers is devoured.

Old Adélaïde does not recount her family's history; this is the task of her grandson, Doctor Pascal, who has inherited only her gaze. In young Charles' death he too sees the need to give back, give men back their royalty. Drowned in the bloodstain are all the kings whose pictures the child has just cut out. Using heredity as a technique for novelistic experimentation should help abolish kings forever. Through the blood of the Rougon-Macquart, the blood of all royal or imperial lines should be consumed in forming the characters which make up the novels; from this ink they are drawn.

In *Le Docteur Pascal* this scene is the direct result and, in a way, the outcome of another, equally extraordinary scene. Just before taking Charles, accompanied by Clotilde, to the Tulettes asylum where he will lose all his blood, the doctor visits his illegitimate uncle, old Antoine Macquart, the family disgrace, at his hideaway where he spends his days drinking.

When they arrive the dog is continually, yet quietly moaning. Several times the doctor calls out "Macquart! Macquart!" No one answers. He opens the door; all is dark, and the kitchen is filled with thick nauseating smoke. He opens the shutters.

> The doctor was astonished by what he then noticed. Everything was in place. The glass and the empty proof spirit bottle were on the table. Only the chair the uncle had probably sat on showed any signs of the fire; the front legs were blackened, and the straw seat was half burned. What had become of the uncle, where had he gone? In front of the chair on the tile floor, stained by a pool of grease, only a small heap of ashes remained; next to it lay the pipe, a black pipe, which hadn't even broken when it fell. All that remained of him was contained in this handful of light ashes. He was also present in the reddish-brown cloud floating out the open window and in the layer of soot which had coated the entire kitchen, a horrible grease of transformed flesh covering everything, viscous and repulsive to the touch.

It is a case of "spontaneous combustion," the finest, Zola tells us, a doctor has ever witnessed. He knows perfectly well he is deep in myth: ". . . and nothing remained of him, not a bone, a tooth or a fingernail, nothing except this small pile of gray dust which the draft from the doorway threatened to blow away."

When Antoine Macquart's will is read, it is revealed that he had assigned his entire wealth to the erection of his tomb, "a superb tomb of marble with two enormous crying angels, with folded wings." Nothing of him remained to bury in it, however.

Far from alarmed by this scene, Doctor Pascal is amazed: "And so he died royally like the prince of drunkards . . . (Once again note this "royally") . . . burning of his own flame, burning away in the blazing pyre of his own body. . . . But this is an admirable death! To disappear and leave no trace but a small heap of ashes and a pipe lying nearby!"

The doctor picks up the pipe in order to keep "a relic," he says, but he picks up something else which his niece, Clotilde, had just noticed under the table, a scrap, a shred . . . a woman's green glove. "Look," she shouts, "it's grandmother's glove, you remember, the glove she couldn't find last night."

Then, they both realize that Félicité Rougon, Doctor Pascal's mother, Clotilde's grandmother and Charles' great-grandmother, had been present at the combustion of old Antoine and didn't attempt to prevent it. She admits this a few moments later when they meet her at the asylum just before the child's death.

This is how the murder of old Antoine took place. This murder, seemingly due to an oversight on the part of his half-sister-in-law Félicité, had, in fact, been planned for a long time. Since he had moved to the hideaway near the asylum she had been giving him presents of wine, liqueurs, brandy in hope of "ridding the family of an objectionable old man." When burying him she would have buried both "old, dirty linen and the blood and mud of the two conquests of Plassans." We know such a burial is impossible. To do away with old Antoine is the same for her as doing away with the writings of her son, Pascal. Unfortunately, at the beginning drink seems to do wonders for its victim by restoring his vitality. After administering the dose she deemed sufficient and then putting a stop to this type of "generosity," she had to face a long wait. However, on that very hot August day when she arrived, all was quiet. She too called out, "Macquart! Macquart!" and entered the dark kitchen: "Her first sensation was only that she was choking on the violent stench of alcohol filling the room. Every piece of furniture seemed to exude this odor; it seemed to permeate the entire house. Then, as her eyes became accustomed to the dim light, she finally caught sight of the uncle. He was sitting at a table with a glass and a completely empty proof spirit bottle on it."

He is sleeping and doesn't hear her. She acts as though he isn't there. She feels warm and removes her gloves. She is thirsty, washes a glass and fills it with water. Just when she is about to take a drink she stops, dumbfounded, and puts the filled glass down next to her gloves:

> She had just noticed that he had probably fallen asleep while smoking his pipe, for the short, black pipe had fallen in his lap. She stood motionless in amazement. The burning tobacco had spilled from the pipe, and his pants had caught fire. Through a hole in the material,

already the size of a one-hundred sous coin, showed his naked thigh, a
red thigh, from which a small blue flame was rising.
At first Félicité thought it was his underwear, his shorts or his shirt
which were burning. However, there was no doubt about it; she clearly
saw the exposed flesh and the small blue flame bursting forth from it,
light and dancing as a flame darting across the surface of a glass of
flaming alcohol. It was hardly higher than a pilot flame burning quietly
yet silently; it was so weak the slightest breeze made it flicker. It was
rapidly growing larger, though, the skin was cracking and the fat was
beginning to melt.

He is still alive; she sees his breathing making his chest rise and fall.
She calls his name, not to awaken him this time but to be sure, if he is
really dying, that there is no chance he will wake up.

Félicité Rougon, reassured that at least this incarnation of the family
shame is dying, drinks down her glass of water in one gulp, then hurriedly
picks up one glove and, thinking she has both, closes the door and flees.

On stage remain the signatures of the two actors — the glove and the
pipe. A feminine article par excellence connected with all the vestiary
symbolism which can be seen in *Au Bonheur des Dames*, the glove covers
the hand and tried to conceal the origins of an act, an event. The
masculine article, the pipe which old Antoine always carried with him,
announces his own death.

Alcohol characterizes the Macquart branch; we know the role it plays
in *L'Assommoir* and *Germinal*. In a way it works against blood by
preventing the hereditary characteristic from emerging. Félicité plies
Antoine with drink to obliterate him from the family. In the same way
employers and their hirelings do everything to encourage alcoholism
among miners, for this is the best way to keep differences, which appear in
certain individuals such as Etienne Lantier, from turning into revolt,
encouraging others to reconquer their royalty and lost humaneness. The
blood flowing from one individual to another within a family is, in one
branch, partially offset by the flow of alcohol in which it is bathed.

However, if destruction of Antoine Macquart, signed by the green
glove, permits concealment of the shame of the Rougon family and,
despite all, strengthening of its reign, the fact that this destruction takes
place in a blue flame by the spontaneous combustion of alcohol will also
destroy this concealment. Once the concealing alcohol has burned away,
the glove which was to conceal the guilty hand becomes incriminating.

In his "royal" death old Antoine becomes a low-burning flame like
old, living Adélaïde. In him a flame secretly smoulders, waiting to destroy
all his alcohol, all that which marks this henchman, this accomplice in
usurpation.

The blue flame burning old Antoine Macquart is in fact but the
harbinger of another flame. This is the flame which will burn Doctor
Pascal in effigy, through his writings, manuscripts and papers, in other

words the *Rougon-Macquart* themselves as novels, in a fire fanned by the angry hand of old Félicité.

> Ah, here they are. . . . Into the fire! Into the fire!
> She had just found the papers. Far in back, behind the pile of notes, the doctor had hidden the blue folders. She was overcome by a fury, a frenzy to destroy the papers she picked up by the handful and threw into the flames. . . .
> They're burning, they're burning! . . . They're finally burning! . . . They're burning, it's so beautiful!

A fire burns in that never cleaned chimney producing at a certain point a rumble like thunder. It awakens poor Clotilde asleep near the corpse of her uncle, and she cries out: "It's as though you just burned your son."

And Félicité answers: "Burn Pascal because I burned his papers! . . . Well, I would have burned the whole town to protect the glory of our family! You know, though, continued the small old woman who seemed to be growing in stature, that I only had one ambition, one desire, the wealth and royalty of our family. . . ."

Like the kitchen of old Antoine the room is full of smoke and soot. Félicité thinks she is victorious once again. Will this fire remain a secret, will it be possible to seal its ashes in the wonderful monument to the Rougons' fortune? Let's see whether we can find a green glove on the table. It stands out so clearly in the untouched family tree that the two arsonists, Félicité and Martine the servant, haven't even thought to look for it there.

Thus the whole wretched family must burn, yet it is from this same family that stems not only genius but this tree, be it a permanent flame or lightning, in which we see the tree of Paradou in *La Faute de l'abbé Mouret*.

> What few people know is that in the garden they had found a spot of total bliss. . . . A place of cool shadows, hidden deep in impenetrable brush, so marvelously beautiful that there you forget the entire world — an enchanted retreat with its enormous tree covering it with a roof of leaves. . . . I was told that a whole life could be lived there in the space of a minute. . . . It is there she is buried. . . . It was the happiness of having sat there which killed her. The shade of the tree has a charm which induces death. . . .

Serge Mouret, who has forgotten his priesthood since entering the garden, interrupts her: "Isn't it forbidden to sit under a tree whose shade has such strange powers?"

Albine says solemnly: "Yes, it is forbidden. Everyone around here has told me it's forbidden."

This is the tree we will find growing in the middle of the new parcel of land in *Fécondité*, the first of Zola's *Evangiles*. Both tree and inhabitants will grow older there together.

While reading the *Rougon-Macquart* all the alcohol which has insidiously begun to flow in our veins must be burned in order to free our blood, yet illuminate it. Thus our revolt will become most effective through calmness, allowing us to immerse ourselves in the baptismal water of rediscovered royalty.

If I have discussed two harmful humours that flow in society's circulatory system, usurpative blood and neutralizing alcohol, I must mention at least two other fluids, beneficial fluids that have an equally important role in the workings of the novels. The first is milk, specifically the milk with which Clotilde, in the last moments of *Le Docteur Pascal*, nourishes that happy family enigma, her son by her uncle. The rôle of milk in the striking chapter on wet nurses in *Fécondité* deserves further investigation. Secondly, and above all, water, the supremely vital medium, seminal water, the sap that flows from the bark of the Paradou tree, bathing it with a "fertile mist," water as mother in *La Joie de vivre*, curative water which effects miracles in Lourdes not because the Virgin wills them, but simply because it is water.

Doctor Pascal, the twentieth-century alchemist who searches for "the universal panacea, the fluid of life which will fight against human debility, the only real cause of all illness, a true, a scientific Fountain of Youth which by providing strength, health and will power, would create entirely new and superior men," after failing with all his extractions of sheep's brain achieves almost miraculous cures with simple injections of distilled water.

Let us look once again at this admirable still life: the pipe on the floor; on the chair the blue flame into which the intoxicated old man is being metamorphosed; the green glove on the table next to the empty bottle of proof spirit and the glass of water.

Now we understand the rôle which water plays. At the death of Antoine Macquart water proves to be the true elixir of long life for his vile "royal" family and for that family's "distinctive characteristic" to which it clung, to which it devoted body and soul and which old Félicité thought she possessed for all time.

It is only the blue flame produced by the combustion not simply of alcohol but of ink, that inexhaustible super-alcohol, that keeps hereditary differences and blood from becoming usurpation. It alone brings the hereditary community — the water — into the light of day.

Zola: The Poetry of Naturalism   Irving Howe*

Each literary generation fashions its own blinkers and then insists that they allow unimpeded vision. My generation grew up with a mild scorn for the writers of naturalistic fiction who flourished in the late nineteenth and early twentieth centuries. Some of them we took to be estimable and others talented: we did not mean to be unfair. Many naturalists had a strong feeling for social justice, and if irrelevant to their stature as writers, this seemed to their credit as men. Zola's great cry during the Dreyfus Affair could still rouse us to admiration. His great cry could stir even those of us who had reached the peak of sophistication where Flaubert was judged superior to Balzac, Stendhal to Flaubert, and all three, it need hardly be said, to Zola—for Zola was tendentious, Zola was rhetorical, Zola was coarse, Zola knew little about the new psychology. With such wisdom, we entered the world.

Everyone had of course read Zola earlier, in those years of adolescence when all that matters in our encounter with a novel is eagerly to soak up its experience. Then *Germinal* had stirred us to the bone. But later we learned that literary judgment must not be defiled by political ideas, and Zola, that damp and clumsy bear of a novelist, became an object of condescension.

It was wrong, hopelessly wrong—like those literary fashions of our own moment which two or three decades from now will also seem wrong. Reading *Germinal* again, and reading it with that emotional readiness which middle age can sometimes grant, I have been overwhelmed by its magnitude of structure, its fertility of imagination, its reenactment of a central experience in modern life.

Still, it should be admitted that if we have been unjust to Zola these past few decades, some of the blame must fall on his own shoulders. He talked too much, he pontificated too much about Literature and Science, he advertised himself too much. We are accustomed in America to bemoaning the redskin dumbness that overcomes so many of our writers when confronted with a need to theorize about their craft, and behind this complaint of ours there is often a naïve assumption that European writers have commonly possessed the range of culture we associate with, say, a Thomas Mann. It is not true, of course. What had Dickens or Balzac to say about the art of the novel? As for Zola, there can hardly have been a modern writer so confused about the work he was doing. Consider the mechanical scientism to which he clung with the credulousness of a peasant in a cathedral; the ill-conceived effort to show forces of heredity determining the lives of his characters (so that a reader of *Germinal*

*This study has previously been published as an afterword to an English translation of *Germinal* (New York: New American Library, 1970). Reprinted by permission of the author.

unaware of the other volumes in the Rougon-Macquart series can only with difficulty understand why Etienne Lantier should suddenly, without preparation or consequence, be called "a final degenerate offshoot of a wretched race"); the willful absurdity of such declarations as "the same determinism should regulate paving-stones and human brains"; the turgid mimicry with which Zola transposed the physiological theories of Dr. Claude Bernard into his *Le Roman expérimental*. About this side of Zola — the journalist preening himself as scientist-philosopher — Angus Wilson has remarked: ". . . he must present his artistic method as though it were a solid intellectual scheme, lend that air of culture and education — of which in reality he knew himself to be deficient — to present as a logical theory what was in fact the form in which his individual genius expressed itself."

Yet we ought not to be too hasty in dismissing Zola's intellectual claims. His physiological determinism may now seem crude, but his sense of the crushing weight which the world can lower upon men remains only too faithful to modern experience, perhaps to all experience. If his theories about the naturalistic novel now seem mainly of historical interest, this does not mean that the naturalistic novel itself can simply be brushed aside. What remains vital in the naturalistic novel as Zola wrote it in France and Dreiser in America is not the theoretic groping toward an assured causality; what remains vital is the massed detail of the fictional worlds they establish, the patience — itself a form of artistic scruple — with which they record the suffering of their time.

In looking back upon the philosophical improvisations of those late nineteenth-century writers who were driven by conscience to surrender their Christian faith and then to improvise versions of rigid mechanism and spiritualized secularism, we like to suppose that their "ideas," once so earnestly studied by literary scholars, were little more than impediments they had to put aside, dead weight on the tissue of their work. You ignore Dreiser's pronouncements about "chemisms"; you agree with Huysman's remark about Zola: "Thank God he has not carried out in his novels the theories of his articles, which extol the infusion of positivism in art." There is of course something to be said for this view of the matter, but less than we commonly suppose, for the announced ideas behind a novel, even those thrust forward by the author as direct statement, ought not to be confused with the actual play of his intelligence. We may judge these announced ideas as tiresome or inert or a mere reflex of fashion; we may be irritated by their occasional appearance, like a mound of fossil, along the path of the narrative; yet in the novel itself the writer can be engaged in a play of intelligence far more supple than his formal claims lead us to suppose. A reductive determinism is what Zola flaunts, as when he places Taine's not very brilliant remark, "Vice and virtue are products like sugar and vitriol," on the title page of *Thérèse Raquin*; but a reductive determinism is by no means what controls *Germinal* and *L'Assommoir*. When we say that a work of literature "takes on a life of its own," we mean in part that the process of composition has brought textural surprises, perhaps fundamental shifts in perspective, which could not have been foreseen by studying the author's original intention.

Even among ideas we regard as mistaken, sharp discriminations must be made when trying to judge their literary consequences. A writer infatuated with one or another kind of psychic charlatanism is hard to take seriously. A writer drawn to the brutalities of fascism rouses a hostility that no creed of aesthetic detachment can keep from spilling over into our feelings about his work. But when writers like Zola and Hardy and Dreiser were attracted to the thought of Darwin and Huxley, or to popular versions of their thought, they were struggling with serious and urgent problems. They may have succumbed too easily to the "advanced ideas" of the moment — precisely the kind that date most quickly. Still, they were grappling with questions that gave them no rest, just as a half-century later Sartre and Camus would be grappling with the questions raised by existentialism, a school of philosophy that may not last much longer than deterministic scientism but which has nevertheless helped to liberate valuable creative powers. As Harry Levin[1] has said in partial defense of Zola: "Surely no comparable man of letters, with the exception of Poe, had tried so hard to grasp the scientific imagination. His contemporary, Jules Verne, led the way for writers of science fiction to tinker with imaginary gadgets. Science for them has been an Aladdin's lamp, a magical fulfillment, an easy trick. . . . For Zola it was much tougher than that; it was behavior under pressure; and the literary experimenter was both the witness of the behavior and the gauge of the pressure."

Insofar as a writer's ideas enter his literary work, they matter less for their rightness or wrongness than for their seriousness. And at least with some writers, it is their seriousness which determines whether the ideas will release or block the flow of creative energies. Zola shared with many late nineteenth- and early twentieth-century writers a lust for metaphysics. Christianity might be rejected, Christianity might be remembered, but its force remained. Among those who abandoned it there was still a hunger for doctrine, a need for the assuagements of system. They wished to settle, or continuously to worry, the problem of their relation to the cosmos. To us this may seem a curious need, since we are more likely to be troubled by our relation to ourselves; but in the last half of the nineteenth century the lust for metaphysics was experienced by people whose moral and intellectual seriousness cannot be questioned.

One large tendency in nineteenth-century literature, coursing through but not confined to romanticism, is an impulse to spiritualize the world, to distribute the godhead among numberless grains of matter, so that in a new if less tidy way, purpose can be restored to the cosmos and the sequence of creation and recreation be made to replace the promise of immortality. Toward the end of the nineteenth century men like Zola could no longer accept transcendental or pantheist derivatives from Christianity, yet they wanted some principle of order by means of which to locate themselves in the universe; whereupon they proceeded to shift the mystery of the creation onto the lawfulness of the determined. What then frightened reflective people was something that we, in our benumbed age, seem to accept rather easily: the thought of a world without intrinsic plan or point.

The transfer from *telos* to causality, insofar as it preserved a premise of meaning, enabled writers like Zola and Dreiser to make their lives into a heroic discipline — heroic because radically at variance with the ideas they expounded. It was almost as if they were reenacting in secular charade the paradox of Calvinism: that a belief in the utter worthlessness of man, living in a world blinded by God's grace, could yet drive the faithful to zeal and virtue.

Zola went still further than those writers who transferred the dynamic of faith into a fixity of law. Like Balzac before him, he yielded to the brilliant impiety of transforming himself into a kind of god, a god of tireless fecundity creating his universe over and over again. The nineteenth-century novelist — Dickens or Balzac, Hardy or Zola — enacts in his own career the vitalism about which the thought of his age drives him to a growing skepticism. Zola's three or four great novels are anything but inert or foredoomed. He may start with notions of inevitability, but the current of his narrative boils with energy and novelty. *Germinal* ends with the gloom of defeat, but not a gloom predestined. There is simply too much appetite for experience in Zola, too much sympathy and solidarity with the struggles by which men try to declare themselves, too much hope for the generations always on the horizon and always promising to undo the wrongs of the past, for *Germinal* to become a mere reflex of a system of causality. Somehow — we have every reason to believe — Zola's gropings into the philosophy of determinism freed him to become a writer of energy, rebellion, and creation.

II

Germinal releases one of the central myths of the modern era: the story of how the dumb acquire speech. All those at the bottom of history, for centuries objects of manipulation and control, begin to transform themselves into active subjects, determined to create their own history.

Now we cannot say that this myth has gained universal acceptance in our culture, nor that those of us who register its moral claims can do so with the unquestioning credence and mounting awe we suppose characteristic of men in ancient cultures. Still, we might remember that insofar as we know Greek myth through Greek drama, we know it mediated by individual artists, and with the passage of time, mediated in directions increasingly skeptical. The myth in *Germinal* — if we agree, however hesitantly, to call it a myth — is one that may have some parallels in earlier cultures, but it takes its formative energies from the French Revolution. It is the myth of the people and more particularly, of the proletariat. They who had merely suffered and at times erupted into blind rebellion; they who had been prey to but not part of society; they who had found no voice in the cultures of the past — they now emerge from the sleep of history and begin the task of a collective self-formation. This, of course, is a schematized version of historical reality, or at least a perspective on historical reality — which may indeed be the distinctiveness of whatever modern myths we have. Where traditional myths appear to us as transhistorical, a frieze of symbolic representation, our own take their very substance from the materials of history, magnifying and rendering heroic the actions of men in time. Some idea of this kind may have led Thomas Mann to write that "in Zola's epic," made up as it is of events taken from everyday life, "the characters themselves are raised up to a plane above that of everyday life."

The myth of *Germinal* as I have been sketching it is close to the Marxist view of the dynamics of capitalism, but to yield ourselves to Zola's story is not necessarily to accept the Marxist system. Zola himself does not accept it. At crucial points he remains a skeptic about the myth that forms the soul of his action. His skepticism is not really about the recuperative powers of the miners, for it is his instinctive way of looking at things that he should see the generations crowding one another, pushing for life space, thrusting their clamor onto the world. His skepticism runs deeper. Zola sees the possibility that in the very emergence of solidarity — that great and terrible word for which so many have gone smiling to their death! — there would be formed, by a ghastly dialectic of history, new rulers and oppressors: the Rasseneurs, the Pluancharts, and even the Lantiers of tomorrow, raised to the status of leaders and bureaucrats, who would impose their will on the proletariat. Zola does not insist that this must happen, for he is a novelist, not a political theoretician. What he does is to show in the experience of the Montsou workers the germ of such a possibility. As it celebrates the greatest event of modern history, the myth of emergence contains within itself the negation of that greatness.

(Is it not this note of prescience, this intuition all too painfully confirmed by recent history, which explains why Georg Lukacs — the east European Marxist critic who always starts with heterodox insights and ends with orthodox dogmas — should attack Zola's work as mechanistic and passive, lacking in revolutionary dynamism? We have here a confrontation between a writer's honesty and an ideologue's tendentiousness, between Zola's myth of a collective entry into consciousness and Lukacs's pseudomyth of "socialist realism." The true myth is a story arising from the depths of common experience; the pseudomyth, a manipulation of that story in behalf of a false collective declaring itself the "vanguard of the proletariat.")

At the center of the novel is the mine. Dramatic embodiment of exploitation, the mine nevertheless makes possible the discipline through which to overcome exploitation. But for the moment, man's nature still bows to his history, personal need to the workings of the market. The mine has a "natural" awesomeness, with its crevices and alleys, depths and darkness: its symbolic power arises organically, spontaneously, and not as a willed imposition of the writer. And then, in a stroke that does not bear the mark of will, Zola creates an astonishing parallel to the miners. The mine-horses share the misery of the men, but without the potential for motivated rebellion; the mine-horses represent, as a gruesome foreshadowing and with an expressionist grossness that defeats critical scruples, what the men may yet accept or sink to.

The mine is voracious and unappeasable, a physical emblem of the impersonality of commodity production. It "seemed evil-looking, a hungry beast crouched and ready to devour the world." It "kept devouring men . . . always ravenous, its giant bowels capable of digesting an entire nation." But this suggestion of a force bursting out of the control of its creators gains its strength not merely from the intrinsic properties of the mine. Here Zola does come close to the Marxist notion that men must beware of fetishizing their predicaments; they must recognize that not in mines or factories lie the sources of their misery but in the historically determined relations between contending classes. And here surely historical associations come into play, associations which even the least literate reader is likely to have with mining—a major industry of early industrialism, notorious for its high rate of exhaustion and accident. As always in *Germinal*, the mythic and symbolic are of the very substance of the historical. And thereby Zola can fill out his myth with the evidence of circumstantiality. The more he piles up descriptions of the mine's tunnels, shafts, timbering, airlessness, and dampness, the more we are prepared to see it as the setting for the apocalypse with which the book reaches its climax.

In a fine piece some years ago William Troy remarked that the great scene in which Etienne and Catherine are trapped in the mine ". . . brings us back to an atmosphere and a meaning at least as old as the story of Orpheus and Eurydice. For what is the mine itself but a reintegration of the Hades-Hell symbol? The immediate and particular social situation is contained within the larger pattern of a universal recrudescence. . . . Etienne emerges from his journey underground to *la vita nuova* of his own and of social experience."

The Orpheus-Eurydice motif is there, Etienne experiences a recrudescence, though of a somewhat ambiguous kind, and the mine is surely the symbolic center of the book. Yet we should be clear as to how Zola achieves these effects. Zola controls his narrative with one overriding end in mind, and that is to show not the way men are swallowed by their work (surely not new) nor how a hero can emerge healed from the depths (also not new) but the gradual formation of a collective consciousness. When Maheu, that superbly drawn worker, begins to speak to the manager, "the words were coming out of themselves, and at moments he listened to himself in surprise, as though some stranger within him were speaking." The stranger is his long-buried self, and this transfiguration of Maheu is at least as morally significant as that of the individual protagonist gaining access to self-knowledge in the earlier nineteenth-century novel.

Etienne reads, Maheu speaks, La Maheude cries out: everything is changed. Gathering their strength and for a time delirious with fantasies of freedom, almost childlike in the pleasures of their assertiveness, the workers become what Marx called a class for itself. And then, with his uncanny gift for achieving mass effects through individual strokes, Zola begins to individualize his characters. He does this not to approximate that fragmentized psychology we associate with nineteenth-century fiction but toward the end of preparing the characters for their new roles: Etienne in the pride and exposure of leadership, Maheu in the conquest of manhood, La Maheude as the voice of ancient grievance, and even the children, led by the devilish Jeanlin, who in their debauchery release the spontaneous zest that the overdisciplined life of the miners has suppressed.

The strike becomes the central action, and thereby the myth of emergence takes on the sharp edge of conflict. The workers are shown in their rise to a noble solidarity and their fall to a brutal mob—better yet, in the ways the two, under intolerable stress, become all but indistinguishable. ("Do not flatter the working class nor blacken it," Zola told himself in notes for *L'Assommoir*.) And nothing is more brilliant than Zola's intuition—it speaks for his powers of insinuating himself beneath the skin of the miners—that after the horrible riot with which Part Five closes, he sees the men continuing their strike, digging in with a mute fatalism, "a great somber peacefulness," which rests far less on expectations of victory than on a common yielding to the pathos of standing and starving together. Defeat comes, and demoralization too, but only after Zola has charted with a precise objectivity the rhythms of struggle, rhythms as intrinsically absorbing for the novelist (and at least as difficult to apprehend) as those of the individual psyche in turmoil.

Again, it should be stressed that the myth Zola employs is not the vulgar-Marxist notion of an inevitable victory or of a victory-in-defeat ending with noble resolves for the future. True, he shows as no other European novelist before him, the emergence of a new historical force, and he reveals the conflict that must follow; but its outcome remains uncertain, shadowy, ambiguous. The more serious versions of Marxism speak of historical choice: freedom or barbarism. It is a choice allowing for and perhaps forming the substance of tragedy. *Germinal* shares that view.

III

A work of modern literature may employ a myth and perhaps even create one, as I think *Germinal* does, but it cannot satisfy its audience with a composed recapitulation of a known, archetypal story. With theme it must offer richness of variation, often of a radical kind, so as slyly to bring into question the theme itself. The hieratic does not seem a mode easily accessible to modern literature. We want, perversely, our myths to have a stamp of the individual, our eternal stories to bear a quiver of nervous temporality.

The picture Zola draws of Montsou as a whole, and of Montsou as a microcosm of industrial society, depends for its effectiveness mainly on the authority with which he depicts the position of the miners. Just as the novel is a genre that gains its most solid effects through accumulation and narrative development, so the action of Zola's book depends on his command of an arc of modern history. If he can persuade us that he sees this experience with coherence and depth, then we will not be excessively troubled by whatever intellectual disagreements we may have with him or by our judgment that in particular sections of the novel he fails through heavy exaggeration and lapses of taste. Two lines out of tune in a sonnet can spoil our pleasure, since a short lyric depends for its success on verbal unity; but in a novel whole episodes can be out of tune without necessarily spoiling our pleasure, since an extended prose fiction depends mainly on such large-scale effects as narrative thrust and character development.

Again we reach an interpenetration of commanding myth and historical material—what I take to be Zola's great achievement in *Germinal*. A stranger arrives, slightly removed from the workers because of superior intellect, yet required to enter their lives and ready to share their troubles. So far, the pattern of the story is not very different from that of much fiction composed earlier in the nineteenth century. But then comes a radical shift: the stranger, now on the way to being a leader, remains at the center of the book, but his desires and reflections do not constitute its central matter. What engages us primarily is the collective experience of the miners, the myth of their emergence. In Part Five of *Germinal*, both the most original and the most exciting portion of the novel, this entry into consciousness is shown in its two-sidedness, and with a complexity of tone that unites passionate involvement and dispassionate removal. In his notes for the book Zola understood that he must remain faithful to his story as archetype:

> To get a broad effect I must have my two sides as clearly contrasted as possible and carried to the very extreme of intensity. So that I must start with all the woes and fatalities which weigh down the miners. Facts, not emotional pleas. The miner must be shown crushed, starving, a victim of ignorance, suffering with his children in a hell on earth—but not persecuted, for the bosses are not deliberately vindictive—*he is simply*

overwhelmed by the social situation as it exists. On the contrary I must make the bosses humane so long as their direct interests are not threatened; no point in foolish tub-thumping. The worker is the victim of the facts of existence—capital, competition, industrial crises.

For this perception to be transformed into a dramatic action, Zola relies mainly on the narrative increment that follows from his myth of the speechless and the symbolic suggestiveness of the mine. In saying this I don't mean to imply that everything which occurs in the novel is necessary or appropriate. The narrative is frequently flawed by cheap and lurid effects. Zola, as someone has remarked, had an overwhelming imagination but only an uncertain—and sometimes a corrupted—taste. That the riot of the miners should be a terrifying event seems entirely right; that it should end with the ghastly *frisson* invented by Zola is a sign of his weakness for sensationalism. Zola tries hard to present his middle-class characters, the Hennebeaus and Grégoires, with some objectivity and even sympathy, but he usually fails. Not, I think, for the reason William Troy gives: ". . . the inherent unsuitability of naturalism, a system of causality based on quasi-scientific principles, to the practice of literature." I doubt that local failures in a novel are ever to be traced so directly to philosophical conceptions. Zola fails because in this novel he is not interested in such people at all. They are there because his overall scheme demands it, because he feels an obligation to "fill out the picture." Sensing as much, we read these inferior portions with a certain tolerance, assuaged by the likelihood that further great scenes with the miners lie ahead. The mediocre intervals come to serve as "rests" helping Zola create or regather suspense. M. Hennebeau, the mine manager, is a partial exception, if only because he is a figure of power and power is always fascinating for Zola. Still, the subplot of Hennebeau's personal unhappiness and his envy of what he takes to be the miners' unsoiled virility is obviously weak—just how weak one can see by comparing it to D. H. Lawrence's treatment of similar material. And again, the immersion of Etienne and Catherine in the mine, once the strike has been lost, is both a scene of considerable power and a scene marred by Zola's lack of discipline when he has the body of Chaval, the girl's former lover, float horribly up to them in the darkness. Zola does not know when to stop.

To notice such flaws can be damaging, and to write as if *Germinal* were not more than the sum of local incidents could be a strategy for dismissing the book entirely. But this seems a poor way of dealing with a novel. *Germinal*, like many works of fiction, depends upon effects that are larger, more gross, and less open to isolated inspection than picking out scenes of weakness would suggest; it depends upon the large-muscled rhythms of the narrative as a whole. We are dealing here with a writer of genius who, in both the quality of his imagination and the occasional wantonness of his prose, can sometimes be described as decadent. One remembers T. S. Eliot's remark that Dickens was "a decadent genius," a remark accurate enough if the noun is stressed at least as much as the modifier. The decadence of Zola, which has points of similarity to that of Dickens, comes through in the excesses of local episodes, the vulgarities of particular paragraphs, the flushed rhetoric with which Zola seeks to "reinforce" material that has already been presented with more than enough dramatic vitality. The genius comes through in the mythic-historical sweep of the narrative as a whole. And at least this once, Zola himself knew exactly what he was doing: "Everyone in the world [he wrote] analyzes in detail nowadays, I must react against this through the solid reaction of masses, of chapters, through the logic, the thrust of the chapters, succeeding each other like superimposed blocks; by the breath of passion, animating all, flowing from one end to another of the work."

If what I have been saying has validity, it follows that there will also be frequent episodes of brilliance — else how could the novelist achieve his large rhythms of narration? And there are, of course, such episodes. Two kinds may be distinguished: those persuading us of Zola's authority as imaginative historian (substantiating detail) and those persuading us of his psychological penetration into a given moment of the action (illuminating detail).

The first kind is to be found mainly in his treatment of the miners at the peak of crisis. Etienne reading a Belgian socialist weekly, hastily and poorly absorbing its contents, seeking to make up for years of waste as he is "gripped by the uneducated man's methodless passion for study" and then overcome by "the dull dread that he had shown himself unequal to the task" — all this bears the thick circumstantiality of the actual. Zola knew the kind of men who were drawn to socialist politics: not merely learned bourgeois intellectuals like Marx and Kautsky, but self-educated workers like Bebel, straining with ambition and stumbling into knowledge. This command of his material is shown even more subtly in the portrayal of the inner relationships among his three radicals: Rasseneur, the most cautious and experienced, clearly on the way to becoming a classical social democrat; Souvarine, also a classical figure, though of the anarchist-terrorist kind who declares the need "to destroy everything . . . no more nations, no more governments, no more property, no more God or religion" and then to return to "the primitive and formless community,"[2] and Etienne, the sincere unformed worker, open to a wide range of possibilities but determined — his aspiring intellectuality prods his ambi-tion — to make a place for himself on the stage of history.

The second and more striking kind of detail shows Zola's imagination at work somewhat more freely, releasing incidents which do not depend directly on the overall design of the novel. On the simplest level there is the pathos of the mine girl Mouquette, hopelessly generous with all she has (her body to the men, her affection to almost anyone, her bared bottom to the strikebreakers), who offers Etienne a dozen cold potatoes to still the hunger of the Maheu household. It is a trifle, but from such trifles affecting novels are made. On a level hard to apprehend in strictly rational terms, there is Etienne finding himself a place to hide, after the riot, in one of the hated mines. But the greatest of such imaginative strokes concerns the strange old Bonnemort, introduced at the outset as a ghost of a man embodying the exhaustion of the workers' lives. He has nothing to say, he is barely alive, until at the strike meeting, amid the predictably rousing speeches

> . . . everybody was surprised to see old Bonnemort standing on the tree trunk and trying to make himself heard. . . . No doubt he was giving way to one of those sudden fits of babbling that would sometimes stir up the past so violently that old memories would rise from his depths and flow from his lips for hours. It had become very quiet, and everybody listened to the old man, so ghostly pale in the moonlight; as he was talking about things that had no obvious connection with the discussion, long stories that nobody could understand, their astonishment increased. He spoke of his youth, told of his two uncles who had been crushed to death at Le Voreux, then went on to the pneumonia that had carried off his wife. Through it all, however, he never lost hold of his one idea: things had never been right and they never would be right.

Without rhetorical strain, this passage summons the losses of the past, the whole unreckoned waste that forms our history. The mode is grotesque, but for readers with a measure of historical imagination, Zola achieves something far beyond the limits of what that descriptive usually suggests.

IV

Zola's style aspires toward a rich and heavy impasto rather than toward a lucid line-drawing, and it is often marred by excess. In *Germinal* the writing is nevertheless effective at two points: first, the passages describing the mine with that wary respect for the power of the actual a novelist must have, and second, the episodes in which he evokes the surge of conflict and the passions of enraged men. In these episodes the prose can be extremely effective, combining mass and speed — as long as Zola stays with his central purpose, which is to depict the sensations of men who have thrown off the discipline of society but not yet discovered the discipline of self. Nor need we succumb to any version of "the imitative fallacy" — that in its internal qualities a style must reflect the matter it is trying to convey — in order to recognize at least some correspondences as proper to the relation between style and subject. One does not write about the collapse of a mine in the style of James analyzing an exquisite heroine.

Zola achieves the effect of speed, but not the light or nervous speed of a Stephen Crane or an Isaac Babel. Especially in Part Five of the novel, his style is that of a rumbling and heavy speed — a leaden speed. The writing is rarely nimble or graceful; the sentences are weighted with qualifiers and prepositional phrases, as well as with accumulating clauses which repeat and magnify the matter of their predecessors. Admittedly, this prose is highly rhetorical: it employs organic metaphors of anger, release, and cataclysm ("Nature," says Zola, "is associated with our griefs"), and it depends heavily on Zola's hoarse and rasping voice. For what he is trying to do seems decidedly risky, even from the vantage-point of eighty-five years later: he is giving dramatic embodiment to a collective as it disintegrates into a mob, and since he must keep his attention mainly on the group, which has of course no individuality of consciousness or will, he finds himself forced to speak in his own voice. That, in the actuality of composition, is the paradox the novelist must face when he tries to dramatize the conduct of a group. His effort to create an action of extreme objectivity, a plot of collective behavior, leads the novelist to a style of extreme subjectivity in which he finds himself driven to "impersonate" the group. At its worst, this kind of writing can seem willed — an effort to do for the action through rhetoric what film-makers try to do for their stories through music. At its best, the writing has a coarse strength and even splendor — what might be called the poetry of naturalism.

Still, it would be foolish to claim for Zola that his prose can yield the kind of sentence-by-sentence pleasure that can be had from the prose of a writer like James or Flaubert. Zola is often careless as a stylist, sometimes wanton, occasionally cheap. His trouble, however, is not that his prose lacks nicety of phrasing or epigrammatic neatness; it is that he does not content himself with a utilitarian plainness but must reach out for the ornamental and exalted, seeking through rhetorical fancy-work to establish his credentials as a literary man. Like other half-educated novelists and journalists of the late nineteenth century, Zola was painfully susceptible to those charms of the "literary" that he claimed to dismiss.

His style, like almost everything else in *Germinal*, is interesting mainly when considered in the large. One then encounters a phenomenon I do not pretend to understand, and which seems an essential mystery of literature. For long portions of the novel Zola yields himself entirely to the passions of the miners, and his prose becomes strongly, even exorbitantly, passionate. We are swept along, as we are meant to be, by the surge of men in revolt; we are with them, the starving and the hunted, and the language heaves and breaks, sweeping across us with torrents of rhetoric. But let us not be frightened by that word "rhetoric": it bears the strength, not only the weakness, of Zola's novel.

Rhetoric, yes; but a rhetoric which accompanies and sustains a remarkably strong evocation. The passion Zola pours out finds its match, its justification, in the incidents he imagines. Yet, as we read into the depths of the book, we grow aware that there is another Zola, one who draws back a little, seeing the whole tragedy as part of an eternal rhythm of struggle and decision. This Zola, as if writing from some timeless perch, is finally dispassionate, withdrawn from his own commitments, and capable of a measure of irony toward the whole human enterprise. Zola the partisan and Zola the artist: for those who like their "commitment" straight such ambivalence is detestable. But I take it to be a sign of Zola's achievement. If there has ever been a novel concerning which one might forgive a writer his unmodulated passions it is *Germinal*; yet precisely here Zola's "scientism" proves to be an unexpected advantage, enabling him to achieve an aesthetic distance that gives the book its ultimate austerity.

There is still another doubleness of response in *Germinal*. Hardly a Zola critic has failed to note the frequency with which images of fecundity occur in the book—repeated scenes in which, along and beyond the margin of his central narrative, Zola displays the unplanned and purposeless creativity of existence. Henry James, in his essay on Zola, remarks: "To make his characters swarm, and to make the great central thing they swarm about "as large as life," portentously, heroically big, that was the task he set himself very nearly from the first, that was the secret he triumphantly mastered."

Now for many nineteenth-century novelists, this "'swarming" can be a source not merely of narrative energy but also of a mindless and pseudoreligious sentimentalism. Everyone has encountered it as a special kind of fictional cant: the generations come, the generations go, etc. Asserted without irony, such declamations often constitute a kind of psychic swindle, convenient enough for novelists who fear the depressing logic of their own work or who need some unearned lilt in their final pages. That Zola does not approach this kind of sentimentalism seems beyond doubt, but again and again he draws back into a baffled stoicism, evading the trap his romantic heritage has set for him. "A black avenging army" is "germinating in the furrows"; "soon this germination would sunder the earth." But even as such sentiments fill Zola's final pages there is no simple assurance—indeed, no assurance of any kind. Despite the sense of a swarming procreation which keeps the race alive, Zola ends on a note of anguish; he does not propose an easy harmony between the replenishments of nature and the desires of men. Etienne, clumsily balancing his idealism and his ambition, goes out into the world. To one reader at least, he enters neither upon personal triumph nor the "final conflict" promised by the dialectic of history, but upon a journey into those treacherous regions of the unknown where sooner or later all men find themselves.

Notes

1. From Professor Levin's scholarly study of French nineteenth-century fiction, *The Gates of Horn*, I have borrowed several citations, and wish here to record my debt to his valuable book.

2. The reader of *Germinal* may be tempted to see Souvarine as a remarkable anticipation of certain contemporary figures, and indeed he does talk as if he belonged to an esoteric New Left faction. But it should be remembered that by the late nineteenth century

the anarchist-terrorist, often a popular stereotype, had become a familiar presence in European culture. Zola was here drawing upon a fund of common material, and what is notable about Souvarine is not the conception behind him but the detachment, even the ironic coolness, with which he is presented.

Ideology and Myth: *Germinal* and the Fantasies of Revolt
Henri Mitterand*

As one delves deeper into the ever more numerous galleries of *Germinal*, one discovers, as in all great texts, more and more of those networks and levels where meanings intertwine, to such an extent that the appreciation — the unravelling — of this text seems destined never to end.

This, moreover, is what casts doubt on the validity of the accepted methods of stylistics, as well as of literary history, and prompts one to seek help from writers who study the mechanisms of signifying in disciplines other than literature. We may attempt any type of interpretation, any type of exploration, or make use of any working hypothesis that the study of humanities suggests. Literature speaks of man, and indeed how could it not do so when its discourse is analogous to that which humanity as a whole uses in other fields where the spoken work is studied; how could a science of literature, a textual analysis, simply do without the teachings of the other sciences of human discourse, psychoanalysis, ethnology, the study of ideologies, etc.?

Indeed, it is no longer possible to be satisfied with a "realistic" appreciation of this work, such as one finds for example in its most complete, most mature, most intelligent form in Auerbach's *Mimesis*: "The serious treatment of everyday reality, the rise of more extensive and socially inferior human groups to the position of subject matter for problematic-existential representation, on the one hand; on the other, the embedding of random persons and events in the general course of contemporary history, the fluid historical background — these, we believe, are the foundations of modern realism."[1]

Such a commentary is no longer sufficient because an interpretation of this novel, based on other key concepts, reveals a permanent break with the real, a crack which extends from one end of the text to the other, a sort of organic deviation from its material, social and mental data. This deviation has long been identified. The problem which modern critics must face is to describe this deviation as precisely and as coherently as possible, by taking into consideration its various occurrences and the role it plays, in an effort to shed some light on the structures which govern the

*From *Le Discours du roman* (Paris: Presses Universitaires de France, 1980), 140–49, by permission of the author and publisher. Translated for this volume by Janice Best.

production of meaning in this work, and to map out what is sometimes called the "space" of the text.

KNOWLEDGE AND DENOTATION

I would like, first of all, as Auerbach has done, to point out that the text of *Germinal* conveys and transmits a *body of knowledge* ["un *savoir*"] that is historical in nature, specific, and determines a field of investigation (the workers' movement), an area of observation (the mining industry), a period of time (the end of the Second Empire). This information produces the entire denotated world of the book: technical descriptions, the analysis of social stratification, observations concerning the emergence of class consciousness, the exposition of political factors, etc.

The text depicts for instance a *décor*, a landscape, with all its indispensable technical denotations, so that its pertinent traits, and most especially those of a technological nature, clearly stand out. Thus the mine appears, at a first level of analysis (that is first in the order of the texts, and first in the order of the meanings that they convey to the reader), as a space hollowed out by man, organised by man, marked by his own work.

MYTHICAL INVESTMENT

But each denotated detail is, so to speak, impure, weighed down by the connotated correspondences invested in it. In the mine, *the rain, the fog, the smell of old metals*, are precise terms destined to define, to particuliarize this *décor*. But they also function equally well as impressive elements, destined to emphasize the inhuman, uncomfortable nature of these places, the contradiction created between basic human needs and human presence in such a place. The text is laden therefore with correspondences between the inanimate world and the human world: ". . . the air became more poisoned and heated with the smoke of the lamps, with the pestilence of their breaths, with the asphyxia of the firedamp . . . At the bottom of their molehill, beneath the weight of the earth, with no more breath in their inflamed lungs, they went on hammering."[2] Several metaphors, mixed together, can be discerned here: metaphors of asphyxiation, of immurement, of the mole or the damned. A code of analogies is gradually established whereby every denotated element (the narrowness of the galleries, the rarefaction of the air, the heat) becomes the signifier of an entire system of connotations which describe less an aspect of the modern industrial and social landscape as some of the forms of the curse that afflicts humanity.

The components of mythical structure are also present: on the one hand we have a description which tends constantly to blend into the narrative sequence: "They went on hammering"; a pictorial form of description (a "tableau") which is perpetually being integrated into the narrative, at the same time as the narrative itself seems to come to a halt in a highly synthetic image; on the other hand, the text itself is built around an exemplar. Here a man if all but lost in the dark, crushed beneath the rock, his breath like fire, hammering away without respite (and the verb *hammer* itself has intransitive connotations). The character is frozen in a gesture which is presented as an eternal one and he becomes an allegory of misery. Concrete reality and rational analysis gradually give way to the fantastic and the fabulous.

If one were to extend this line of research beyond a brief example to include all of the passages which describe the subterranean world, a complex and correlative system of explicit connotations would be revealed:

— The mine, as a subterranean space, refers to the concept of burrowing and burying (the miners are insects, they are also buried alive, prisoners of the grave), to the concept of suffocation (the galleries become narrower and narrower, poisonous gases are given off), to the concept of devouring (Le Voreux devours, wolfs down its daily ration of miners, is an insatiable belly).

— The organisation of this subterranean space calls to mind buried cities: its labyrinth refers to the concept of wandering, of disorientation, of deliberately concealed exits.

— The mine, as an area of shadows, is the place where instinctive impulses — hunger, sex, murder — which daylight normally censures or controls, break loose freely and violently. This is the place where man reverts to beast.

Thus, the constituent elements of this space lose their inertia and become mythical elements, since this set of correspondences is the result of the system of correlations established between these elements and man, between the inanimate and the animate. Earth, rock, water, fire are the natural instruments of persecution against man, and the coordinates of what in *Germinal* is called "that horizon of misery, sealed like a tomb."

A multitude of myths spring forth within this profusion of analogies. It is not at all surprising that several of these are created by the discourse of the miners themselves: the myth of the Torrent (a water-dream), the myth of the Tartaret (fire), of the Black Man (night, sexual and homicidal violence), etc. As for Zola himself, he makes myths out of myth. The miners' labor, in its various stages, tells the tale of a myth of immurement.

But things are not quite that simple.

TWO PARALLEL WORLDS

The mine is but one of the two poles of a structure which establishes equivalent relationships between the two societies above- and below-ground, between the surface and the pit, day and night, bosses and workers, the haves and the have-nots, etc.

The structure of the entire novel is based on this relationship between the "superior-tive" and the "inferior-tive," which may be presented on a chain of substitutions in the following way:

$$\frac{\text{Surface}}{\text{Pit}} \sim \frac{\text{Bourgeoisie}}{\text{Proletariat}} \sim \frac{\text{Haves}}{\text{Have-nots}} \sim \frac{\text{Light,}}{\text{Night}} \text{ etc.}$$

This chain of relationships can take on multiple forms, the complete inventory of which remains to be drawn up. But the system appears to be totally coherent. A categorical, paradigmatic opposition between the Bourgeoisie and the Workers, the Haves and the Have-nots exists. And each one of the terms of this opposition is linked to the other terms of the same level by a syntagmatic correlation. A vertical reading defines the core of the code of meaning and the kernel of the myth, a horizontal reading defines the narrative text. Here are two examples: the relationship between the wealthy and the starving is the same as that between the devouring god and the devoured population, as it is between the feast and fornication. If the bourgeois eat, the miners go hungry, and if the miners indulge everywhere and at any time in the pleasures of copulation, Hennebeau is constantly in despair because of his own frustrations. Scenes with the Grégoires or the Hennebeaus at the table occur with the same frequency as sexual scenes with the miners in their habitual haunts. On the vertical axis, a relationship of equivalence is thereby established (Lévi-Strauss has pointed out that in many myths an analogy between *eating* and *copulating* is evident; this is one of the outstanding characteristics of *Germinal*): on the horizontal axis, one finds a relationship of contiguity. Connotation circulates along both of these vectors. Each element is determined by its relationships with the others.

Thus the articulation of the novel appears to resemble closely that of the myths by which the "savage mind" organises its interpretation of the world.

And it is here that ideology breaks through. The social structure is thus correlated organically, in the textual universe, to natural structures (light and darkness, the surface world and the subterranean one) and to biological structures. The division into two classes is a natural and eternal phenomenon, not a social and transitory one. It is a fact of nature, not of culture. There is, in the nature of things, no antagonism inherent in such a division. If such an antagonism does appear, the system, on the contrary, will absorb it and neutralize it.

STRUCTURE AND NARRATION

For myth is dynamic, just as it appears to be in the original titles that Zola considered for the novel. Of course, the opposition between two of these titles, *L'Assiette au beurre* [*The Soft Life*] and *Les Affamés* [*The Hunger-Stricken*], reflects the static nature of this structure. But others introduce the idea of a dynamic transformation: *La Maison qui craque* [*The Break-up*], *Le Sol qui brûle* [*Eruption*]. Here, the chain of substitutions is transformed into a chain of transformations. From the depths of the underground world there bursts forth the explosion which destroys the home, the tabernacle for which it was the foundation. The hungry come out of their holes and destroy the universe of the rich. From the purifying destruction of the old world, a new world will spring forth.

In this way the basic principle on which the previous structure is founded, one of homological parallelism, is undermined by the narration itself. The rebels invade the territory of the wealthy, in order to destroy it, and in so doing they substitute a relationship of contiguity for a relationship of equivalence and attempt to upset the order of the world.

But the remarkable fact is that this attempted overthrow is dealt with in a mythical mode, and in several different manners, all of them forms of travesty. I shall give but two examples:

The Simulacrum.—We must now turn to three scenes in the novel: the castration of Maigrat, the murder of the little soldier, the strangulation of Cécile Grégoire by Old Bonnemort. Three scenes of sacrifice, of magical and not practical action. In each of these cases the working class does not attack the real power of the bourgeoisie, but believes it can modify the order of the universe by means of a ritual sacrifice, which moreover is carried out by marginal officiants (women, children, old men). In each case, the victim is an intermediate being who, by nature, represents the possible connecting link between the two worlds. The grocer, the soldier, Cécile, are *ambiguous*. They are the ones designated by the narrative to serve at the same time as expiatory and propitiatory victims. When Bonnemort raises his hand against Cécile a connection between the two worlds is established. Once Cécile is dead, the gods must fill in the empty space by establishing social justice, a reward on which the miners secretly, unconsciously, have been counting. But all of this is mere dream, magic, sham. . . . The revolution fades into fantasies. The metonymical journey has failed.

The Metaphorisation of Revolt.—The narrative of the strike makes use of all the images accumulated in previous passages of the text:

> It was the red vision of the revolution, which would one day inevitably carry them all away, on some bloody evening at the end of the century. Yes, some evening the people, unbridled at last, would thus gallop along the roads, making the blood of the middle class flow, parading severed heads and sprinkling gold from disembowelled coffers. The women would yell, the men would have those wolf-like jaws open to bite. Yes, the same rags, the same thunder of great sabots, the same terrible troop, with dirty skins and tainted breath, sweeping away the old world beneath an overflowing flood of barbarians. Fire would

flame; they would not leave standing one stone of the towns; they would return to the savage life of the woods, after the great rut, the great feast-day, when the poor in one night would emaciate the wives and empty the cellars of the rich. There would be nothing left, not a sou of the great fortunes, not a title-deed of properties acquired; until the day dawned when a new earth would perhaps spring up once more. Yes, it was these things which were passing along the road; it was the force of nature herself, and they were receiving the terrible wind of it in their faces.

> A great cry arose, dominating the *Marseillaise:*
> "Bread! Bread! Bread!"[3]

In this passage, the proletarian uprising is likened to the unleashing of a troop of brutish creatures, a pack of ferocious beasts, the over flowing of a mighty stream, the reappearance of characters from the Reign of Terror, the resurgence of ancient *jacqueries*. In all of these comparisons, the author makes use of a-historical and non-rational concepts which are borrowed sometimes from the order of natural catastrophes (floods, earthquakes, fires), sometimes from the order of instinctual behaviour (passionate anger, violence, the thirst for rape, fire and blood).

A type of magical transformation occurs here as well, but it is the author's doing: human actions are naturalised, treated as if they formed an integral part of physical determinism. Historical and social denotation is overwhelmed, submerged by biological and natural connotation. The narrative leaves history behind to inject social tragedy into the series of cataclysms which periodically affect the order of the world and are constituent elements of this order.

IDEOLOGICAL SIGNIFICANCE

So it is up to the reader to work out his own method of deciphering this decipherment, his own interpretation of this interpretation. The author's interpretation of the event is a mythifying travesty. But this interpretation points directly to the ideology which underlies it and which it denotes. The mythical structure is deeper than the superficial structure of the events related. But the ideological structure is even deeper than the mythical structure(s). It is at this level that we must seek the minimal sentence of the narrative. As Hjemlslev put it, denotative semiology subsumes connotative semiotics.

On all levels, we have isolated the process of naturalisation and immobilisation in the eternal. This process is also one of reversal and of idealisation. Marx wrote in *The German Ideology*: "Social power appears as an outside force, a force in itself, independent of will and of human development." History vanishes and gives way to nature. Elaborating on one of Marx's ideas, Barthes wrote in his *Mythologies*: "The status of the bourgeoisie is particular and historical: the man it represents will be universal, eternal." One can easily apply this statement to *Germinal*, a novel which, seen as the union of historical fact and of a mythified version of social history, refracts the middle class ideology of the end of the 19th century, a mixture of lucidity and of the inability to take a rational view of social evolution. By depicting the society of miners as a primitive society, as a world of nature, and not a world of culture and of history, Zola helps us to understand what Althusser somewhere calls "the discourse of the unspoken desire of the bourgeoisie."

But, without knowing it, he also applies a precept of Marx, who, in his *Critique of Hegel's Philosophy of Law* exclaimed: "We must represent each sector of German society as the shameful part of German society. We must shake up these fossilized conditions by singing their own tunes back to them. We must teach the people self-horror, in order to instill courage in them." This explains the ambiguity of the lessons offered by this work and the availability of meanings that it has maintained, well outside the social structures which gave rise to the author's reflections and dreams.

Notes

1. [Editor's note: Eric Auerbach, *Mimesis: The Representation of Reality in Western Literature*, trans. Willard R. Trask (Princeton, N.J.: Princeton University Press, 1953), 491].

2. [Editor's note: Emile Zola, *Germinal*, trans. Havelock Ellis (New York: Dutton, 1951), 50–51; original date of this translation: 1894.]

3. [*Ibid.*, p. 368.]

Mother's Day: Zola's Women   Naomi Schor*

On the striking cover of Jean Borie's *Le Tyran timide* a black and white reproduction of Lucas Cranach the Elder's *Hercules and Omphale* furnishes immediate commentary on the puzzling oxymoronic title and its equally ambiguous subtitle *Le Naturalisme de la femme au XIXe siècle*. Omphale, it will be recalled, was the queen of Lydia, "in whose service Hercules, dressed as a woman, spun wool and performed other womanly tasks for three years to appease the gods" [Webster's New World Dictionary (New York: New World Publishing Company, 1966), p. 1024]. In this treatment of a theme repeated with variations by Cranach and his workshop, Hercules is depicted as a Renaissance Gulliver, a bear of a man

*Review of: (1) Jean Borie, *Le Tyran timide: Le Naturalisme de la femme au XIXe siècle* (The timid tyrant: The naturalism of woman in the XIXth century) (Paris: Klincksieck, 1973), and (2) Anna Krakowski, *La Condition de la femme dans l'œuvre d'Emile Zola* (Woman's condition in Emile Zola's works) (Paris: Nizet, 1974). Reprinted from *Diacritics* 5 (Winter 1975):11–17, by permission of the journal.

held in thrall by four lovely women who are armed only with the tools of spinning. While the great Hercules is tied down by a single diaphanous wool thread, two of the smiling women are covering his head with a cloth (metonym for his feminine attire), and two are pinning his left arm back with the distaff. In this hyperbolic representation of man's castration by woman, the supreme mythical figure of masculine strength is condemned to perform the lowliest woman's work. The subliminal message of this cover is clear: the male / female relationship is a variant of the master/slave relationship, with the male as the indentured slave of a female master. In order to appease the gods, the aggressive, imperialistic male must serve the Queen.

But who then is the timid tyrant: humble Hercules in drag? or his seductive subjugators? Taken as a liminary sign-system, this cover points up the essential confusion which mars this rich and often brilliant work. The identity of the timid tyrant is unstable: now woman is the Queen and man her slave, now man is the King and woman his slave. Like Borie's remarkable earlier study, *Zola et les mythes* [Paris: Seuil, 1971], *Le Tyran timide* consists of two parts: a Marxist prolegomenon and a central Freudian-thematic analysis (in this instance of a single novel, *La Joie de vivre*). This methodological and metalinguistic split accounts for our uncertainty as to the gender of the tyrant: if in a Marxist perspective men are the oppressors, in the Freudian perspective adopted by Borie the oppressors are women. The title and the painting clash: the one raises expectations of univocity which orient our reading and are frustrated, the other suggests a "dialectic of sex" which is never articulated, making a final synthesis impossible.

In his introductory chapters, Borie debunks the nineteenth-century cult of woman-as-nature by demonstrating that both in the "bachelor discourse" of an Alfred de Vigny and the liberal-feminist discourse of a Michelet (surely the demi-urge of nineteenth-century French "gynéco-mythie,"[1]), manifest worship of women hides their latent exploitation. Balzac's cynical remark, quoted by Simone de Beauvoir, might serve as an epigraph to this section: "the married woman is a slave whom one must be able to set on a throne" [*The Second Sex*, trans. H. M. Parshley (New York: Bantam, 1970), p. 103]. To be the prime mediator between man and Nature (Muse), or even the equivalent of Nature (Mother), lowers woman's status while appearing to raise it, for woman is thus held within a chain of equivalences which, in the Victorian era, links women, the lower classes, the body, and the colonies. All these share a common fate: oppression, repression, or colonization at the hands of bourgeois white males. Still, according to Borie, the cult of woman as earth-mother, as angel of the hearth, hypocritically masks her relegation to a subordinate role in society, one strictly determined by the political and economic changes ushered in by the French Revolution. Under democratic liberalism and its concomitant, free enterprise, the family—centered on the wife and mother—

provides a bulwark against loneliness, anomie, and revolution. Men tied to their wives' apron strings are likely to stay off the streets and the barricades; in this structure, Nature (= Woman) and History (= Man) are binary opposites. Borie commendably strips away the trappings of woman-worship in the Victorian era, showing that a certain stage of capitalism is founded on the domestication of female sexuality, the loss for women of the "privileges of passion" [p. 118].

Given this useful analysis of the status of women in nineteenth-century France it is all the more disappointing to find that, in the second half of the book, Borie falls victim to what Deleuze and Guattari have aptly termed "the analytic imperialism of the Oedipus complex" [Gilles Deleuze and Felix Guattari, *L'Anti-Oedipe* (Paris: Editions de Minuit, 1972), p. 30]. By Borie's own admission, the Oedipus complex dominates *Zola et les mythes:* "In an earlier work devoted to Zola we attempted to demonstrate that naturalism is necessarily, historically, the most Oedipal literary discourse extant" [Borie, p. 12]. This article of faith accounts for Borie's choice of *La Joie de vivre* — one of Zola's most neglected novels — as the focus of his study: this is the novel *par excellence* of the nuclear family and, what is more, the "novel of ambivalence" [p. 102] toward the maternal imago. *La Joie de vivre* could have been entitled, in homage to Zola's friend Turgeniev, "Mothers and Sons." Indeed, Borie's longest sub-section is entitled "The Mothers," and all the females in the novel (including the cat!) are mothers. One passage in this section exemplifies the dangers inherent in Borie's approach, and, beyond Borie and Zola, in any form of psycho-criticism or text-analysis practiced by a son on the fiction of a son using a methodology devised by a son. These are the ravages of unchecked oedipal imperialism: "There is not, strictly speaking, any mother who is not domineering [abusive], since women only seek after maternity so obstinately in order finally to affirm their completeness and avenge a lack. Conversely, the male child who abdicates his virility in favor of his mother cannot expect the latter to put it to good use. The phallic mother exists both in and of herself and as a phantasm willingly enthroned by the son [. . .] The couple constituted by a passionate mother and her *only* son is a tight little hell" [p. 105].

To borrow Barthes' question (with reference to Flaubert's irony): "*Who is speaking?*" [Roland Barthes, *S/Z* (Paris: Seuil, 1970), p. 146]. It can hardly be Zola; there is no evidence that he ever wrote anything of which this could be an updated paraphrase. Freud? Certainly not. His statements on the subject of the mother / son relationship would seem to indicate that, when dealing with this sensitive relationship, even the most hard-nosed and brilliant male scientist may be caught fantasizing out loud: "A mother is only brought unlimited satisfaction by her relation to her son; this is altogether the most perfect, the most free of ambivalence of all human relationships" [Freud, "Femininity," p. 133]. Furthermore, to my knowledge, Freud never affirmed the existence of the phallic mother outside of dreams and phantasies. Borie's sweeping generalization is, then, an expression of his own point of view, implicitly linked to Zola on the one hand (context), and to Freud on the other (metalanguage). Now, if there is any critical praxis which calls for some degree of self-awareness on the part of the critic, some acknowledgement of where the critic stands, it is psychocriticism. If such criticism is, in Barthes' words, a "projective test" [*Sur Racine* (Paris: Seuil, 1963), p. 161], which "proceeds by identification" [Serge Doubrovsky, *La Place de la madeleine* (Paris: Mercure de France, 1974), p. 153] and succeeds when the neuroses of the author and the critic mesh, then it is crucial that the critic implicate himself in the analytic process. As Doubrovsky states: "Any analytic situation, involving either a man or a work, entails its own transferences" [loc. cit]. This leads to a second objection to Borie's use of psychoanalysis: he treats the characters as though they were patients on the couch, and not constructs of language, referring, for example, to "Madame Chanteau, in the secret of her unconscious" [p. 109]. The literary and fictional status of the neuroses under analysis is ignored.

In the end, however, Borie's discussion of motherhood in *La Joie de vivre* suffers most from a lack of connection with his opening chapters, where he exposes the ideological functions of family-life. Borie's rather literal application of Freud is sorely lacking in historical awareness. The naturalism of women in the nineteenth century — so scathingly revealed as a self-serving male construct in Chapters I and II — is proposed as a model of eternal femininity in Chapter III: woman-as-nature becomes woman's nature. How is it that Borie, who convincingly unmasks the prime practitioners of the contemporary cult of woman as muse / mother, suddenly loses sight of the historical context in which characters such as Madame Chanteau and Pauline Quenu (the main mother-figures in *La Joie de vivre*) are operating? While there is cause to question a certain feminist strategy which dismisses Freud's depressing and / or infuriating remarks about women by viewing them as obsolete products of *fin de siècle* Vienna, some connection must surely be made between Zola's domineering women and their socio-economic predicaments. Indeed, not to make this connection is to gloss over the information Zola provides us, suggesting that both Madame Chanteau and Pauline are frustrated by their socially determined roles as women, their inability to act on and in the world except vicariously, through the mediation of men, and singularly ineffectual men at that. Perhaps the most poignant words in the novel are uttered by Pauline, who has sought to convince her feckless cousin Lazare to study medicine: "if she were a man, what she would find most exciting would be to cure the world" [*Les Rougon-Macquart* (Paris: Pléiade, 1964), III, p. 842]. Both Pauline and Madame Chanteau, the would-be doctor who has to be content with "playing doctor" and the former schoolteacher who has to be content with tutoring a niece, are eloquent testimonies to the waste of human potential which results from confining women to the home. The tyranny they exert on the men in their lives is proportionate to the exiguity of their empires.

Mme Chanteau is not unique in Zola's fiction. She belongs to a "type" of female character which recurs throughout the *Rougon-Macquart*, a "type" which Anna Krakowski classifies under the rubric "the ambitious women" [p. 140]. Any notion that, by virtue of birthright, every female critic is automatically a feminist is quickly dispelled by a reading of this exhaustive inventory of Zola's female characters. Krakowski's sketch of the ambitious woman in Zola can serve as a companion piece to Borie's characterization of the domineering mother: "In opposition to the ideal wife, who is never her own master because she belongs entirely to her husband and her children, the ambitious woman is very egotistic. She subjugates her husband and is often aggressive and shrewish with him because he has proved incapable of fulfilling her dreams of grandeur. In her, vanity and envy have supplanted goodness, generosity, and the spirit of justice, and she lacks scruples whenever it is a question of satisfying her appetites" [p. 140].

Despite the considerable differences in their styles, both Borie and Krakowski resort to the same form of paraphrase-summary to disguise their interpretations of Zola's texts. Krakowski's hostility to this type of female character becomes overt when she remarks, with reference to Félicité Rougon, upon the power behind *La fortune des Rougon:* "We have no alternative but to recognize that she is endowed with a spirit of initiative and an innate sense of responsibility; it is thanks to these gifts that she attains the maximum of her power" [Krakowski, p. 142; italics mine]. The designing woman and / or domineering mother characters are the acid-test for critics dealing with images of women in fiction. Borie's and Krakowski's negative valorizations of these "types" betray their personal preferences for the "good mother" and / or the "ideal wife," as well as their distaste for female characters endowed with those highly prized "masculine" qualities— ambition, energy, and egoism— which are the hallmarks of Zola's male protagonists.

The key word in the passage from Krakowski quoted above is "ideal"; her constant preoccupation is to abstract and delineate Zola's *ideal* woman. The following passage, which concerns the protagonist of *Au bonheur des dames,* reveals Krakowski's fundamental assumption and her vision of Zola: "Denise Baudu inaugurates the series of the ideal women [. . .] As a moralist, the latter [Zola] emphasizes and underscores what he sees as excellent and strong in this well-balanced young woman. He does so in order to oppose her to her entourage, a prey to debauchery. The triumph of wisdom over the folly of the senses is most certainly not a commonplace event, but, while allowing the author to end his novel on a pathetic note, it remains in keeping with the general line which characterizes this type of heroine" [p. 96].

In other words, whereas Borie deplores the domestication of female sexuality, Krakowski sees it as Zola's greatest contribution to renewing traditional representations of women. If Zola depicts "negative female types" [p. 241], it is only in order to offset his "positive heroines" [p. 123]; if he depicts vice, it is the better to teach virtue. That classical alibi is invoked constantly, and it does serve to remind us of Zola's very real moral purpose. However, Krakowski goes too far in promoting her central thesis. Nowhere is the reductionism inherent in her approach more flagrant than in her remarks on Nana, that troublesome incarnation of female sexuality on the loose. In keeping with her moralistic bias, Krakowski reduces *Nana* to a tract against the courtesan: "The final impression we retain from reading it is in no way favorable to the obscene courtesan" [p. 197]. Krakowski is so bent on proving that Zola repudiated the Romantics' glorification of the courtesan and sexual passion that she completely overlooks Nana's mythic quality, her demonic dimension. Of Nana's "three faces" [Chantal Jennings, "Les trois visages de Nana," *French Review*, 44, Special Issue No. 2 (1971), 117–28], she sees only the reassuring one. Following in the footsteps of a previous generation of Zola scholars, Krakowski consistently reads Zola's works in the light of his stated intentions, with little regard for his eventual realizations. Unencumbered, in her fidelity to the author's pronouncements, by a critical position or language of her own, Krakowski writes a respectful work about Zola, to whom she revealingly refers as "the *father* of the *Rougon-Macquart*" [p. 246; italics added].

Yet *La Condition de la femme dans l'oeuvre d'Emile Zola*, despite its Manichaean view of femininity and lack of critical sophistication, is a worthy pioneering effort at dealing with a subject whose time has come. A solid base for a critically and ideologically self-conscious treatment of Zola's women emerges from the accumulation of information about Zola's and his contemporaries' views on women and from the plot summaries of all of Zola's woman-centered novels (though the majority of Krakowski's examples are drawn from the *Rougon-Macquart*; important works such as *Thérèse Raquin*, at one extreme, and *Fécondité*, at the other, are almost completely neglected). Moreover, by inadvertence, Krakowski raises some important and difficult questions about interpreting women and/in literature, questions which pertain directly to the position of the woman as critic and to the elaboration of a feminist hermeneutics. Perhaps the most troublesome should be faced first: should feminist criticism be evaluative? More specifically, how relevant to the study of women in a given author's works is that author's feminism and / or misogyny? The question of Zola's feminism arises early on in Krakowski's book and she answers it by saying that Zola was no more a feminist than a socialist, he was above all a humanitarian: "He treats feminism just as he does socialism, he serves it without joining the official ranks" [p. 24]. However, Krakowski then muddies the issue by seeking to prove that Zola was a friend to women, concluding that he was a man ahead of his time, in short, a fellow-traveler of feminism. In existing examples of feminist criticism, the assumption of a certain evaluative posture is undeniable: it suffices to recall the essays on literature in *The Second Sex*, or to compare Krakowski and Chantal Jennings[2] on Zola's women. If an evaluative stance is predictable and inevitable in the early stages of a criticism which emerges from a fundamentally ideological position, then Zola promises to pose as many problems for the feminists as he has for the Marxists. Like the Marxists, feminist critics will have to devise subtle strategies for dealing with Zola's contradictions, in particular those between his theories and his practice, his early and his late works.

A case in point is Zola's "sticky" ideology [Barthes, *Le Plaisir du texte* (Paris: Seuil, 1973), p. 52] of woman as earth and hearth mother. Both the Freudian and the non-Freudian converge on this point, lending it the quasi-scientific status of objective fact: "Zola's heroine is first and foremost physically and psychologically a mother" [Krakowski, p. 148]. If she strays from her assigned place in the home—commits adultery or gets a job—she brings tragedy down on the heads of her nuclear family: "fundamentally, in Zola's works mothers are forbidden to go out" [Borie, *Zola et les mythes*, p. 147]. Zola's bourgeois women (and as Krakowski points out, "all the ideal heroines are bourgeois women" [p. 36]), are under house arrest. Yet as we noted earlier in regard to the mother figures in *La Joie de vivre*, by virtue of his faithful mimesis of social reality, Zola subverts his code with his message. This convenient example of the home-bound woman can hardly reflect the sum of Zola's contradictions, the extent of his ambivalence on the question of women's proper place; it is only meant to suggest a type of opposition which solicits further attention from critics. The example also lends weight to the hypothesis that Zola's feminism and his socialism run parallel courses. One of the logical consequences of the equation posited by Borie between women and the lower classes is that both socialism and feminism are infused with an identical strain of still another -ism: paternalism. Indeed, Zola's heroes, from *La Confession de Claude* through *Travail*, make the same "special type of object choice" analyzed by Freud ["A Special Type of Object Choice Made by Men," *Sexuality and the Psychology of Love* (New York: Collier, 1970), 49–58]: they are all saviors bent on *rescuing* women. Zola's Messianic politics, centered on a Christ-like leader, are mirrored in his sexual politics. And, just as Zola's paternalistic brand of socialism does not win high marks from Marxist critics [see Frederick Ivor Case, *La Cité idéale dans "Travail" d'Emile Zola* (Toronto, University of Toronto Press, 1974)] his paternalistic brand of feminism is hardly likely to win an endorsement from N.O.W.

But surely feminist criticism does not want to go the way of the N.A.A.C.P. on *Huckleberry Finn* or B'nai Brith on *The Merchant of Venice*; evaluative criticism ceases to be a worthwhile or legitimate academic pursuit when it turns into censorship. The polemical, attention-getting stage of feminist criticism, perhaps best typified by Kate Millett's

Sexual Politics, seems to be giving way to its necessary counterpart and corrective: a feminist formalism, concerned with the images of women in fiction, the linguistic codes used to describe female characters, the narrative structures engendered by the specificity of the feminine destiny.[3] Notwithstanding the claim of at least one feminist critic, namely that formalism is a form of (male) chauvinism [Fraya Katz-Stoker, "The Other Criticism: Feminism vs. Formalism," in *Images of Women in Fiction*, ed. Susan Koppelman Cornillon (Bowling Green, Ohio: Bowling Green University Popular Press, 1972), 313–25], feminism and formalism are not irreconcilable: formalism offers feminist critics the necessary instruments for the precise and objective analyses they need to produce if Women's Studies are to be accepted as a serious academic discipline. Semiotics and ideological criticism can be complementary. Combined, they give rise to the tone which distinguishes the best efforts in this field: a tone of controlled rage, a kind of in-rage.

Besides the question of evaluation, Krakowski's book, by its title alone, poses another and potentially more serious question: how legitimate is it to deal exclusively with Zola's (or any other authors') women, without reference to their men? No doubt one danger to be avoided is that of imposing a polarized view of the male / female relationship on the study of fiction. Feminist critics have tended to accept, as a basic premise, an *a priori* opposition / distinction between male and female which leads to studies of images of women in isolation, with little or no reference to the corresponding images of men. While this hard and fast opposition may indeed be operative in certain authors and periods, to apply it automatically would be to miss perhaps the most significant contribution made by nineteenth-century French novelists to a theory of sex. Zola is part of a long line of authors, extending from Stendhal to Proust, who imaginatively grappled with what was to become one of the central stumbling blocks in Freud's theory of sex: the elusive criteria for defining the psychological differences between male and female. Rejecting conventional equations of maleness with activity and femaleness with passivity, Freud's thought—as mythical thought does—moved away from binary opposites toward their mediation, in the form of bisexuality. Though problematic, because it must be reconciled with Freud's phallocentrism, the "factor of bisexuality" [*Three Contributions to the Theory of Sex* (New York: Dutton, 1962), p. 77] is a cornerstone of Freud's reflections on sex and one with wide-ranging applications to the study of literature. It is particularly illuminating to keep this in mind when reading Zola, one of Freud's contemporaries and favorite authors. What is revolutionary about Zola's women is that it is so hard to tell them apart from his men. His work embodies one of the contradictions / denegations characteristic of his period which, according to Carolyn Heilbrun, "superseded all others in finding confusion between the sexes terrifying" [*Toward a Recognition of Androgyny* (New York: Harper, 1973), p. 29]: it insists on the specificity of woman's procreative function while / because it attests to a breakdown of difference between the sexes. Zola protests too much and his "masculine protest" is suspect, significant in ways which seem to escape both Borie and Krakowski. Both touch lightly on aspects of the breakdown of difference, but only in passing; if anything, Krakowski, the non-Freudian, because of her thoroughness, attributes more importance to this aspect of Zola's work than does Borie. Quoting Zola's remarkable note to himself in his *Différences entre Balzac et moi* "As for me, I see no difference between men and women, while recognizing the natural differences" [Zola, *Les Rougon-Macquart* (Paris: Pléiade, 1967), V, p. 1737]—further evidence that the problem of *difference* haunted him—Krakowski comments: This "attribution to the feminine sex of the faculties and the disposition of the masculine sex is the basis of his entire conception of women" [Krakowski, pp. 16–17]. Here, Krakowski comes perilously close to asking the important questions: given the breakdown of difference between male and female, what is the significance of Zola's choice of female protagonists for several of his novels? what specific function(s) do his women serve? what specific women serve them best? The problem of sex difference and the problem of the female *persona* of a male author are inextricably linked.

If the "riddle of femininity" [Freud, "Femininity," p. 116] is seen as one of Zola's central preoccupations, then *La Joie de vivre* offers an excellent "case" in point; it is, as Borie contends, a pivotal novel. The events are few and banal; the characters, ordinary people living out their lives in a provincial backwater. Pauline Quenu, the orphaned daughter of the prosperous *charcutiers* in *Le Ventre de Paris*, is taken in by her aunt and uncle, the Chanteaus, who live with their only son Lazare in a godforsaken fishing village on the coast of Normandy. When Pauline arrives she is ten years old and due to inherit a fair sum of money on coming of age. Her life will consist of a series of self-sacrifices, compensated, as Borie rightly emphasizes, by the gratifications of imperialism (Pauline makes herself indispensable to the Chanteaus). Pauline, who has inherited her parents' avariciousness along with their money, allows her fortune to be plundered, squandered by the Chanteaus; Pauline, who falls in love with her good-for-nothing cousin, gives him away in marriage to Louise, a rich young heiress; Pauline, who is built to bear children, ends up nursing the sickly son of Louise and Lazare.

The relationship of Pauline and Lazare is the consummate elaboration of a type of erotic relationship which recurs throughout Zola: the idyll, always "sterile and deadly," as Angus Wilson, the first Freudian commentator on Zola, has noted [*Emile Zola* (London: Mercury Books, 1965), p. 58]. The question is this: why are the rites of passage from adolescent to adult love blocked by insuperable obstacles?

Read along the syntagmatic axis (as opposed to Borie's paradigmatic reading), the story of Pauline and Lazare is the fictional transposition of a man's anguishing discovery of sexual difference—the shattering of what

Luce Irigaray calls "an old dream of symmetry" [*Speculum* (Paris: Editions de Minuit, 1974), p. 7]. This "fall" is allegorized in Lazare's musical composition, a solemn march based on the expulsion of Adam and Eve from Paradise. In its early stage, Pauline and Lazare's relationship is that of two siblings, but *male* siblings: "Lazare, from the very first day, had accepted her as a boy, a younger brother" [Zola, III, p. 838]. As long as their "boyish camaraderie" [III, p. 848] lasts, the two cousins are inseparable companions, working and playing together; this is the idyllic phase of their relationship and it is strikingly similar to other real or pseudo-fraternal relationships depicted by Zola. Thus, in *La Fortune des Rougon*, young Silvère's feelings for his playmate Miette are those of an older brother: "He watched her jump over the wall with the satisfaction of an older brother watching the exercises of one of his younger brothers" [Zola, *Les Rougon-Macquart* (Paris: Pléiade, 1963), I, p. 193]. Other variants of this male / (fe)male idyll could be adduced, but these two should suffice to suggest that for Zola, happiness is when "a little girl is a little man" [Freud, "Femininity," p. 118]. However, to both Pauline's and Lazare's surprise and distress, in due time they find out that they are not Same, not brothers, but Other. Pauline's menstruation—a particularly gory and traumatic event—forever sunders the fraternal tête à tête; this reminder of woman's "castration" brings the "intersexual" [Wilson, p. 58] idyll to an end: "So, this little girl, this younger brother was definitely a woman? One could not graze her without her moaning, one ought not even count on her at all times of the month. With every new fact they were surprised, as at an unexpected discovery which embarrassed and moved them both, in the midst of their boyish camaraderie. Lazare's reaction seemed to be only one of annoyance; it would no longer be possible to work together since she was not a man and a mere nothing disturbed her. As for Pauline, she was left with a feeling of malaise, an anxiety which gave rise to a delightful charm" [Zola, III, pp. 867–68].

With the fall from intersexual innocence, the expulsion from the Paradise of non-difference, shame makes its appearance. In a perhaps unintended parody of Virginie's drowning at the end of Bernardin de Saint-Pierre's *Paul et Virginie*, the archetypal eighteenth-century tale of an interrupted fraternal idyll, Pauline nearly drowns when her bathing suit springs a tear while she and Lazare are out swimming. Unlike Virginie, Pauline survives, but she is denied the fulfillments of a "normal" woman: marriage and motherhood are conferred instead upon Louise. In Pauline, femininity is reduced to its lowest common denominator, its smallest semantic component: lack. The logic of the subtext requires the reduplication of the initial lack by the lack of the compensatory baby; redundancy insures the reader's perception of the line that divides the characters in the novel, what Barthes has termed "the axis of castration" [S/Z, p. 42].

In the nineteenth-century French novel, woman's lack, her empty space, functions as a blank screen onto which male authors can project any monstrosity ranging from the love of death to the loss of reason. Seen in this perspective, Gérard de Nerval's *Aurélia* is not an unclassifiable *hapax*, but only a border-line case: "Castration is, in fact, the constitutive, constituent experience of *Aurélia*. If Nerval examines himself, his madness under a feminine title, it is because woman symbolizes that empty space around which delirium crystallizes. *Aurélia* is not, in truth, the female protagonist of the narrative, but the nominal form of an absence, the signifier of loss" [Shoshana Felman, " 'Aurélia' ou 'le livre infaisable': de Foucault à Nerval," *Romantisme*, 3 (1972), p. 49]. There is no female *persona* of a male author who does not bear, Minerva-like, the imprint of her maker: when Baudelaire dubbed Emma Bovary a "bizarre androgyn" [Charles Baudelaire, *Oeuvres complètes* (Paris: Pléiade, 1961), p. 652], he was in effect describing most of the memorable heroines of Stendhal, Balzac, and Zola as well. Pauline's very name, composed as it is of a masculine root and a feminine suffix, recapitulates her genesis. Krakowski duly records that the greater feminization of Zola's heroines coincided with a withdrawal of his personal investment in them: "It is only with Clotilde (1893) that women are no longer the main spokesmen for his ideas. Women become more feminine, are less identified with the person of the novelist" [p. 27]. Surely it is no coincidence that Caroline Hamelin—the female character about whom Zola's note, "embody myself totally in her" [*Oeuvres*, V, p. 1248], recalls Flaubert's self-identification with Madame Bovary—is, like Pauline, conspicuously sterile.

What indispensable role do Zola's minimally female, maximally androgynous heroines play? The metamorphosis of the beloved younger sibling into a woman short-circuits the strong homosexual undercurrent which pervades so many of Zola's novels. Zola, that fearless iconoclast, drew the line at overt representations of male homosexuality. Whereas in *Nana*, he titillates the reader with descriptions of a lesbian restaurant, and takes Nana's relationship with Satin to its logical conclusion, in *La Débâcle*, his war novel, he narrowly averts the consummation of corporal Jean's deep feelings for soldier Maurice, by introducing Maurice's look-alike twin sister Henriette as an object onto whom Jean can transfer his love. We know, furthermore, from Zola's *ébauches* for *La Débâcle*, that he had originally set out to write a novel without female protagonists, but found the project unviable. Thus Zola's women are connected with the author's (latent) homosexuality in two ways: first, male homosexuality is transcoded into female homosexuality; second, the women separate the men from the men. Thus, while I would agree with Julia Kristeva that women in the modern psychological novel are a "pseudo-center," I would qualify her statement that, in this center, "man seeks man" [*Le Texte du roman* (The Hague: Mouton, 1970), p. 160]. Women are not merely go-betweens, but at the same time obstacles, natural barriers, so to speak, who serve to prevent unnatural acts from taking place. Take away the women and you are back on the raft with Huck and Jim. To this raft, Zola preferred the perils of the *Raft of the Medusa.*[4]

This pictorial allusion brings us full circle, back to Borie, Cranach and *Hercules and Omphale.* In the end, while Borie does not reconcile his Marxist and Freudian analyses, working within the Freudian framework, he does account for the timid tyrant's unstable identity. The root of the problem lies in the tyrant's ambivalence, hence the oxymoronic title of the book: "Lazare would like both to love and destroy, enslave and serve. His own ambivalent feelings are reflected, by projection, in his partners: Mme Chanteau, devoted and tyrannical, Pauline, generous and sacrificed and, at the same time, possessive and imperial" [Borie, pp. 153–54]. This recognition of the contradictions, the split within Zola's female characters, can ground a much more persuasive reading of the condition of women in Zola than that of Krakowski, who argues to the very end that Zola transcended the stereotypical polarization: woman as angel vs. woman as demon. In support of Borie's interpretation, one might note that, of all Zola's heroines, only two have endured, have become eponymous: Gervaise and Nana, the hyperbolic victim and the *femme fatale.* Beneath *Hercules and Omphale,* one may imagine the outlines of an earlier painting, as though a process of pentimento had taken place; that painting is Cranach's dyptich representing those two antithetical, yet complementary images of woman in antiquity, Lucrecia and Judith. In Zola's fiction, these archaic images of woman as object either of terror or of pity, have not really been expunged, only papered over, so to speak. Pauline is double not only in her contradictory nature, but also in her mythical heritage. Zola's entire effort at transcending archetypes results only in the transformation of the tragic into the melodramatic: when Pauline, Lucrecia-like, takes up her scissors to plunge them into her breast, the gesture is pure parody; when Pauline, Judith-like, dreams of being a savior, her dream is pure fantasy. However dim or degraded, the outlines of the tragic models are still legible in Zola's text. This conversion of the great female figures of antiquity into bourgeois characters which occurs throughout Zola's fiction, points up the need to relate any future study of Zola's women to Zola's work as a whole: the isolationist, thematic approach must be replaced by a totalizing project which would stress the exemplary quality of woman's destiny. Thus, what Elizabeth Hardwick has called "the death of sex as a tragic, exalted theme" [*Seduction and Betrayal* (New York: Vintage, 1975), p. 218], symbolized by Nana's death, is, in fact, part of a larger picture: the death of tragedy itself.

Notes

1. Cf. Pierre Fauchery, *La Destinée féminine dans le roman européen du dix-huitième siècle 1713–1807. Essai de gynémythie romanesque* (Paris: Armand Colin, 1972).

2. See her "Zola féministe?, "*Les Cahiers naturalistes*, No. 44 (1972), 172–187 and No. 45 (1973), 1–22.

3. See, for example, Nancy Miller, Gender and Genre (Unpublished Dissertation: Columbia University, 1974).

4. In the course of their tour through the Louvre, members of the wedding party in *L'Assommoir* do actually stop in front of Delacroix's painting; it is thus explicitly included among the cultural artifacts which serve as referents in *Les Rougon-Macquart* (Zola, *Les Rougon-Macquart, II*, p. 444).

Oedipus at Médan   Philippe Bonnefis[*]

"Melancholy, from Médan, Zola watches
                              his name go by" (Ph. Viollet).

From the balcony at Médan, a melancholy Zola watches his name go by. Yet, what is he thinking about? Perhaps he is thinking the same thing as the Young American who had just left his mark on a New York subway train and astonished Norman Mailer with his mania (his instinct) for writing his name, saying: "You have to put in the hours to add up the names. You have to get your name around."[1]

Yes, perhaps Zola is ruminating on the same thing. Edmond de Goncourt, already suspecting him of as much, wrote in his *Journal* on 14 December 1880: "Here is a man who spreads his name throughout the world, whose books sell by the hundred thousand, who has caused more of a stir than any other writer during his lifetime: and yet, because of his morbid disposition, his depressive frame of mind, he is the most disconsolate of people, gloomier than the most abject of life's failure's!"

Every novel of the *Rougon-Macquart* series reproduces Zola's name a hundred thousand times. A new economic phenomenon, no doubt. But that is not exactly what interests me, unless the phenomenon is described in terms of a quite different economic system, with Zola as the manager of his name. But his name? — The problem is knowing what the bearer understands in his name, what it is in his name that appeals to him and would ring out in your ears as you uttered it, as long as you heightened the voice a little, placed your tongue closer to your teeth, rounding the palate, trilling the *l* and making it sound twice: Zolla! Thus the patronymic name is restored in the original spelling as it appears in the archives of the Republic of Venice where Emile's father, Francesco, was born on the 7th

*This article was first published in the *Magazine littéraire*, no. 132 (January 1978): 28–30, and the material has been incorporated in the author's recent book *L'Innommable: Essai sur l'oeuvre d'Emile Zola* (Paris: SEDES, 1984). Translated for this volume by David Baguley. Reprinted by permission of the *Magazine littéraire* and the author.

of August, 1795. But *zolla* in Italian (i.e. in the father's language, in the language of his own name) means "clod of earth."

This being so, how could Zola not have interpreted his name as a message, whatever its derivation? A personal message, of course, one which would say in no uncertain terms something like this: in all etymological seriousness your father is nothing more than this detached piece of his mother's body; and that is where you in turn originate, in direct lineage, from that amorphous matter, that primordial clay from which life issued forth at the Genesis of the world. Just find your beginnings. Go back to your roots, to see . . .

All of that in a name? That and much more. In fact I would consider Zola's work to be an exploration of that unfathomable noun whose homonymy the son parades all the more derisively because he is a writer and as such, as M. Blanchot writes, "he only possesses the infinite, he misses the finite, limits escape him."

Various circumstances will lead Zola to investigate the life and personality of his father. From the scattered chapters of this biography, to which the text of Zola's novels refers and, at the same time, from which it keeps its distance, there emerges the fascinating profile of a father who works with fire and moulds clay, an anal figure, a Titanic figure, blasting rocks, releasing the vast waters of the mountain down into the city. We know that François Zola was commissioned to dig and construct the water supply canal in Aix-en-Provence, an event which young Emile will later celebrate by erecting the votive monument of a long poem in the manner of Victor Hugo. But it is particularly interesting to note that, of his father's many activities, Zola only retains the "gigantic struggle" of his excavations: new docks sunk in the port of Marseilles, the mounds of the Paris fortifications shifted, an embanking machine invented, a railway line in Austria laid out, a treatise written on surveying. A whole life spent digging up the earth or filling it in; creating the image of a father lost in body and in name in this earth where he burrows away like a mole; and here is his son, following in his footsteps, an indefatigable Telemachus, as if it is his duty to find for his father's remains a final resting-place.

We have only to reread his open letters to the municipal authorities of Aix: "A year ago I went along every street of the town and I looked in vain for my father's name on the walls. . . . Such is their ingratitude that they have not even written my father's name on the Rotonde fountain." It is as if proof were missing, proof of — a death. As if, in the absence of the dead man's body, at least signs are being produced to confirm his passing, to record the fact, reiterate it for eternity: a memorial inscription, a plaque in the street, an epitaph: Here Lies François Zola, his name attests to the fact, the effigy of a name which, through the monumental presence of its engraved letters, is a safer seal than the laminations of a tomb. . . .

The Aix Affair is resolved to the plaintiff's satisfaction. François Zola has his street. And yet the name still does not stick. Zola seems condemned constantly to go back over the letters of a name that inevitably comes to nothing again (falls beyond the realm of the sign, like an object): "It is a fact that the *Mémorial d'Aix*," he writes, "has not yet tried to efface my name from the cover of my books." The insinuation is not a mere matter of pique. It expresses the very real fears of someone who feels threatened by a kind of perpetual absence. We only have to look at his works: all that ink and paper as if to overcome the fear that the name "Zola" might simply fade away. And all that effort, resulting in nothing more than the extravagant fabrications that we know. For, in order successfully to live up to the trademark, this symbolic death that a son owes to his father would have to take place. On the discharge of this duty depend the exercise and legacy of the paternal function and it is that duty that determines the sum of the impossible debt.

We can now begin to see, no doubt, the particular importance that the genealogical "motor" will take on in the functioning of Zola's text; the *motor*, in effect, and not simply the formal structure—in the sense, for example, that one speaks even today of a "cybernetic motor" (Michel Serres). The linking of generations, the capture and channelling of genetic forces, their distribution determined by an inextricable network of relationships represent the model to which Zola, having learnt the art of interesting history in his fate, systematically ascribes any circulating flow of forces. This is also why there can be no immediate political solution to the concrete problems encountered in *Germinal*, *L'Argent*, or *La Débâcle*. The social question is the case in point of a broader question which will only be resolved through the fiction of a family novel. Thus it becomes clear that the order of the *Evangiles* merely complies with the programme: *Fécondité* first, then *Travail*. Only when *Fécondité* (fertility) has restored the blocked flow of genealogy is *Travail* (work) conceivable.

Let us compare, from this point of view, the *Evangiles* and the *Rougon-Macquart*.

In the realm of genealogy the transmission of a name is the symbolic act by which what is transmitted is transmissibility itself, the power of the son to transmit in turn. The founder of a family is not strictly its originator. In this arrangement the Father merely represents the point at which a link is established with the source; he is not really the source itself. It is here, at the outset, that a sterile force, derivative, divided, subdivided, and rapidly dispersed, is transformed into a useful force, useful for as long as it remains caught up in the complex web of alliances, for as long as it makes its way by many a devious route, from relays to intersections, without ever encountering an obstacle, without ever being checked or disconnected. The system is therefore destined to develop *ad infinitum*. This expansionist tendency is illustrated by the imperialism of the *Evangiles*, "the teeming fertility of the conquering Froments;" after the family, the race; and after the race, "there is humanity, endless expansion." If, in Zola's last novels, the names pile up in apparently interminable lists in which the reader runs the risk of getting completely lost, is it not for the pleasure of making sure that the line is never broken, of checking that the current is flowing freely at all points of the network? For, at the slightest obstacle, there is a blockage. In *Les Rougon-Macquart* a lack of paternity puts the whole system out of operation. The genealogical *circuit* gets clogged like a sewer that cannot be drained. The child, a force made flesh, becomes no more than wasted energy; consanquinity promotes a process of alienation; the being is diffused among its offspring. There is only one solution, but it is a desperate one: the desire for a salutary stability in death (*La Faute de l'abbé Mouret*, *La Joie de vivre*. . .).

According to Freud a preoccupation with genealogy represents the will to know about God, and therefore about the true father, because he is the fatherless father, the perfect name, neither transmitted nor transmittable, a holograph writing of the Name, a signature of enormous and insurmountable particularity. There is no chance that in *Les Rougon-Macquart* genealogy could satisfy such a fancy. There is, it is true, an ancestor present throughout the whole work, a single character who alone blocks further ancestry (and descent); but it is a mother and not a father— Adélaïde Fouque, who very soon became a widow and is never called Madame Rougon, mother or mamma, and who is referred to by a dubious nickname which, typically, does not establish any family link: Aunt Dide.

If we now go to the last novel of the cycle, *Le Docteur Pascal*, we see that, by means of a sudden short cut, the beginning and the end are brought face to face, Aunt Dide and Little Charles, the ancestor and her double (At the top of the genealogical tree which Zola includes with his novel we read the following entry on this last offshoot of the family: "A throwback by three generations. Moral and physical resemblance to Adélaïde Fouque"). The origin thereby returns from afar but it (re)turns back upon itself, after branching off in many directions, merely to bring about this recapitulation. However, to connect the same with the same creates a problem. "See how they should be finished off," Zola asks himself in his preparatory sketch for the novel. "Could Aunt Dide strangle Charles, then die afterwards? . . . I rather like the idea of strangling." In fact he will choose haemorrhaging: Charles bleeds himself white. But the writer's hesitation was worth noting. It shows that in this kind of circulatory mechanism the same result can be obtained by blocking the current or opening up the sluices. In point of fact the two movements are tried out one after the other, within the space of a few pages. Effusion: the source is reflected in the source and the mirror empties itself out. Then constriction: Pascal dies of angina pectoris: "Instead of the normal spurt of blood, only a red trickle came out of the aorta. Behind, the veins were swollen with black blood, the choking increased, the suction pump, the force-pump that was regulating the whole machine was slowing down."

Hereditary character, according to the imagination, is carried in the blood, here in this thin black blood, in this venous stock, handing down the blood of the ancestress to all her descendants. From his first plan for the *Rougon-Macquart* series, Zola defined his purpose this way, then, subsequently, respected his own directions to the letter: "*Degeneration* in the family of an ancestress who turned out badly, and nature's terrible logic in putting a little of this woman's blood in the veins of every member of the family." By virtue of this share of the ancestral blood bequeathed to every child, he or she will be a carrier of evil "maternity." Evil indeed, for there can be no good "maternity." As far as woman is concerned, the requirement is the same as for Luce Irigaray: her red blood must promote resemblance, without a blemish. Hence the dream that Zola fosters of a lineage without a genetic source, a flow of reproduction (of resemblance: *qualis pater talis filius!*) finally purified of the menstrual flow.

Yet there is doubt about the effectiveness of this agitated symbolism. If not, why would there be a need for the strange acts of exorcism that the sons will later perform in the womb of the basilica of Montmartre (see the end of *Paris*, the last of the *Trois Villes*)?

How can one pass from one form of anality to the other: from filth (matter, the taint, woman . . . *Zolla*) to its sublimated forms, exchange, circulation, the connection of hereditary forces over vast geographical and historical ensembles? — Each of Zola's novels is consumed with this question. In this respect, each of Zola's novels resembles *Au Bonheur des Dames*, in which the store, despite all the floral extravagance of its decorations, rests on a corpse, a dead woman whose presence is never forgotten, for Octave and the reader are frequently reminded of it. On the one hand there is this *thing*, on the other these wares — those goods, this commerce.

Hoarding — coining: the contrast applied to the difference between gold and silver: gold piles up, is buried, is hidden; silver is spent openly, it circulates. Octave Mouret is obsessed with the fact that the same sum of money keeps coming back, three times, four times, ten times in the year, for the round gets faster and faster. Any interruption in cash flow, any impediment to the circulation of bank notes would favour the rise from the foundations, from down below, of the thing in the crypt, that "artificial subconscious" which serves as a basement to the whole literary and commercial edifice (I am purposely confusing the book and what it describes), the secret trunk that contains the *word-thing* itself: *Zolla.*

The depressing moment for Octave each day (and we can deduce from it Zola's own anguish) proves to be closing time in the stores. Then the product of the day's sales stagnates, becomes dense, a dull mass, that large pile of gold which at the fateful hour the chief cashier places on the manager's desk.

From the balcony of Médan, a melancholy Zola watches his name go by. Yet, etc.

Note

1. Norman Mailer, "The Faith of Graffiti," in *Pieces and Pontifications* (Boston-Toronto: Little, Brown and Company, 1982), p. 136.

The Narrator's Fantasies   Henri Mitterand*

Let us say, for the sake of simplicity, that there have been three ages of French studies on Zola. First of all there was the age of indifference in French society and universities (with some notable exceptions: André Gide, Albert Thibaudet, Henri Barbusse, Heinrich Mann), a time when a few Médan regulars and Zola's descendants published memoirs and biographies, and paid homage each year to the militant fighter of the Dreyfus Affair. As for the Sorbonne, that modest and prudent old dame, she kept the troublemaker at a safe distance.

Then there was the second period, after World War II, when the working classes gained access to the affairs of the State, when university education was made to be relatively democratic, and the sociopolitical novel and film came to the fore; the Zola continent emerged from the screen of mist and silence that had been built around it. Biographical investigation became more precise. In the universities young scholars, trained in the historical methods of Lanson to study the genesis, the documentary evidence, the sources of texts, seized upon the sketches, plans and dossiers of the *Rougon-Macquart* novels kept at the Bibliothèque Nationale. They were preceded by English and American researchers, by the works of Hemmings, Lapp, Niess, Walker, Salvan, etc., with their elements of structural and thematic analysis derived from American New-Criticism. The success of the *Rougon-Macquart* in the paperback Livre de Poche shows that there had never been a lack of popular interest in Zola, but now he began to force his way into middle-class libraries, with the Pléiade edition of the *Rougon-Macquart* and *Contes et Nouvelles* [short stories], and the fifteen volumes of the *OEuvres complètes* published, with a certain boldness, by Claude Tchou.

Then the Structuralist wave comes to France. Not only does Zola hold up well to it, but it provides him with a new lease of life. There are new perspectives on his work; historical studies give way to immanent analysis; there are explorations of his thematic, symbolic, mythic universe (Jean Borie, David Baguley, Naomi Schor, Auguste Dezalay, Roger Ripoll, Michel Serres, Philippe Bonnefis); the logic of his narrative system is

*From the *Magazine littéraire*, no. 132 (January 1978): 17–19. Translated for this volume by Davd Baguley. Reprinted by permission of the journal and the author.

scrutinized (Philippe Hamon); and there is revealed, beneath the complications of his plots and the discourse of his characters, the workings, sometimes conscious, sometimes unconscious, of the ideologies of his age (Aimé Guedj, Jacques Dubois, Claude Duchet, Françoise Gaillard). In short, over a period of fifteen years, there emerges a Zola "poetics", which demolishes *Naturalism* as the author of the *Rougon-Macquart* built it up to be — for external consumption — and as the text-books in literary history, for sixty years, never failed to present it.

At the same time, however, there are considerable advances in historical and scholarly research. More and more links are forged in the novelist's biography (with the works of Colette Becker and the Polish critic Halina Suwala). In ten years, the treasure-trove of the *Correspondance* goes from 600 known letters to more than 3,000. In 1973 the CNRS establishes a research team entirely devoted to Zola. Only the Inspection Générale des Lettres resists: there has been no Zola novel on the agrégation programme since 1954; the centenary of *L'Assommoir* went unnoticed by the candidates in 1977. But this is the exception that confirms the tendency. Zola has even won over Cerisy, the land of the *happy few* of new criticism, who in 1976 organized a colloquium on Naturalism.

Here then is a totally new Zola, a Zola liberated from the positivist or radical-socialist stereotypes, still fervently read by the general public and, with an unshakable sturdiness, providing for all the different interpretations of an ultra-sophisticated age: Bachelardian and Marxist, psychocritical and Lacanian, 'Tel Quel-ian' and semiotic, anthropological and ideological. . . . In the face of all that he holds firm, by a combination of mass and subtlety. What a revenge over Brunetière!

THE DISCOURSE ON METHOD

They expected to find Claude Bernard, and they find Rabelais instead. Yet Zola had never failed to adapt his language and his working methods to those of the positivist revolution. When, in 1860, he begins his career at the age of twenty, everywhere around him the imperious voice of the natural sciences is reverberating. What Cuvier was for Balzac, Darwin, Claude Bernard and Taine will be for him. *Observation, analysis, experimentation, determinism*, these are the catchwords of the day. A whole section of the French intelligentsia, the one that Zola will join when he goes to work for Hachette, has embarked upon the huge enterprise of sorting out and making available to the public vast areas of knowledge. Pierre Larousse publishes his *Grand Dictionnaire Universel du XIXe siècle*, Littré his *Dictionnaire de la langue française*, Hachette his *Bibliothèque des merveilles*, Jules Verne his *Voyages extraordinaires*, Duruy his laws on the extension of public education. These are just a few examples among hundreds. Zola, then, writes *Thérèse Raquin* in 1867, begins the *Rougon-Macquart* series the following year, and joins the field, to practise a literature of knowledge and didacticism, dedicated to the investigation of the natural world and of society, obeying the deep pressures of economic expansion.

In doing this, Zola — with undoubted excitement — accepts the challenges of a fight. The articles and studies that, fifteen years later, will go to make up *Le Roman expérimental* all have a polemical function. The idealistic tradition forbade any discourse on the Body, and on the class struggle. But Naturalism, in the name of the duties and liberties associated with human knowledge, brings sexuality and social struggles into general circulation, telling, narrating, offering such things out of principle to the vast public of readers of the novel, for whom the genre itself will act in part as a substitute encyclopedia. But this does not come about of its own accord. It represents a redistribution of the ideological stakes of literature and a restructuring of the systems of meaning and expression in the novel. We should not be surprised that the opposition was harsh and we should measure carefully the strategic importance of Zola's critical ideas in relation to the change in the intellectual climate which was starting to occur towards the end of the Second Empire.

The same is true of his methods of composition. Until now the preparatory dossiers of his novels have been studied as a fund of information on the chronology of his work on a given novel, and on its "sources": what he knew, saw and read. The *Notes* taken at Anzin amid the miners for *Germinal;* the reports from Sedan, for *La Débâcle*; the notes from a reading of Doctor Magnan's book *L'Alcoolisme*, for Coupeau's *delirium tremens*. . . . Such is the vulgate of Zola research. Yet such studies are far from being completed and have been, in fact, far too limited and cautious. There is a book to be written which would reproduce, with an appropriate taxonomy, all that Zola saw, all that is buried in the archives of his novels. Then there would emerge the most extraordinary perhaps the only — ethnographic discourse on itself that XIXth Century France has left behind: Emile Zola, or the Lévi-Strauss of the tribes of Paris around 1870. . . . But finally, by means of the documentary notes and plans for the *Rougon-Macquart*, there should also be an effort to apply a combination of two models that are equally symptomatic of a prevalent "climate" in Zola's time: a didactic model, involving the distribution of knowledge, and a narrative model, involving the distribution of suspense. Zola's narrative art is expository in nature, marked by the new encyclopedic spirit; guided by the narrator, and through the eyes of the character, the reader explores the coal-mine, or the painter's salon. Who would deny the efficiency of the pleasure of learning through the act of reading? In this respect Zola's novels are akin to those of his contemporary, Jules Verne; they are related to the *Magasin pittoresque* and *L'Illustration;* hence their success with the people, with dreamers and with poets. Inversely, Zola's didactic art is narrative in nature, sending knowledge into orbit along all the vectors of the story; the document becomes fiction; the documentary notes disappear into the impeccable machinery of the plans, in their three versions: the *Ebauche* [Outline], the *First Detailed Plan* and the *Second Detailed Plan;* the man of science becomes the story-teller, fulfilling the dream of an age of pedagogy and fiction.

Consequently we should not underestimate the documentarist and constructivist side of Zola's genius. It forms a language in itself, in which the explicit — a normative theory of the novel — is less important nowadays than the implicit: its puritanical, ethical implications which impose on the writer the duty to teach and on the reader the duty to learn. It is the creed of Jules Ferry. Each person is master of his own destiny; let him have the will to construct his life on the basis of study and work, and he will escape the inevitable misadventures of the body and of history. It is hardly surprising that the public version of "Naturalist" discourse — in Zola's articles — says nothing about the role of the imaginary and its deviations, nor of the privileges or the enticing lures of narrative fiction. If, by force of circumstances, the novelist is a story-teller, an inventor, the fact is already evident in the working plans, but is not rightly to be stated. Zola spent his whole life creating an image of his work calibrated according to the canonic law of the neo-Kantian ethic in which the founders of Republican civic principles were steeped. There is his well-known declaration intended to embarrass politicians not rigorous enough for his liking: "The Republic will be Naturalist or will not exist." The terms of the statement could easily have been reversed: "Naturalism will be Republican or will not exist." It is a dated ideology and, as such, its characteristic features have still to be defined. It would be a way of reconciling with a single critical approach the objectives and techniques of the history of texts and the analysis of discourse.

RITUAL AND STRUCTURE

Knowledge, as it relates to Zola, must be understood with two meanings, or on two different planes: the level of the document and the level of what I would call, borrowing the expression from the field of generative grammar, competence: i.e. a set of rules that can be systematized, that are permanent, innate or acquired from the origins, that are prior to any "performances," and are beyond all circumstantial objectives; a kind of cultural and narrative grammar, that is identical for any novel whatever its subject, and strongly determines the process by which occasional documents are put to use. In *Germinal* knowledge involves the technical details relating to the mining of coal; the *competence* is the profound intuition that provides that basic phrase, the key phrase of the *Ebauche* of *Germinal:* "This is the novel about the workers' uprising, about the nudge given to society, which cracks for just a moment: in short, the struggle between labour and capital." Zola is a great novelist because he has at his disposal this extraordinary store of knowledge, this network of controlling images, which sustains his work from below and feeds its surface documentation.

There are several models. There is, as previously mentioned, an ethnographer in Zola. Then there is Zola the anthropologist, an admirable judge of human and social life perceived in its elementary aspects, where need and ritual, survival and magic are always associated. The opening of *La Fortune des Rougon* — which is also the foundation of the *Rougon-Macquart* series — provides such an example. The text begins with the description of a disused cemetry abandoned at the edge of the town. Zola notes all the signs of the taboo which both excluded and preserved the ancient dead of Plassans: remoteness, the walled enclosure, solitude. One day the money-grabbing town wished to reclaim the land. The wall was knocked down, the land dug up, the graves opened, and the bodies transported to the other side of the town: transgression. The rule of money precludes respect for the sacred. The punishment is not long in coming: in their journey across the town the coffins, which are being carried on carts, scatter here and there bits of flesh and bones, and the urchins of Plassans hang them on the doors of the bourgeois houses of the town. . . . The dead take hold of the living. At the end of the novel the blood of Silvère, the young Republican insurgent against Louis-Napoléon Bonaparte's *coup d'état*, who is shot down on a stone in the old cemetry, will spatter over the salon of the Rougons, his relations, originators and beneficiaries of the *coup d'état* in Plassans, which sets the seal on their *Fortune*. At one and the same place, ritual, myth and history converge. Above and beyond the historical document (the Republican insurrection in the Var district in 1851) the text reveals itself to be a monument on which can be read — as long as the "excavation" penetrates far enough into the depths — a true cultural archeology.

Yet the functioning of other "competences" needs to be located as they run through the novelist's work, direct its sometimes eccentric course, and give it its peculiar stamp: for example, narrative competence and rhetorical competence, inherited also from the distant past and subsuming all manner of models. Balzac's and Flaubert's, of course, but also those of the Romantic serial novel or of *l'écriture artiste*. What Zola has to say about the working classes, about the class struggle, he says through, among others, one of his characters, Etienne Lantier, who owes his status as "leader" to the social obsessions reverberating through Zola's discourse, but who also owes his roles as "quest-hero" — in search of Woman and Justice, Love and Revolution — to twenty centuries of tragedies, epics, tales and novels. Contemporary discourse links up with achronic, or pan-chronic structure, and it holds true, even a hundred years later. . . .

THE DRIFT

In Zola's work neither the document, nor the monument is innocent, neutral, silent. There is no realism. Coupeau is not an alcoholic, but rather the fictitious projection of a set of views of the age, and in several respects also. The discourse of the alienist on *delirium tremens* meets up with the language of the social moralist, his views on the "bad worker"; and each one of them merges into the fantasies of a narrator occupied in writing twenty novels about madness. Saccard is no less mad than Coupeau, who is no less mad than Nana. Here we see the dimensions of ideology and of myth—two products of the imaginary—permanently intersecting with the dimensions of knowledge and of the story, and forming together the fabric of the *Rougon-Macquart*. That also is censored, repressed, by Zola's theoretical monologue, but it bursts forth everywhere in the text of Zola's novels and an analysis of it would also help us to answer the question: what is it that excites his readers?

It is apparent that Zola invents tightly structured plots that reveal an obsession with numbers and symmetry. In fact each of his novels also drifts off on a tangent, becoming progressively invested, and travestied, by dream-like and figurative elements, the latter, in particular, undergoing numerous transformations. Nightmare figures in *La Bête humaine*: the locomotive stuck in the snow, the swallowing up by the mountain, the burying alive, the crazy train ride at the end. Orphic figures in *La Fortune des Rougon* and *Germinal*: just as Silvère, watching over and waking the dead souls of Plassans, will not be able to save Miette from the death that awaits her under the tombstones of the old cemetry, Etienne Lantier will return alone from the hell of the flooded galleries of the mine where he left behind his Eurydice. Even the signifiers of proper names agree metonymically with the great roles that they designate: we can discern meanings in the names Saccard, Rougon, Macquart, Coupeau, Chaval, La Croix-de-Maufras. . . . Even the structure of Zola's novels follows the shape of ritual and symbolic modes. In *Germinal*, the women of the miners of Montsou kill and castrate Maigrat, the rapacious and salacious grocer; Jeanlin, the vicious throwback, cuts the throat of the sentry who is on watch over the mining village during the army's occupation; Bonnemort, the old demented miner, strangles Cécile, the young daughter of the shareholding couple. Three murders whose perpetrators and victims are all marginal participants, outsiders even, in the main confrontation. Isolated murders, removed from the collective struggle, and, one could even go so far as to say, ritual, fetishistic murders. It is as if the anger of the working class, reinterpreted by the social fears of the narrator or of those who speak with his voice, was transformed into pure, blind, delinquent violence; as if it needed expiatory victims and sacrificial priests. In their way, these three murders, which form a series closely analagous to the story of the strike, show the uncanny, panic-stricken vision that the French intellectual bourgeoisie conceives of the class struggle, fifteen years after the Commune.

This is why, if we take into account the imaginary in Zola's works, we cannot limit ourselves to a symbolic or mythical analysis *sub specie aeternitatis.* If the themes and schemes of his narrative works draw upon a reserve of archetypes that are as old as literature itself — and that, in part, is the secret of his lasting success — they are also characterized by a relationship to the history of modern society, by a whole subconscious social level that is perfectly historicized. The *psycho*-analysis of figures and myths in Zola's works can only be completed as *socio*-analysis. The nightmare of being swallowed up, which reaches gigantic proportions with the demolishment of Le Voreux, derives no doubt from a distant and quite personal obsession; but it also leads to the conclusion, from the depths and echoes of the text, that Nature holds sway over History and the latter is only Nature in disguise: every civilisation is swallowed up in the end, but is reborn again thereafter, in a cyclical and cataclysmic evolutionary movement, over which human intelligence, when all is said and done, has little control. Here, then, is a way of seeking reassurance, at the dawn of the workers' movement, towards the end of this XIXth Century.

But there is nothing that is univocal in Zola's symbolic discourse. Rationalist and mystical, sceptical and imbued with faith, tragic and carnivalesque, he puts forth both a historical epitome and one of the greatest fables of the XIXth Century. He has expressed and at the same time shifted, turned upside down, all the received ideas of his age, to the extent to being taken for Scandal incarnate. In addition, he calls into question our own conception of historical and critical knowledge. He forces us to admit that his text is rich in resources, that it is multiply "encoded." The problem of Zola's aesthetic, moral and social ideas, the problem of Naturalism, these are false problems, an academic *trompe-l'oeil*, since, in the double network of Zola's theoretical and narrative discourse, we become aware of a questioning of positivism by the positivist himself. The conceptual infrastructure is dated, but we have to break through the shell; then there spill out *fabulous* contents that still have much to say to us, for they are a source of questions and discoveries for today's reader, as long as he rids his mind of the empiricist problematics in which academic criticism encloses him, with its deference to the tradition of overt Naturalism. Faced with Zola, knowledge must also be enriched by the imaginary.

The Myth of Médan

Alain Pagès*

This study entitled "The Myth of Médan"[1] deals with *Les Soirées de Médan*, the collection of short stories published in April 1880 by Zola and his Naturalist friends and treats in particular the problem of the genesis of the volume, the conditions in which it appeared. The reader of this

*From *Les Cahiers naturalistes*, no. 55 (1981): 31–40. Translated for this volume by David Baguley. Reprinted by permission of the author and the journal.

collection is immediately faced with a question prompted by the very title of the work: *Les Soirées de Médan*.[2] Here then is a group of stories about the Franco-Prussian War, written ten years after the event, in 1880, that disguises its main subject and proposes something different: *evenings* — but what evenings? — and a *place*, not at all a well-known place, whose pronunciation, *Médan* for *Medan* has been changed in any case. There had to be an explanation and it was Maupassant who provided that explanation to the readers of 1880 in a long article published in *Le Gaulois* at the precise time when the volume appeared, recounting the birth of *Les Soirées de Médan*.

In the following extract from that famous account Maupassant tells how during the summer of 1879 Huysmans, Céard, Alexis, Hennique, and himself, were all together with Zola in the countryside, at Médan:

> As the nights were magnificent, warm, full of the fragrance of leaves, we would go over to the *large island* opposite, every evening, for a walk.
> I took everybody in my boat, *Nana*. Now, one night, by a full moon, we were talking about Mérimée whom the ladies described as "a charming story-teller," whereupon Huysmans declared in more or less the following terms: "A story-teller is a gentleman who, because he can't write, talks a lot of pretentious nonsense."
> Then we went through all the most famous story-writers singing the praises of those of them who could tell a good story out loud, the most marvellous of them being, to our knowledge, the great Russian writer Turgenev, an almost French literary master. Paul Alexis claimed that a short story is very hard to write. Céard, the sceptic, gazed at the moon and murmured: "Now here's a lovely romantic setting, it should be used. . . ."
> Huysmans added: ". . . for the telling of sentimental stories." Zola thought that it was a good idea, that we should tell each other stories. The suggestion amused us and we agreed that, to make things more difficult, the frame chosen by the first would remain the same for the others, who would use it for different adventures. . . .

The article ends with a summary of the stories by Huysmans, Céard, Hennique and Alexis.

Critics, of course, rushed to show that this account of the origins of the volume is *false*. During the summer of 1879 Zola was otherwise engaged. He did write a work in collaboration with Céard and Hennique, but it was a play, an adaptation of *La Conquête de Plassans*, that was to be entitled *L'Abbé Faujas*. And his remaining energies were devoted to his novel, *Nana*, which would occupy him entirely until the beginning of 1880. Thus *Les Soirées de Médan* was not created at Médan, nor was it produced during the summer, but probably during a meeting in Paris in November 1879 with Zola and his Naturalist friends. Apparently the contents of the book came about by chance, by virtue of a bit of opportunism: Zola, Huysmans and Céard had already written a story on the Franco-Prussian War; they therefore urged Alexis, Hennique, and Maupassant to do the same. However, nobody was really enthusiastic over the project: Zola was toiling over *Nana* (there is not a single mention of *Les Soirées de Médan* in his correspondence during the years 1879–1880); Alexis had a lot of trouble finishing his story; Maupassant, in writing his, had utmost in his mind some added publicity for the collection of poems that he was publishing at the same time; Charpentier, the publisher of the collection of stories, was slow in having the volume printed.

In short, a very ordinary set of events, characterized by chance, indifference, haste, so that what is important is not the historical reality associated with the volume, but the projected, the studied reality suggested by the title, a tale, a myth, a seventh story besides the six in the volume itself, and just as important as they. A myth is an imaginary construction which satisfies certain expectancies, fulfils a moral or religious desire. Why then did Zola and his disciples in 1879–1880 feel the need to gather together, tell about themselves, tell *us* a story, construct a *myth* about themselves, a myth with its characters—the group of six friends—and a *place of action*—Médan?

1. A GROUP OF FRIENDS

Zola in 1879 is a solitary writer. His solitude is due to his material success, after the publication of his novel *L'Assommoir* and the theatrical adaptation of the same work by William Busnach, a degree of success that sets him apart from his fellow writers. He adds further to his isolation by his campaign in *Le Voltaire*, the newspaper that the Naturalists are trying to invade. He attacks the person of Hugo whom Gambetta's triumphant Republic is glorifying as a national hero with eulogies for performances of *Ruy-Blas* and *Hernani*; he attacks his fellow-writers, the successful novelists of the day, Jules Sandeau, Octave Feuillet, Victor Cherbuliez, Léon Cladel . . . , exposing their mediocrity. Zola is therefore alone, not belonging to a school or a group. But, in the late nineteenth century, literary groups are an essential part of the writer's life, for writers like to meet and be seen in salons and at dinners, not only for the company and for the ideological discussions, but because such groups link the writer to the literary institutions of the time. They put the author in touch with the press, the machinery of propaganda and publicity, affording him *celebrity*; they put him in touch with political power, the means to rewards and honours, affording him *recognition*.

There is also the fact that Zola's isolation is due to his break with groups to which he formerly belonged. There is, first of all, the group of friends from his early years, from the "Boeuf Nature" dinners, writers, poets, painters, belonging more or less to his own generation, Numa Coste, Marius Roux, François Coppée, Paul Bourget. Then there is the group of founders of Realism, the group of Five, those who were at the famous dinner of the "auteurs sifflés,"[3] as they are called, Flaubert and Goncourt, Daudet and Turgenev. With Flaubert ill, the unity of the Five breaks up; Daudet and Goncourt are opposed to Zola, Goncourt especially, for he is jealous of the growing importance of the author of the *Rougon-Macquart*. He writes in his *Journal*: "Zola has a *clique* of young *faithfuls* whose admiration, enthusiasm, and fervour the crafty writer fosters and feeds by providing them with contacts for articles in foreign journals, by lucrative openings in the newspapers over which he reigns supreme, by all kinds of material favours."

Indeed, Zola, the solitary writer, is beginning to surround himself with a group, but it is only just forming. Goncourt's comments date from May 28, 1879, and he makes no precise mention of Huysmans, Céard, Hennique, Alexis and Maupassant, for the future Médan group is still undefined. In fact we now have to reject the too hasty, traditional dating of the origins of the Médan group as going back to the famous Trapp dinner of April 1877. At that time, Alexis, Céard, Hennique, Huysmans, Mirbeau and Guy de Valmont (who is not yet called Maupassant) are admirers of Goncourt and Flaubert as well as of Zola. But, in 1879, the situation is different: Alexis, Céard, Hennique, Huysmans rally around Zola alone, Maupassant is hesitant, and Mirbeau is out of the picture. The boundaries of the newly forming group are unclear. One might even identify *several* naturalist groups in the literary life of this time. There is first of all, in a broad sense, the set of *friends* who are at all the major events like the opening of *L'Assommoir* at the Ambigu theatre in January 1879 or the *Assommoir* ball at the Elysée-Montmartre in April; the complete list would be very long indeed and would include such diverse personalities as Félicien Rops, Nadar or Adolphe Belot. Then there are those who approach Zola to offer him their services and to ask for his help, young novelists like Edouard Rod, Elémir Bourges, Alexandre Boutique, those who aspire to be his *disciples*. Finally there are those who claim to be in favour of the new literature, who try to benefit from the glory and scandal surrounding Naturalism. But Zola does not know them and has no dealings with them; they are *pseudo-disciples*, like Vast and Ricouard, founders of the so-called "realist" review, or like the team of young writers who run the so-called "modern," "Naturalist" review, *La Revue réaliste* and *La Revue moderne et naturaliste*.

In short, all this is very indeterminate, as the errors of the journalists prove as soon as they begin to write about the future Médan group, but make up different lists.[4] And, if the group is not clearly defined in the public's perception, it is no more so in its intrinsic structure, for the Five are far from enjoying the same status as a quick survey of their relative situations shows, in 1879 during the months before the publication of *Les Soirées de Médan*.

Huysmans is the most established writer of them all, because he belongs fully to the Naturalist mainstream as defined by *L'Assommoir*. The

critics who, in February 1879, pour scorn on *Les Soeurs Vatard* have no
difficulty classifying the newcomer, for he also writes regularly for *Le
Voltaire* like Zola and his "salon," in June and July 1879, causes an uproar.
Thus Huysmans seems like a special disciple, a second Zola. The new
edition of *Marthe* in October even suggests that the disciple has upstaged
the master, having already written the life story of a prostitute before
Nana.

As for Céard and Hennique, they are clearly in a subordinate role and
Zola has no hesitation in asking favours of them. In January he has them
working on a parody of *L'Assommoir* that he wants to put on with
Busnach. Then, from June onwards, he sets his two disciples on to the
considerable task of writing *L'Abbé Faujas*. In addition, we know that
Céard takes on the role of Zola's substitute, attending the opening nights
of plays for him and then sending him notes so that he can write his weekly
drama reviews. If Huysmans is a second Zola, Céard, by contrast, is a kind
of shadowy double.

Though he has been a friend of Zola's longer than the others, Alexis is
somewhat separate from the group, an object of their jealousy, with a
reputation for laziness, but busy at work. His is the role of biographer, a
field in which he can make good use of his personal relations with Zola.
He begins what will later become his *Notes d'un ami*, publishes a chapter
in *Le Gaulois*, and, above all, performs the enormous task of synthesizing
and defining the conception of Zola held by foreign critics. He is another
of Zola's doubles, even more inclined to imitate the master.

The most isolated of the group, however, is Maupassant, whom they
all treat with a certain amount of condescension. They know that he has
already written some poetry and that he wishes to make a career of
writing poetry, but they do not think highly of his prospects. He is aware
himself of the ambiguity of his position, complaining to Flaubert that
Zola's "little gang" is "dropping" him as he is not "Naturalist" enough for
them. There is considerable truth in this, for he pretends to despise
Naturalism of the Zola kind and prefers to look elsewhere for support, to
Goncourt and especially to Flaubert.

As we see, it is a very mixed group, each member fulfilling a different
function and finding it difficult as well to succeed. The team of Huysmans, Céard, Hennique, and Alexis, working together on the newspaper
Le Voltaire, sees its efforts fail; the collaboration only lasts for one
summer. In the face of such contingencies, of such a dispersal of individual
and social relationships, what precisely is the myth that *Les Soirées de
Médan* seeks to convey? It tells the story of an imaginary group, of an
exclusive group, the chosen Five, a group which includes Maupassant but
chooses to leave out Vast and Ricouard, Mirbeau, and the rest. It tells us
that, after Zola of course, the Five are all equals, since Zola's name
appears at the head of the list, but the others follow with identical status,
as the revealing anecdote confirms, according to which the Five drew lots

to determine the order in which their stories were to appear in the collection; chance conferred equality. Finally, it tells us that the Five fulfill the same functions, are endowed with the same degree of talent, show the same potentialities for success; hence the unity of the genre that they choose, the short story, the beginner's genre (Zola purposely chooses a form that is decidedly secondary in importance to him); hence too the unity of content, the—arbitrary—reference to the Franco-Prussian War.

Thus is established the first aspect of the myth, the vision of a collectivity, the ideal of unity, the principle of equality, Huysmans the novelist, Céard and Hennique the dramatists, Alexis the biographer, Maupassant the poet. . . .

2. MEDAN, A PLACE

The second aspect of the myth concerns the place and the man at its centre, Zola, on whose life the unifying, totalizing function of myth is now focused, for, with the success of the novel L'Assommoir, of the play L'Assommoir and of Nana behind him, he must now comply with the biographical scrutiny of the press and be written up, described, explained. There is enormous interest in biographical narrative in the nineteenth century, the documents of the past and of the present are avidly sought and preserved; every writer knows that in his letters and diaries he is preparing himself for posterity to read about himself. Journals are more than ready to publish biographical introductions to famous figures of the day and weeklies like Les Hommes d'aujourd'hui, Les Contemporains, spring up with their mixture of caricature and biography.

Zola knows perfectly well what is at stake and readies himself, fully aware that his novels, by their incursions into the literary field, leave him open to slander and insults. At this particular time he keeps in mind Balzac's fate, and the fate of Berlioz whose correspondence he is carefully reading, two exemplary figures, artists of genius, ignored, attacked during their lifetime and achieving recognition too late after their death; he identifies himself with their fate. Moreover he keeps a careful watch at an early stage for errors of detail that the journalists make about him. He points out to Anatole France, for example, that he was not born in Aix but in Paris. He makes it clear to Félicien Champsaur that he did not graduate from school, that he has not been decorated, that Alexandrine [his wife] was never a laundress . . . Such corrections as these allow him to put a stop to future distortions. But these are only passive reactions. The biographical myth, since there is no escaping it in any case, has to be more actively orchestrated, controlled, and given unity. And this is where Médan plays its part, in this search for coherence and for a version of the truth that can be communicated and explained, as a defence against the journalists pulling the writer to pieces. Médan will be a unifying factor, in which Zola finds a symbol, an image of himself, a focus of descriptive metaphors.

Two typical articles of this period illustrate the way in which Médan has become the focal point of commentaries on Zola. They appear in the fall of 1879, at the time when *Nana* is about to come out. Zola anticipates the attacks that it will provoke and takes precautions, by means of an article by Alexis, first of all, in *Le Gaulois* [15 October 1879]. It describes a day at Médan, tells how the writer came to buy the property, gives an account of the peaceful life he leads there. Zola himself drew up the plan of the article for Alexis in one of his letters: "Here is the outline that I advise you to adopt: a short description of Médan, a brief account of the purchase of the small house and the building of the large one, the life of your heroes [*sic*] as you know it, and a conclusion that deals with the real character of the man as opposed to the legends that are attributed to him." A fine example this, of a discourse full of foresight and justification.

The second article, published in *Le Figaro* on 12 October 1879, is by Albert Wolff, who sets out to tell the story of *Nana* before any instalments of the novel have appeared, a difficult task and one that could possibly lead to controversy. How is the author of such a scandalous novel to be presented to the public? Wolff does precisely what Alexis did, situating it in the seductive framework of Médan, a place from which only accept- able, normal, reasonable literature can issue forth. Thus the article begins: "I have known the plan of *Nana* for more than six months now; Zola told it to me one spring morning in the little garden at Médan where, from morning until night, this literary revolutionary, this most bourgeois of all bourgeois, watches the western trains go by as they shake his house to its foundations." The choice of this place is particularly significant, for we know from the correspondence between Wolff and Zola that the interview between the two men took place in fact in Paris!

Médan, in short, possesses mythical powers of explanation, is the culminating point of a process of literary creation whose boldness is a source of concern, the culminating point of a career of surprising diversity. The myth of Médan provides an answer, suggests a unified solution to all the objections and contradictions that make up a life. The unity that it establishes is of a temporal kind; thus we learn how the past and present merge, how from the poor young Romantic poet evolved *Zola*, the successful, well-established bourgeois. But a spatial unity is also estab- lished; thus we learn that for Zola Médan is the obverse of Paris and that the alleged pornographer is in fact a home-loving writer who shuns worldly values and avoids the company of others. By means of these contrasts a consistent biographical picture is elaborated, the image of an author who, within the spatial confines of Médan, watches the river Seine flow by — a symbol of eternity — and watches the trains go by — symbols of the bustle of modern life. Within the temporal confines of Médan, the inviolable timetable for each day is adopted, the image of a well-organized author, who rises at a prescribed hour, novelist in the morning, journalist in the afternoon. . . . But in this space of time, where each moment is accounted for, there remains however a period of freedom, the evening. Here the myth unfurls its fictitious account, as an epilogue, presenting us with an image of Zola after his day's work is complete, at the capital moment of the day, surrounded by his disciples, guiding them, listening to them declaim the literature of the future . . . the *Soirées de Médan*.

A writer's life-story, says Roland Barthes, is often made up of "a few tenuous details"; it is "a mere plurality of charms," "a discontinuous ballad of compliments." Thanks to Médan, Zola's life, on the contrary, strikes us by its coherence, authenticated by all the objects that surrounded him and all the documents, like his correspondence, that show us traces of that life, a more stable, more incontrovertible biographical reality than psychological facts. Zola, a hundred years ago, apart from his works, is made up of all the paraphernalia of Médan: the boat "*Nana*," christened as such before the novel of the same name is written, the boat that Maupassant rows up in from Bezons; the colossal fireplace in the study, where, according to Alexis, "a tree would roast a lamb whole"; the window showing "Mes Bottes" that Céard has had made in Paris by Baboneau, the master in stained glass, which will decorate the entrance to the kitchen. . . . Through the discontinuity that comes with time, and the dispersion of objects that goes with it, Médan rises up as a place of recognition and of understanding.

This is why, beside the most precise interpretations and the most detailed of chronologies, the myth of Médan holds a special interest. The account of the genesis of *Les Soirées de Médan* that Maupassant wrote in April 1880 for *Le Gaulois* possesses its own kind of truth, a synthetic truth that denies the contingencies of past time and constructs a memorial, a durable history. *Les Soirées de Médan* remains important to us, not for the contents of a collection of stories put together, but for the myth that clings to it, a myth in which dreams and desires are projected, the dream of a united group, the dream of a writer, master of the future.

It is this dream, this imaginary reality, which really counts, for it is an expression of the very *will to exist* of the group which came, one hundred years ago, to Médan.[5]

Notes

1. For the purposes of publication in *Les Cahiers naturalistes* we have avoided overloading this study with detailed commentary. The historical documentation from which it derives may be found however in volume III of Zola's *Correspondance* in the edition directed by B. H. Bakker, C. Becker, H. Mitterand (Montréal: Presses de l'Université de Montréal; Paris: CNRS, 1982), with A. Pagès and A. Salvan as collaborators on that volume; there precise references and more detailed information may be sought and the validity of

allusions and interpretations may be verified. Needless to add, at the basis of this meditation on the "myth of Médan" there is also the magnificent book by Etiemble, *Le Mythe de Rimbaud* (Paris: Gallimard, 1961), an exemplary work of historical analysis, but one which, perhaps, goes too far in the direction of *de*-mythification. There seems, on the contrary, to be considerable advantage in heeding the lessons of mythical accounts and combining the necessary process of deconstruction with the equally historical gesture of reconstruction, of *re-mythification*.

2. [Editor's note: Though the individual stories of Zola and Maupassant have been translated, there is no English translation of the collection. The English title would probably be rendered as M*édan Evenings* or *Evenings at Médan*, but the word *soirée* can also suggest "evening gathering" and the definite article is significant in the French title referring to the specific meetings of the Médan group.]

3. [Editor's note: The group met on numerous occasions supposedly to celebrate their lack of theatrical success, all five claiming that their plays had been hissed (*sifflées*); the first such dinner took place on 14 April 1874.]

4. E. G. Montjoyeux writing in *Le Gaulois* in December 1878 lists Huysmans, Hennique, Céard and Alexis, but ignores Maupassant; Harry Alis, in *La Revue moderne et naturaliste* in May 1879, still only mentions Huysmans, Hennique, Alexis and Céard; Charles Bigot, in *La Revue des Deux Mondes* in September, speaks of Hennique and Huysmans, but includes in the group of Naturalists Vast and Ricouard; Félicien Champsaur, in October in *Le Figaro*, deals rapidly with Maupassant and Céard, concentrates on Huysmans and Hennique, and also mentions Vast and Ricouard.

5. [Editor's note: This article was originally an address delivered in October 1980 at the annual pilgrimage of the Société littéraire des Amis d'Emile Zola, held at . . . Médan.]

Zola's Ideology: The Road to Utopia

Brian Nelson*

The central social theme of the early Rougon Macquart novels is the rush for the spoils that followed Louis-Napoleon's coup d'état of 2 December 1871. Zola's moralizing satire is directed against the predatory greed and brutal self-interest of the Rougons. He exposes the sterility of bourgeois life and lays bare the materialist foundations of bourgeois ideology, of which the Second Empire was for him the epitomized political expression.

La Curée (1872), the richest and most representative of the early novels, focuses on the rebuilding of Paris by Haussmann, which attracted to the capital large numbers of unscrupulous speculators and fortune-hunters who wished to exploit the economic possibilities offered by the new Imperial regime. Zola's protagonists, Saccard and Renée, embody the two major preoccupations of Second Empire Paris: money and pleasure.

*This essay has been prepared specifically for this volume and is based upon the author's *Zola and the Bourgeoisie* (London: Macmillan, 1983). Material from the book is reproduced by permission of The Macmillan Press Ltd. Translations from the French are by the author, except where indicated otherwise.

Moreover, the "psychological" theme of Renée's incestuous passion for her stepson not only counterpoints but interlocks with the "social" theme of property speculation, for the novel's narrative structure centers on Renée's ensnarement in the ruthless financial machinations of her husband. The novel portrays the falsification and distortion of human relations produced by the cash nexus and, as such, may be regarded as an aggressive critique of an alienating society.

The long descriptive passages round which *La Curée* is built do not simply reproduce but help to define the social reality with which the novel deals. The descriptions of houses, furniture, and social gatherings are not merely documentary but portray an individual crushed by things, alienated from her environment. The opening pages, which introduce us to Renée, establish an equation between "the fulsomeness of luxury" (1:328)[1] and "the void of her existence" (1:324): the outward splendour of her life contrasts with her inner sense of futility. Exhaustive descriptions of material objects, of the sumptuous physical décor of bourgeois existence, express a vision of a society which, dominated by the profit motive, reduces people to the status of things. Zola's stress on description means that the natural order of things is reversed: objects become the real protagonists of the novel and the human element is displaced. If we adopt the Lukács / Goldmann theory that the essence of the novel as a genre is the search for authentic values in an inauthentic society, then we will conclude that Renée's climactic sense of self-awareness signifies her recognition of the inauthenticity of Second Empire society and her awareness of her own reification. She realizes that, in the eyes of society, she is seen and valued in commercial terms, as a mere marketable commodity, another glittering artifact; she exists in a society that eliminates human values and denies her separate existence as a person.

La Curée thus proclaims the falseness and hollowness of a society governed by money. The mainspring of the novel, however, is the theme of dissipation. Zola's satire of speculative frenzy and sexual excesses is grounded in his horror at the futile and uncontrolled expenditure of energy. The novel's descriptions are characterized by constant impressionism of detail, and the essence of Zola's impressionism is movement and instability. Throughout the novel the motifs of frenetic movement and dizzy excess correspond to the motifs of flux and dissolution. Recurring water imagery suggests both movement and dissolution, and combines with the play of light which decomposes surfaces, objects, and buildings. The volatility of the phenomenal scene creates a sense of swarming multiplicity. Even inanimate things seem to be set in motion, to vibrate with a dynamic inner life. The themes of money and pleasure are linked by the motifs of movement, *débandade*, and waste. Renée's sensual and financial extravagance, and the massive scale of Saccard's speculations, are characterized by a total lack of control. They both embody excess; and dizzy excess corresponds to perpetual movement: "Saccard left the Hôtelde-Ville and, being in command of considerable funds to work with, launched furiously into speculation, while Renée, in mad intoxication, filled Paris with the clatter of her equipages, the sparkle of her diamonds, the vertigo of her riotous existence" (1:339). An unstable world moves with increasing speed toward destruction.

To excess and movement corresponds a kind of manic delirium in the characters. The key words and the general lexical tone of *La Curée* reflect a sense of madness and instability: "It was pure folly, a frenzy of money, handfuls of louis flung out of the windows" (1:436). Images of movement, fever, and freneticism combine with recurrent images of fire and heat to evoke Saccard's frenzied speculative activity: "this dance of gold which it [Paris] had led off" (1:418); "its violent fever, its stone-and-pickaxe madness" (ibid.); "this burning and insatiable Paris" (1:419). Saccard's very name evokes both money ("sac d'écus") and the idea of destruction and ruin ("saccage"). His precarious fortune, like his house, is built on a void: "companies crumbled beneath his feet, new and deeper pits yawned before him, over which he had to leap unable to fill them up" (1:463). Saccard, though dynamic, is a figure of total disorder. The linguistic character and thematic structure of *La Curée* focus on the destructive consequences of activities that are subject to no control or constraint; the novel, viewed as a coherent totality, conveys a vision of appalling waste.

The theme of "la curée" corresponds in the early novels to the motifs of food and eating. In *Le Ventre de Paris* (1873), focused on the central food market of Paris, Les Halles, Zola attempts to create the impression of a social class obsessed with food; he establishes a symbolic equation between mountains of food and bourgeois complacency. The fat Lisa Quenu, a prosperous pork-butcher's wife, smugly supports the Government and the Church, for they maintain order. Zola sharply attacks the sterile parasitism of the Quenus, who are the first of a series of "respectable" bourgeois families to be found in later novels: the Campardons in *Pot-Bouille*, the Grégoires in *Germinal*, the Charles in *La Terre*, and the Mazelles in *Travail*.

If Lisa represents the parasitism of the *petite bourgeoisie*, Nana (*Nana*, 1880) symbolizes the decadence of the *haute bourgeoisie* and aristocracy. The actress / prostitute is seen as both the product of a corrupt society and the catalyst of its destruction. Her body, like her house, swallows up both men and their fortunes. Her death coincides with the outbreak of the Franco-Prussian war, and the projected vision of the future looks forward to the ending of *La Bête humaine* and the imagery of *La Débâcle*. The atmosphere, heavy with a sense of foreboding, carries with it intimations of apocalyptic destruction, with the nightmarish image of the swelling crowds in the streets below the hotel room in which she dies, "like flocks of sheep driven to the slaughter-house at night" (2:1480).

Although the novels that followed *Nana* are less specifically concerned with anti-Imperial polemic, they nevertheless describe or allude to the rottenness of the social fabric: the hypocrisies, guilt, and perversions of bourgeois sexual life portrayed in *Pot-Bouille* (1882) are seen as part of a general social malaise; *La Bête humaine* (1890) contains telling references to the corruption of the magistrature; *L'Argent* (1891) links the dissipation of Imperial society to a sense of social collapse; the retributive disasters of *La Débâcle* (1892), which describes the French defeat at Sedan and forms the historical conclusion to the cycle, are seen as the inevitable consequence of uncontrolled energy, dissipation, and the moral corruption of the representatives of social and political order. The *Rougon-Macquart* as a whole depicts the breakdown of a society doomed to dissolution because of its reckless individualism and its uncoordinated use of human energy. Running through the cycle is the theme of degeneracy, both social and pathological. The frenzied excesses of the Rougon-Macquart family contrast with the mute immobility of its foundress, Tante Dide, who incarnates the fatal permanence of heredity, as if waiting at the lunatic asylum at Plassans for her corrupt race to destroy itself in wild agitation. The driverless train hurtling blindly through the night in *La Bête humaine* becomes an epic symbol of catastrophe. Full of singing soldiers bound for the crushing defeat of the Franco-Prussian war, the runaway train represents the nation rushing headlong toward destruction. It becomes, in other words, a striking figuration of the main motifs of Zola's indictment of Second Empire society: a destructive lack of control, radical instability, an absence of social leadership.

What solutions does Zola propose to the problems of social anarchy and sterile materialism highlighted by his portrayal of Second Empire society? While he saw the bourgeoisie as a class as unfit to rule, he had little faith in the ability of the workers to help themselves; Zola was deeply skeptical of mass class action, revolutionary idealists, and professional social reformers. He portrays socialists and revolutionaries as either naive utopian dreamers or cynical opportunists. The problems of proletarian leadership are posed with particular acuity in *Germinal*, in which Etienne Lantier, the leader of the miners' strike, appears as a meddler with things beyond his understanding and beyond his control. Zola's conception of the proletarian social reformer is at once patronizing and dismissive: ineffectual or incompetent, his revolutionaries are seen as inadequate leaders both of their own class and, potentially, of society. On the other hand, he was deeply concerned by the mediocrity of republican politicians: nowhere was his distaste for organized bourgeois politics more visible than in *Une Campagne*, the series of articles he wrote for *Le Figaro* in 1880–81.

Zola was not a systematic political thinker. He was indeed less interested in dogma than in the efficient management of national affairs. He thus advocated the application to social problems of the positivist spirit, which was founded on a passionate faith in science. The use of the scientific method, he argued, would produce a form of government based not on dogma or on a priori principles, but on the objective "laws" evolved from empirical experimentation and observation. Moreover, this "technocratic" form of government, based on social engineering, would involve an elitism by which the nation's most able men of science and the arts would be called upon to assume the responsibilities of office.

There is clearly a tension between Zola's positivist ideology, which leads to an optimistic vision of a well-ordered society based on science, and his detailed observation of the anarchic nature of a society based on the survival of the fittest. Zola's scientific faith, in other words, is at odds with his Darwinian view of humanity. The whole of his fiction may in fact be read as an attempt to reconcile the themes of Darwinism and social responsibility. The motif of "la curée" and the persistence in modern man of a primordial "bête humaine" reveal his recognition of the Darwinian aspects of human behavior and his pessimistic awareness of the disruptive presence of instinctual appetites; it is precisely this awareness that leads him to realize the need for some form of enlightened social leadership.

Despite the evidence of both his fiction and his journalism, Zola's preoccupation with social leadership has been obscured — probably by his intervention in the Dreyfus affair and the humanitarian eloquence of *L'Assommoir* and *Germinal*, which have tended to promote a simplified view of Zola as champion of the oppressed and spokesman of the workers rather than an advocate of responsible bourgeois leadership. For Zola's skepticism about the workers' capacity for self-determination is matched by clear indications that his conception of the social role of the bourgeoisie is less negative than has been supposed. His positivist faith in progress through science is accompanied in *Les Rougon-Macquart* by a latent messianism that is fully realized in *Les Quatre Evangiles*. This latent messianism takes the early form of fascination with power and admiration of energy. Early prototypes of the messiah are social adventures and figures of power like Saccard I (*La Curée*), the Abbé Faujas (*La Conquête de Plassans*), Eugène Rougon (*Son Excellence Eugène Rougon*), Octave Mouret (*Pot-Bouille* and *Au Bonheur des Dames*), and Saccard II (*L'Argent*) — all of them variations on a single character type, and all of them members of the bourgeoisie. The defining characteristics of these leader figures (which makes them stand out in stark contrast both to Zola's ineffectual revolutionaries and to the corrupt types of bourgeois in *Les Rougon-Macquart*) are an obsessive will to power and ruthless determination: they are all remarkable individualists.

Zola's latent admiration of Faujas, Eugène Rougon, and Saccard I develops into explicit approval of the Octave Mouret of *Au Bonheur des Dames* and Saccard II. This approval is connected with Zola's attempt in *Au Bonheur des Dames* and *L'Argent* to reconcile his Darwinian view of life with a need for responsible social leadership. In these two novels, and also in *Germinal*, Zola specifically addresses himself to the world of capitalism, portraying the general economic structures of society through the careers of the dynamic entrepreneur Mouret and the arch-capitalist financier Saccard.

Au Bonheur des Dames (1883) is an important text, for it marks Zola's desire to broaden his social perspective and embrace the whole of socioeconomic reality through his description of the establishment of the first great Parisian department store. Far from advocating a radical reform of the capitalist foundations of society, Zola writes lyrically of private enterprise and the bold new forms of capitalism: the department store, though it destroys the old-fashioned little shops around it, is seen as an inevitable product of progress and economic modernization; and its creator, Octave Mouret, the quintessential "self-made man," is admired for his imagination and energy. The marriage between Octave and one of his shop assistants, Denise Baudu, is a piece of artificial social symbolism that nevertheless marks a significant step in the development of Zola's social vision toward the utopianism of his late novels. For the price of Denise's hand is the internal reorganization of the store along humanitarian lines — which looks forward to the Fourieristic system of social cooperation which will form the basis of Luc Froment's ideal community in *Travail*. *Au Bonheur des Dames* thus represents an attempted marriage between bourgeois individualism, rationalized efficiency, and the common good.

In *Germinal* (1885) Zola attacks the exploitive nature of capitalist society. But though his compassion for the miners is beyond question, the bourgeois representatives of capitalism are far from being uniformly evil. The mine managers are not presented as cynically exploitive monsters but as victims of economic circumstance. Zola stresses the divided responsibilities of Hennebeau, the salaried manager of the big Montsou company. Hennebeau's nephew, the engineer Négrel, is an antiproletarian cynic, deceitful, and gruffly authoritarian, but he keeps the respect of the miners because of his energy and physical courage. After the collapse of the mine he risks his life to save the trapped miners; his courage is clearly contrasted with the inhumanity of the anarchist Souvarine. But the most sympathetic bourgeois in *Germinal* is Deneulin, the progressive, hard-working, paternalist owner of a small colliery. Like Négrel, he is respected for his energy and courage. Although authoritarian, he is an excellent manager of men: "He did not sit on a distant throne in some unknown temple; he was not one of those shareholders who pay managers to fleece the miners and whom the miners never saw; he was an employer, he had other things to lose besides his money — his intelligence, his health, and his life" (3:1392–93). He is allied with the miners not only through the compassion he shows toward them but through the fact that, like them, he is crushed by the big company of Montsou. Although Zola wished to base his novel on stark contrasts, the bourgeoisie is not presented as monolithic; there are conflicts within the bourgeoisie as well as between the classes. The contrast between the idle Grégoires and the energetic, enlightened Deneulin emerges with particular clarity at the great dinner held at La

Piolaine to celebrate the engagement of Cécile and Négrel after the failure of the strike. The dinner quickly turns into a celebration of the victory over the miners; the smugness of Grégoire is contrasted with the melancholy of Deneulin, whom the strike has ruined. Zola laments the triumph of conservatism and egoism, ironically juxtaposing the defeat of the man of energy with the victory of the selfish Grégoire, thus underlining his condemnation of parasitic elements in the bourgeoisie and his approval of entrepreneurial vigour.

Through his account in *L'Argent* (1891) of the remarkable rise and dramatic fall of a banking company, Zola attempts to grasp the mechanisms of the social life of contemporary France and to present the Bourse as a paradigmatic representation of the capitalist system itself. But his depiction of Bourse activity, focused by the epic power struggle between Saccard, a modern tycoon, and Gundermann, a Jewish financier, may be seen in allegorical terms as well as in documentary and sociological perspectives, for the novel is arguably less concerned with exploring the structure of capitalism than with depicting the interplay of vital forces. It dramatizes a tension between energy and order, showing the ineluctable defeat of the reckless, passionate Saccard by the prudent, methodical Gundermann.

Although Saccard's passion and profligacy do lead to disaster, he possesses a number of redeeming features and emerges as a far more positive figure than his distant precursor in *La Curée*. In *La Curée* Zola stresses Saccard's venality and corruption, whereas in *L'Argent*, though his cynicism is still strong, he is invested with a heroic and messianic quality. His messianism is complemented by benevolent and humane impulses, which contrast with his cold ruthlessness in *La Curée*. Furthermore, his dynamic energy and inspirational abilities correspond to his "Darwinian" vision of money; although a source of exploitation and misery, money is also a vital, fecundating force. The chaotic and destructive character of capitalism is seen as inseparable from its value (allied with science) as a powerful humanitarian instrument. The ambitious schemes of the engineer Hamelin for the creation of a new industrial society in the Middle East anticipate Luc Froment's "cité idéale" in *Travail*, while the pattern of manager / technician (Saccard / Hamelin) looks forward to the partnership between Luc and Jordan.

Saccard is thus not just a figure of waste and folly, but also a symbol of progress and creation. The crux of *L'Argent* is the problematic nature of human vitality as embodied in the character and conduct of its protagonist. The novel dramatizes the catastrophic effects that ensue from a radical dissociation of human energies from moral responsibilities and proper constraint. The close relationship between Saccard's passion for money-making and the themes of philanthropy and creative energy suggests that his energies might be harnessed for the general benefit of society. It is the bourgeois Saccard rather than the tubercular socialist dreamer Sigismond Busch or the ineffectual philanthropical aristocrat Princess d'Orviedo who is presented as offering the possibility of social progress. Zola's stated desire that his novel should articulate an optimistic view of life is embodied in the character of Saccard's mistress, Mme Caroline, who, within the allegorical framework of the novel, represents a moral conscience and the bourgeois ethic of moderation. The ideal the novel expresses (a balance between energy and order, a reconciliation of dynamism with the demands of moral and social equilibrium) is fully realised in the stable and harmonious society created by Luc Froment in *Travail*.

Zola suggests, then, that the answer to the problems of France is not revolution but conservatism. Although he had a strong sense of social justice and responsibility, his vision is conservative in its impulse toward order and rationality, and in the considerable respect he implies for authority. And faith in the traditional bourgeois values of self-discipline, hard work, and moderation is allied to a messianism whose germs are already visible in the early novels of the Rougon-Macquart series. Zola was a sharp critic of the anarchy and inhumanity of uncontrolled capitalism, but was unable to accept the remedies of utopian socialists; on the other hand, he did not globally condemn the bourgeoisie: his satire is directed against the bourgeois as parasite, while he implicitly sees hope for the creation of a new social order in certain bourgeois figures who, though partly presented in a framework of satire, are admired for their energy, enterprise, and leadership. *Les Rougon-Macquart* reflects the development of Zola's attempt to combine dynamism with responsibility and rationality, to reconcile his worship of the will with his desire for a satisfying moral and social order. The myth of leadership is fully developed in his late works, *Les Trois Villes* (1894–98) and *Les Quatre Evangiles* (1899–1903).

Although Zola's work represents a defense of certain bourgeois values, he became increasingly hostile to the established forms of bourgeois religion. His work from *Le Docteur Pascal* (1893) onward represents a systematic attack on the obscurantism of the Church, its hostility to science, and its ability to come to terms with the deepening social problems of the modern world. The utopian fiction of his last years, partly focused on anticlerical themes, makes discursively explicit the evolving social patterns of *Les Rougon-Macquart*. The diagnosis of social abuses is now replaced by the prescription of humanitarian remedies. The organizing principle of *Travail* (1901) — and the matrix of Zola's fiction — is the theme of fecundity, which shapes Zola's sense of community and his vision of human relations. Work is equated with fecundity, which becomes both a moral imperative and a principle of social organization. The basis of Luc Froment's utopian community, La Crècherie, is man's creative energy, the use of the human passions within a harmonious and rationally organized society. The idea of a harmonious city means greater efficiency in that Luc's rational exploitation of the human passions along Fourierist lines entails the elimination of waste and the suppression of all nonproductive, parasitic elements: "It would suffice to reorganize work in order to reorganize the whole of society, of which work would be the one civic obligation, the vital rule. . . . A town, a commune, would become an immense hive in which there would not be a single idler and in which each citizen would contribute his share toward the general sum of labor necessary for the town to live" (654). The expansion of Luc's organic community and the cooperation between enlightened bourgeois and willing workers spell the disappearance of all capitalist middlemen, represented by the greedy little retail traders, and of all parasitic, nonworking bourgeois.

The lessons of bourgeois degeneracy in *Travail* are that idleness is a sin, class exploitation is wasteful, and parasitism subverts the efficiency and humane organization of the working community. Zola suggests, however, that collective action by the workers offers no hope of social reform. He stresses the irresponsibility, conservatism, and inertia of the workers, who play a negligible part in the social transformation represented by La Crècherie; and his critique of their political apathy is matched by explicit disapproval of the (collectivist and anarchist) ideologies of revolutionary activists. The corollary of Zola's lack of faith in the workers as a force for social change is Luc's status as a patriarchal leader. Zola's utopian hopes of human redemption correspond to his myth of a New Man; and the New Man—the Messiah—who comes to restore order, to rebuild and redeem, arrives in *Travail* not as a working-class militant but as a bourgeois reformer.

It is feasible that this emphasis on Luc's status as a "man of destiny" was reinforced by Zola's own spectacular demonstration of the efficacy of individual initiative by his intervention—as a leader of opinion—in the Dreyfus affair. But this contingent historical factor must not obscure the continuity of Zola's fiction. For the individualism so apparent in *Travail* and the later novels is prefigured, as we have seen, by Zola's general interest in characters of outstanding determination, energy, and enterprise; in particular, the thematic structure of *L'Argent*, with its stress on the themes of leadership, energy, and responsibility, points to the links between the Napoleonic Saccard and the charismatic Luc. The term *charisma* is not misapplied, for it denotes Luc's inspirational role in the construction of the new community, his patriarchal authority, and the virtual hero worship of which he is the object:

He was everywhere at once, encouraging the men in the workshops, promoting brotherliness between one and all at the community-house, and watching over the management of the cooperative stores. He was constantly to be seen in the sunlit avenues of the new town, amidst the women and the children, with whom he liked to laugh and play, as if he were the young father of the little nation now springing up around him. Thanks to his genius and creative fruitfulness, things arose and grew methodically; it was as if seeds fell from his hands wherever he went. (761)

Luc's prestige as the founder, benefactor, and benign ruler of the perfect city-state merely increases with the passing years.

The presence of Luc's three female companions heightens his patriarchal status. The self-abnegating Suzanne and Soeurette provide him with moral support and practical assistance in his social task, complementing Josine, the revered mother of his numerous children, who, in their turn, provide dynastic continuity. The self-abnegation of Suzanne and Soeurette (for their relationship with Luc is noncarnal) is matched by Josine's placid willingness to share her husband with two other women in the interests of his cause; the transcendence of personal claims by the glory of service to their master underlines their essential subservience. This subservience (which would hardly commend itself to feminist readers of Zola) is accompanied by a pervasive rhetoric of adoration. Female veneration is most marked in the case of Josine, rescued by Luc from a life of hunger and degradation; their love, described entirely in terms of Luc's ineffable compassion and Josine's undying gratitude, is presented less as a personal relationship than as a piece of social symbolism which reinforces Luc's messianic project and his superior role as redeemer of society. Zola's sexual politics thus mirror the patriarchal social structure of his utopia: his ideal woman is a good wife and mother. All of his ideal heroines in *Les Rougon-Macquart* are or become bourgeois women, his delineation of the ideal feminine type reflects his approval of the bourgeois values of work, moderation, and order, and throughout most of his career he believed in the stabilizing influence of marriage and the bourgeois family ideal; Luc Froment, though he does not believe in the bourgeois institution of marriage, does believe in fidelity and responsible parenthood.

The reader is informed that the economic organization of La Crècherie is based on profit sharing and worker participation. Although Zola provides no practical details concerning the distribution of wealth and rewards, capitalist economics, in the form of shares and profits, are retained; this is illustrated by the nature of the economic association between La Crècherie and the neighboring farmers of Les Combettes. The constantly repeated formula used to denote the economic structure of La Crècherie is Capital, Travail, Talent: "Jordon would provide the money required, Bonnaire and his mates would provide the labor, and his [Luc's] would be the brain that plans and directs" (670). The ideal that La Crècherie fulfills is that of capitalism with a conscience, an ideal that reinforces Luc's bourgeois philanthropism. The question of worker participation, however, is more problematical. Although little is said of the political structure of Luc's organic society, it is plain that it is deeply

paternalistic. Zola's brand of socialism in *Travail* is one in which govern-
mental organization, unions, and political parties hardly figure at all. The
workers do not seem to share in the administration of the city; Luc
remains the dominant figure, and power seems concentrated entirely in his
hands. The only character whose prestige is comparable to Luc's is Jordan,
the gifted technician who embodies the fact that Zola's scientific faith is
central to his millenarian dreams. Thus, whereas the predominant viewpoint in *Germinal* is that of the exploited workers, in *Travail* it is that of
the bourgeois reformer, the isolated individual. The working classes, far
from occupying the center of *Travail*, figure most schematically in the
novel. The vision of society implicit in *Travail* relates only marginally and
obliquely to contemporary socialism. Although the novel's point of depar-
ture is the apocalyptic expectations resulting from the crisis of industrial
capitalism, the ideological basis of the social reforms advocated is not
scientific socialism but a form of bourgeois paternalism.

Zola's ideology is informed by a preoccupation with creative energy
and the organization of vital forces. The governing pattern of his work
may be defined as a concern with social purpose, social order, and
responsible social leadership. Much of his fiction shows the pernicious
consequences of misdirected human energies, and what his work develops
toward is the rationally organized utopian society described in *Travail*, in
which human energies are coordinated and regulated, and put to produc-
tive use in the service of a stable and integrated social order. The essence of
Luc Froment's ideal community lies in the principles of social equilibrium
and natural harmony; Zola's final vision of the ideal society corresponds to
class collaboration and a rearranged bourgeois hierarchy. *Travail* describes
a radical reform of institutions and managerial personnel rather than a
proletarian revolution. The bourgeoisie as an exploitive, property-owning
class is consigned to extinction in Zola's utopia; but although *Travail*
describes the collapse of the old bourgeois order and the abolition of
economic privilege, the principles of bourgeois leadership and authority
are both retained and affirmed. Zola sees the ideal bourgeois as a leader
and an organizer, as a kind of inspired technocrat seeking to organize and
to rationalize rather than to bring about violent revolutionary change. The
propertied bourgeoisie of the capitalist variety is eclipsed by a new
managerial elite. Zola's social outlook may thus be described as conservative in the sense that he makes it clear that society is held together by
hierarchy and authority. Moreover, his ideal society (like the social
criticism voiced in *Les Rougon-Macquart*) is grounded in the traditional
bourgeois values of work, moderation, and order, as well as in his faith in
the natural forces of fecundity, scientific progress, and a liberal education.
Zola spoke wiser than he knew when he said in the preface to *L'Assommoir*: "If they only knew how much the blood-thirsty creature, the
ferocious novelist, is a worthy bourgeois . . ." (2:374).

Note

1. All references to *Les Rougon-Macquart* are to the Pléiade edition, edited by Henri Mitterand, 5 vols. (Paris: 1960–67). References to *Travail* are taken from vol. 8 of the *Œuvres complètes*, also edited by Mitterand (Paris: Cercle du Livre Précieux, 1966–70). The translation of *La Curée* (*The Kill*) by A. Teixeira de Mattos, first published in 1895 for the Lutetian Society, has been used for quotations from that novel.

Zola: Poet of an Age of World Destruction and Renewal
Philip D. Walker*

No writer has been more caught up than Zola in the process of world destruction and renewal that has marked our age. On 2 June 1860, just as he was setting out on his career, he wrote his friend Baille, "Our age is an age of transition: emerging from an abhorred past, we head towards an unknown future." With deep emotion, he went on to note the impatience of their epoch, its immense curiosity to discover what the future held in store, its feverish activity in science, commerce, art, politics, and religion, its technological progress, exemplified by the railroad, telegraph, steamship and balloon. He evoked the vast popular uprisings, the movement of the empires toward unity, the collapse of the old religions, and the need for a new faith more suitable to the new world about to be born. He likened society to a runner racing up the path of the future, straining to see what lay ahead. He compared the nineteenth century to a mother big with child and admonished those who wanted to take refuge in the past: "The fools! with their scorn for our age, such a fine, holy age! When a mother still bears her child in her womb, people bow down before her: bow down therefore, you beasts, before our century so full of promise for your descendants."[1] Throughout the remainder of his career, he paraphrased, developed, and elaborated these observations over and over again. The historical vision behind them was, with him, a veritable obsession.

By his mid-twenties, it had already become one of his major journalistic themes. "We are in the midst of a state of anarchy, and, to me, this anarchy is a curious and interesting spectacle," he confessed in *La Revue contemporaine* of 15 February 1866. "This unceasing and obstinate procreation of our age is not sufficiently admired. . . . We are witnessing a profoundly human labor . . . we are creating bit by bit a new world."[2] At about the same time, he dreamed of writing a vast series of newspaper articles chronicling the drama of change and upheaval as a Parisian

*This essay has been written specifically for this volume, with certain passages based upon the author's article "Zola: Poet of an Age of Transition," *L'Esprit créateur* 11 (Winter 1971): 3–10, and reproduced by permission of the journal.

reporter like himself could observe it unfolding: "the great battle of our century . . . this clash of all interests, human and divine . . . this laborious birth of a new society." In doing so, he would not only, he pointed out, be satisfying his own and his contemporaries' need to keep track of the transformations taking place around them; he would also be recording for their descendents the world of the future, "how they were born, in the pain and travail of giants" (13:47).

Although his attempts to interest an editor in this project as originally conceived proved fruitless, the idea behind it kept on haunting him for the rest of his life. Indeed, his three major series of novels, whatever else they may be, are a realization of it in fictional form. This is not to say that each and every work included in them, when considered apart from its larger fictional context, would seem to be concerned with the theme of world destruction and renewal; but when we stand back and view Zola's fiction, beginning with *La Fortune des Rougon*, as a whole — as a single giant fresco — what may impress some of us above all is the vision that emerges from it of the metamorphosis of an entire civilization. Through Zola's eyes, we look out upon this spectacle just as, almost from the start, he had envisaged it, the titanic conflict between the forces of the past and future, the convulsions, the catastrophes, the birth out of the chaos to which the old world had returned of a new heaven and a new earth.

To be sure, he would seem in his earliest plans for the *Rougon-Macquart*, drawn up in late 1868 or early 1869, to have conceived of this first and greatest of his fictional series as primarily a demonstration of its physiological thesis, but it must be noted that even in these initial groping outlines he went out of his way to specify that the fortunes of his central family were to be determined not only by its members' inherited traits, but also by their environment, and that what characterized their environment was above all the momentous changes and upheavals going on within it. "To summarize my work in a sentence," he wrote, "I wish to depict, at the start of an age of freedom and truth, a family which makes a rush for the wealth at hand and goes off the rails, carried away by its own momentum, precisely because of the murky lights of the time, the fatal convulsions of the birth of a new world."[3]

As his plans for the series advanced, the historical theme gained in importance, and in *Les Rougon-Macquart* itself it is quite as persistent and central as the physiological theme, if not more so. In fact, the volume that has generally been considered Zola's masterpiece, *Germinal*, does not, as he admitted, really turn on physiological problems at all. Yet none of his individual novels more powerfully sets forth a major aspect of the transitional drama that Western society was undergoing in his time. As for the other volumes of the series, one after the other treats directly or figuratively other aspects of the same drama. Already, in *La Fortune des Rougon*, the overturelike first volume, the reader is fully plunged into it; for the social and political conflict at the heart of this novel involves far more, of course, than just a clash between a band of republicans and a few supporters of Louis-Napoléon Bonaparte in a remote French province in December 1851. The insurgents represent the republican spirit itself and, more generally, the whole emergent world of the future. Pierre Rougon, his ambitious, grasping wife, Félicité, and the novel's other conservatives and reactionaries, stand for the forces of the past.

La Curée, the second volume of the series, resumes the same general cosmogonic theme, concentrating in particular on the rise of modern finance, embodied in the financier Aristide Saccard. The third volume, *Le Ventre de Paris*, exalts Les Halles and through them the advent of modern architecture, predicting even more revolutionary structures to come — "a brave task, go to it," as the artist Claude Lantier observes, "and one which is still only a timid revelation of the twentieth century" (1:799). Volume 5, *La Faute de l'abbé Mouret*, symbolically evokes the destruction of traditional religion by one of the most widespread of the new secular faiths competing to replace it in the nascent modern world, a highly romantic cult of nature. Volume 11, *Au Bonheur des Dames*, is about the rise of modern commerce, symbolized by Octave Mouret's brash new department store, towering above the old-fashioned drapers' shops that have been ruined by it, "presenting its upstart face to the showy and sunny side of the new Paris" (3:761–63).

Germinal, the thirteenth novel, portrays, as we know, the awakening of the modern industrial proletariat and the commencement of modern economic class warfare — "the jolt given to a society that has cracked," to be followed inevitably by "other jolts until the final collapse occurs."[4] *L'Œuvre*, the next volume, recounts the birth of modern art. *La Terre*, Volume 15, depicts the peasantry, still barely touched by modern ideas. *Le Rêve*, which immediately follows, transports us into a remote, still-surviving corner of the past, a provincial Cathedral town. But with *La Bête humaine*, *L'Argent*, and *La Débâcle*, Volumes 17, 18, and 19, we are once again introduced into the thick of the tempest of change, in particular the rise of modern technology and, again, finance, symbolized by the locomotive, the Prussian cannon, and Saccard's Banque Universelle. The final volume, *Le Docteur Pascal*, fittingly exalts science, the chief agent of change. It shows the physician Pascal Rougon battling against the forces of reaction (embodied here principally by his mother, Félicité) and converting the younger generation (his niece-mistress Clotilde) to his new vision of reality. As those who have read this novel will recall, the possibility is raised at the end that Pascal and Clotilde's infant may be the New Messiah.

In *Les Trois Villes*, *Les Quatre Evangiles*, and most of Zola's other later writings, the theme of world destruction and renewal plays an even more dominant role than in *Les Rougon Macquart*. The tension between traditional and modernizing forces during the early Third Republic or an imaginary twentieth century is at the very core of *Lourdes*, *Rome*, *Paris*,

Fécondité, *Travail*, and *Vérité*. Physiological considerations are of minor importance. It is not surprising that around 1900, only two years before his death, Zola conceived the project of a series of plays, to be entitled *La France en marche*, in which he would once again treat the same cosmogonic theme. "I want to do for the Third Republic what I did for the Second Empire," he wrote. "On the one hand, the forces of the past, the monarchical spirit, the clerical spirit, acting, taking advantage of Republican freedom to reverse the progress made. On the other hand, all the forces of progress . . . the struggle between yesterday and tomorrow . . ." (15:843–44).

The same preoccupation with the drama of transition can also be seen in the chief distinctions that governed Zola's choice of characters and settings. It has been too seldom noted that the hundreds of figures and decors depicted in his fiction fall into three major categories. The first — far larger than those who have read only his most famous novels may suspect — consists of vestiges of the past: priests, nobles, peasants, old bourgeois, academic artists, small merchants, old-fashioned soldiers. We may recall, for example, poor Uncle Baudu, the draper, shaking his fist at the big, new modern department store driving him out of business, in *Au Bonheur des Dames*, or the once beautiful Comtesse de Beauvilliers, in *L'Argent*, weeping endlessly in her bare, impoverished room as the expanding modern French capital slowly swallows up her decaying country estate. Nor must we overlook the multitudinous priests depicted in Zola's fiction, including the heroes of no less than five novels and such unforgettable supporting figures as the majestic old Cardinal Boccanera of *Rome*, lifting his voice in prayer: "O powerful God, may Thy will be done, then! May everything die, everything crumble, everything return to the night of chaos! I shall remain standing in this ruined palace, I shall wait to be buried under the rubble. . . . O powerful God, sovereign Master, I am at Thy command, make of me, if such is Thy plan, the pontiff of destruction, of the death of the world!" (7:972).

A second major group appears in *Les Quatre Evangiles*: the inhabitants of the future, Zola's mythical twentieth century. But the largest, most varied category, the one upon which Zola chiefly focuses the spotlight of his fiction, is the one that has to do with the ephemeral, often fetal or monstrous products of the present — those institutions, places, and people who belong neither so much to the past or to the future as they do to the process of transition itself: the Satanic factories and mines, crowded, expanding cities, swollen slums, vulgar, lavish new mansions, swarming stock exchanges, giant barks and soaring iron and glass markets — all those things that are destined to disappear or be surpassed in their turn when the world of the future arrives. Zola's best, most memorable characters are, with some notable exceptions, from this category — his proletarians, new bourgeois, avant-garde artists and writers, labor leaders, financial and commercial pioneers, social, political, and religious reformers and visionaries — and, behind them all, the crusading engineers and the scientists, who, as the revered chemist Bertheroy in *Paris* points out, are the only true revolutionaries.

Nor can we help but be impressed, furthermore, by the comprehensive depth and sweep with which Zola has developed his vast theme of world destruction and renewal. On the one hand, he shows all the major forces making for change or resisting change. He brings onto the giant stage of his fiction a host of the historical figures playing prominent roles in the transitional changes and upheavals of his time — from Napoleon III, Wilhelm I, and the aging Leo XIII on down. He recounts not only the major transitional events of his epoch, but also, in the process of doing so, the private dramas of the little people caught up in them — the Serge Mourets and Pierre Froments, the Lazare Chanteaus, the Etienne Lantiers, Maheus, and Jean Macquarts. He depicts the history of his epoch as it might have been observed (or ignored) by representatives of every major social group involved in its unfolding.

Moreover, there is hardly an important aspect of his epic historical subject matter, political, social, economic, intellectual, or psychological, that he was not explored. Indeed, the better one knows Zola, the more one may be struck by the richness with which he has portrayed, among other things, the metaphysical and religious mentality of middle and late nineteenth-century French society, its frantic metaphysical questioning, its attempts to cope with the painful skepticism provoked by the Enlightenment and scientific progress, its widespread longing for a new and better faith, its immense spiritual instabilities, tensions, and confusions.

In fact, no author might better serve to illustrate Carl Jung's remark that contemporary man is "living in what the Greeks would have called the 'right time' for a metamorphosis of the gods — that is, of the fundamental principles and symbols."[5] On page after page, Zola takes us into the fiery furnace in which the old gods were (and still are) being melted down; he shows us the old traditional visions of reality disintegrating, the old doctrines flickering out — in Clotilde Rougon, for example, or Abbé Pierre Froment, the troubled priestly hero of *Les Trois Villes*, witnessing within his own soul "the supreme collapse."

> It was the end, science was victorious, nothing remained of the old world. (7:1002)

> His faith was dead for ever, even his hope that the faith of the crowds could be used for the common salvation. He denied all, merely awaiting now the final, inevitable catastrophe, the revolt, the massacre, the fire, which were to sweep away a guilty, condemned world. (7:1178)

But Zola also conveys to us the awareness of thousands of his contemporaries, which, as we have seen, he shared, that they were living in a time of extraordinary spiritual change comparable in magnitude to that of the first centuries of the Christian era—in, for example, this remark by Sandoz, in the final chapter of *L'OEuvre*: "Ah! indeed! I assert nothing, I am torn myself. Only it seems to me that this final convulsion of the old religious fright was forseeable. We are not an end, but a transition, a beginning of something else . . ." (5:733).

He shows us, in these and other characters, new doctrines dawning. He suggests the clash of religious or pseudoreligious ideas, tendencies, and movements competing to replace Christianity, the countless cults of science, of history and progress, the social religions, the metaphysical religions, the occult and neopagan religions: the pantheistic naturalism undermining Serge Mouret's Catholicism, Lazare Quenu's Schopenhauerianism, Etienne Lantier's socialistic humanitarianism, Sandoz's cult of the Great Mother, Pascal's creed of science, work, progress, and life, Pierre Froment's Religion of Science, the religions of fecundity, work, truth, and justice preached by the Messianic heroes of *Les Quatre Evangiles*—not to mention the pseudoreligions depicted in *L'Assommoir* or *Au Bonheur des Dames*. Père Colombe's bar, as Zola portrays it, is an infernal altar dispensing the salvation of death to its despairing communicants. Octave Mouret's department store, whose architecture "was like," Zola tells us, "a tabernacle and an alcove" (4:1016), "bringing forth," he goes on to say, "a new religion, the churches that a wavering faith was gradually deserting were replaced by his bazaar, in souls henceforth unoccupied" (4:1038–39).

Zola's preoccupation with the theme of world destruction and renewal is also strongly reflected in his imagery and symbolism. Over and over again, he contrasts objects associated with the past with objects associated with the present or future: for example, Saccard's showy new mansion in the Parc Monceau and the dark, sober, silent old house of Renée's *vieux-bourgeois* father on the Ile Saint-Louis; Les Halles and the adjacent Church of Saint-Eustache; the locomotives thundering by above the Cimetière de Saint-Ouen and the droning Latin of Claude's interment; or the new electric lights twinkling here and there, struggling to shine, to stand out, among the dim gaslights and dark ruins of the old quarters of the Holy City as seen by Pierre Froment from the Pope's apartment: "Rare constellations, brilliant stars sketching out mysterious and noble figures vainly sought to struggle and break free. They were drowned, obliterated in the confused chaos of the dust of an old star that would have broken up there, losing all its glory, reduced henceforth to being no more than a kind of phosphorescent sand" (7:914).

Or we may recall the numerous symbolic sunrises and sunsets in Zola's fiction—in *Germinal*, *La Débâcle*, *Paris*, or *Travail*, for example. Toward the end of *La Débâcle*, it seems to Jean, ". . . in this slow nightfall, above this city in flames, that a new dawn was already breaking. . . . It was the inevitable rejuvenation of eternal nature, of eternal humanity, the promised renewal to those who hope and to those who work" . . . (6:1121).

Nor must we forget Zola's numerous evocations of passages from Genesis or Revelation or of classical creation myths: Adam and Eve (*La Faute de l'abbé Mouret*), the Biblical deluge (*Germinal*), Jacob and the angel (*L'Œuvre*),[6] Sodom and Gomorrah (*La Débâcle*), the Red Whore of Babylon (*Nana*), or the Great Final War and the advent of a New Messiah (*La Débâcle, Travail*); Chronos, Furies, Titans, Tartarus, the wars between the gods, the classical flood, Deucalion and Pyrrha, etc. (*Germinal*).[7]

Zola's fiction, in its grand outlines, is a vast cosmogony. In his youth, he dreamed of being a modern Lucretius; but it would be more apt to compare him to Hesiod. Zola is the Hesiod of the contemporary world.

But the overwhelming impression that Zola's writings can give us of being caught up in the birth of the contemporary world is heightened by our awareness as we read him of his own personal involvement in the same momentous process.

This involvement may be seen in many aspects of his life and personality, but nowhere better than in his philosophical and religious thought. Like numerous other French intellectuals of his period, he was deeply affected by the crisis provoked by the impact of science and other modernizing forces on traditional beliefs. When, in an article composed in 1879, he remarked regarding Renan's youthful loss of faith, "it is always the same story: the first quiver of doubt, then the painful struggles, then the final wrench" (10:1212), he could not but have had himself in mind as well; for he too, while still in his teens, had broken with traditional religion and experienced the anguish that often accompanies disbelief. He shared throughout his life the hunger for infallibility which is one of the major traits of nineteenth-century thought and, like many other intellectually and spiritually insecure thinkers of his epoch, found it in science and little, hard facts—"naked, living reality," which, as he wrote in an early essay, "this life of sufferings, of doubt," makes one love "with a deep love" (10:74). Hence his embrace of, first, in his mid-twenties, the pseudopositivist philosophy of Taine, then, in his late thirties, the pure philosophical positivism of Littré and Bernard. But no more than Littré himself was he capable of remaining satisfied for very long with the cautiously limited truths that positivism admitted; he suffered intensely from the metaphysical anxiety that was so widespread in the thinking of his time. He frequently succumbed to one or another of the various forms of pessimism then circulating in France. He also participated in the general desire of many thousands of his contemporaries for a new, more satisfactory faith and from his late adolescence on expended enormous amounts of energy trying to invent one.

As what was left of his childhood religion crumbled, a confusing array of tentative, more or less nebulous new cults, creeds, and full-fledged "new religions" or philosophical religion substitutes took shape in his mind: the Michelet-like religion of love that he began elaborating while still enrolled at the Lycée Saint-Louis; the "new belief, philosophical and religious belief" based on geology that he may already be found developing in early 1860;[8] the romantic pantheism that he described in a *Causerie* published in the spring of 1868 (13:112–17); the creed expressing absolute faith in life, humanity, work, science, and progress that he professed in *Le Figaro* of 5 September 1881 (14:650–55); the religion of work that he gravely, some observers thought morosely, propounded in an address delivered at a banquet of the Association Générale des Etudiants in May 1893 (12:677–83) and set forth again, more briefly, in a letter, dated 29 May 1898, to his friend Louis Delpech (14:1497–98).

Unfortunately, none of these new faiths permanently satisfied him. Nourished by thinkers as diverse as Hugo, Michelet, Taine, Renan, Claude Bernard, Sainte-Beuve, George Sand, Cuvier, Darwin, Lucas, Letourneau, Pelletan, and Schopenhauer, he never managed to reconcile his clashing notions of God, man, nature, and history. After the solid Catholic cosmos of his youth had disintegrated, his philosophical and religious thought remained up to his death, in 1902, essentially chaotic, characterized by what Paul Bourget had called in 1883 that "anarchy of a unique kind" which, by that time, "has set in among all those who think."[9] Beyond the little hard facts and real or supposed scientific truths to which Zola clung, like a shipwrecked sailor clinging to a rock in the midst of a stormy sea, there was nothing but the metaphysical chaos into which he had been born and which he helped perpetuate.[10]

Inevitably, his awareness of the radically transitional nature of his epoch, his self-identification with the forces of the future, and the highly transitional nature of his own thought had an immense impact on his conception of his role in life. From almost the outset of his career, Zola was determined to be the one who would create and impose the formulas of the art of the future. "There are no masters, no schools any more," he proclaimed in the preface to *Mes Haines*. "We are in the midst of a state of anarchy, and each one of us is a rebel who thinks for himself, who creates and fights for himself. . . . And deep down in each new fighter there is a vague hope of being the dictator, the tyrant of tomorrow" (10:27). In one after another of his early journalistic articles, penned long before the Naturalistic battles of the late seventies and early eighties, he can be found already struggling to attain this goal—in, for example, his campaign of 1866 in behalf of Manet and the Impressionists. Nor could the success of his literary and artistic doctrines at the peak of his literary career satisfy him, as we know from his desperate journalistic efforts in his later years to retain his grip on a public tired of naturalism and win over to his own aesthetic doctrines a younger generation marching to a different drummer.

But to be merely the artistic lawgiver of the nascent new world was by no means all that Zola wanted. From his late adolescence on, he was driven by an even more audacious goal. He wanted to help create the entire world of the future—champion all the great modernizing forces as he defined them, shape the new society, contribute to the formation of the new political and economic structures, formulate the religion of tomorrow. In short, he dreamed of being the prophet, perhaps even the new Messiah for whom his contemporaries were waiting. For him, as for Hugo, his first great literary hero, poetic creation and world creation were barely distinguishable. It was not purely by chance that, when he was only twenty, he had posed for his Provençal artist friend Chaillan as Amphion, the son of Zeus and Antiope, who, by the music of a magical lyre given him by Hermes, walled the city of Thebes. "The role of the poet is sacred; it is the role of the regenerator," he wrote Baille on 25 July 1860. "He is committed to progress."[11] A few days later, he added, in another letter to the same boyhood friend: ". . . fundamentally, prophets, artists [have] the same brows marked by the finger of God."[12]

His prophetic ambitions grew more compelling, if anything, with the years. In the fall of 1868, just as he was beginning to plan *Les Rougon-Macquart*, he adjured Mistral: "Poet, do not belie your mission. You are one of those inspired spirits who must divine and preach the future" (10:763). In January 1869, as the series continued to take shape in his mind, he announced, somewhat coyly (for what was he describing but his own self-appointed mission?): "There is at the present time a patrimony of work and struggle to be taken up, the patrimony of the Victor Hugos and the Lamennais. And not one of us has yet risen up to claim that dazzling and painful succession" (10:778). In *La Cloche* of 12 April 1872, he affirmed, "when you live in the nineteenth century, you must have the courage to enter into the realities, into the toil, into the immense and grandiose spectacle of this age which is surely in the process of giving birth to a new world" (10:947).

As a journalist, he fought indefatigably, year after year, to realize his prophetic aims. On the one hand, he bombarded in a host of articles everything that in his opinion stood in the way of progress—Louis Napoléon and his political supporters, the Salon Juries, the bourgeoisie, the capitalist system, the jingoists responsible for Sedan, the conservative and reactionary deputies of the early Third Republic, the perpetrators of the crime against Dreyfus. Above all, he concentrated his thunders on traditional religion, not sparing the Protestants, but aiming in particular at the Roman Catholic Church—Veuillot, Dupanloup, the Jesuits and other teaching orders, the Vatican itself. He was deadly serious when he wrote in 1879: "I can understand that practicing Catholics do not like us, for we hack into their beliefs" (10:1389). He did not even hesitate to attack the basic doctrines of Christianity, pointing out the failure of Christ's attempt to save the world, deploring the Sermon on the Mount, and referring, in March 1902, to the Gospel, "which has been stifling us for eighteen centuries . . . eighteen centuries of suffering and lies" (13:745).

On the other hand, he eloquently supported science, democracy, the republic, the separation of church and state, state-run schools, Dreyfus, socialism, and everything else that he associated with progress. His energy and passionate commitment to these causes never flagged. "Action! action!" he exhorted his future son-in-law, Maurice Le Blond, on 1 December 1900. "All of us must act, all of us understand that it is a social crime not to act, at such a grave hour, when the baneful forces of the past engage in the supreme battle with the forces of tomorrow' (14:1532).

From his youth on, moreover, he struggled to realize his ambition to be the prophet of the new religion of the future—and this despite his failure to find a faith in which he himself could permanently believe. While still only nineteen, in December 1859, he planned what would have been, if he had ever completed it, his first "Gospel"—a long story demonstrating "that there is a god for lovers."[13] *Paolo*, one of his major adolescent poems, is a strongly evangelical work. So also, apparently, if we are to judge from the first eight verses, would have been *La Genèse*, the unfinished epic that he started seriously elaborating in 1860. In October 1865, when he was in his mid-twenties, he solemnly proposed his "new faith" based on geology to the middle-class readers of *Le Salut public* of Lyons (10:99–101). "La Démocratie," one of the concluding articles in *Une campagne*, has a strongly prophetic, evangelical ring (14:650–55). So also do his address at the annual AGE banquet on 18 May 1893, proposing his religion of work (12:677–83), and his article of 23 May 1896, in *Le Figaro*, exalting procreation as the supreme religious act (14:785–90). *Messidor* and more than one of the other opera scenarios that he wrote in his last years for his friend and composer Alfred Bruneau are also Zolaesque "Gospels."

Zola's novels strongly reflect this whole transitional side of his nature: the spiritual and intellectual thinker caught up in the metamorphosis of fundamental principles and symbols provoked by the rise of contemporary civilization; the would-be dictator of the new artistic formula; the prophet, the world creator.

This may be seen in the numerous autobiographical elements in Zola's fiction—all those many characters who are in large part more or less faithful or imaginary self-portraits: for example, the Claude of Zola's first novel, the spiritually troubled young Zola bereft of his childhood religion, passing through the dark night of the soul, then finding God, reaffirming his cherished reveries, in an impassioned leap of faith; Pascal Rougon, a reflection of Zola's ideal image of himself as crusading physician, bringer of the new religion; Lazare Chanteau, the neurotic, doubting, despairing Zola; Pauline Quenu, Zola as he would like to be, the strong-nerved positivist, the selfless healer, the stubborn affirmer of life's value; Claude Lantier, Sandoz, complementary avatars of Zola the inventor of the new artistic formula, Zola the twentieth-century Jacob (as he liked to think) struggling at the dawn of a new world with the angel of nature, reality, truth; Pierre Froment, the spiritually tortured priest rejecting Catholicism, searching for a new faith, and finding it in the cult of science and social progress; Guillaume Froment, Zola the scientific social reformer torn between evolutionism and catastrophism, anarchism and trust in the revolutionary power of science; Mathieu Froment, Zola the apostle of fecundity; Luc Froment, Zola the Christ-like prophet of the new religion of work, the New Messiah, the founder of a new Jerusalem on earth; Marc Froment, Zola the teacher, the triumphant champion of truth, the Zola of the Dreyfus affair fictionalized, apotheosized, magnified into still another Zolaesque New Messiah.

But if Zola's involvement in the process of world destruction and renewal as it was going on in his day is reflected in many of his characters, it may also be discerned in many of the distinctive thematic, stylistic, and structural traits of his fiction. Among other things, many of the most frequently remarked excesses of Zola's novels must be ascribed at least in part to his determination to use his novels as weapons in his campaign to be the artistic dictator of the future. *L'Assommoir*, with its deliberate attempts to push naturalism to the limit, displaying all that the new movement had to offer while assaulting the aging literary conventions that still stood in its way, is Zola's *Hernani*. *Le Ventre de Paris* is Zola's answer to Hugo's *Notre Dame de Paris*, which it simultaneously emulates and undermines. *La Terre* must, on one level, be appreciated as a ferocious anti-*Mare au Diable*, the coup de grace directed by a triumphant Zola to the vitals of sentimental romantic idealism.

It can hardly be stressed too much, moreover, to what a great extent Zola's fiction, like his journalism, issues from his ambition to help shape the whole world of the future. Not only *Les Trois Villes* and the final "gospels," but also *Les Rougon-Macquart* have a cosmogonic mission. All twenty *Rougon-Macquart* novels (except perhaps *Une Page d'amour*, *Le Rêve*, and *La Bête humaine*) testify to his determination to help destroy everything that, in his opinion, obstructed progress, hasten the advent of the future, and make it comply with his own prophetic visions. For example, we may recall his numerous attacks, commencing with *La Fortune des Rougon*, on the bourgeoisie as represented by Pierre and Félicité Rougon in *La Fortune des Rougon* or the Grégoire family in *Germinal*, much as it would be by the Duvillards in *Paris* or the Qurignons in *Travail*. Or we may remember the anticlericalism implicit in, for example, the portrayals of Abbé Faujas, the sinister central character of *La Conquête de Plassans*, the rushed, perfunctory priests in *L'Assommoir*, and the uncharitable Abbé Joire and wild-eyed Abbé Ranvier in *Germinal*. Or we may think of the attacks here and there throughout *Les Rougon-Macquart* on more than one of the basic doctrines of traditional religion: for example, *L'Assommoir*'s rebuttal, through its account of Gervaise's misfortunes, of the central Judeo-Christian doctrine of Divine

Providence, evoked in Mme Lerat's song at Gervaise's saint's day celebration.[14]

Even Zola's frequently criticized tendency to focus on the horrors of life — all those repulsive things symbolized by the dirty linen (in the literal sense) that he airs in *L'Assommoir* — is, as he more than once protested, largely motivated by his desire to hasten social change by arousing the conscience of his public and thus inducing it to make needed reforms.[15] *L'Assommoir* not only recounts the story of a laundress, it is itself a laundry, and the same might be said of *Les Rougon-Macquart* in its entirety and its giant fictional sequels.

Yet the demiurgic thrust of Zola's fiction, including most of the *Rougon-Macquart* novels, is still more evident in their tendency to glorify nearly everything that Zola associated with the future: scientists, engineers, republicans, socialists, daring industrial and commercial entrepreneurs, avant-garde artists and writers; iron and steel architecture; the bicycle, the automobile, the electric motor; France (the Messianic nation, the sacred country of the Revolution), Paris (the capital of the Revolution, the wine vat in which the future was being brewed); republicanism, socialism, the nineteenth century (blessed among all centuries for the new world that it bore within it), and all those other modern heroes, physical objects, or values that Zola revered and liked to think would be honored by the society of the future — nature, love, life, fecundity, force, work, truth, justice. (Few critics have remarked to what a great degree the fundamental themes, characters, and settings of Zola's fiction are dictated by precisely these same Zolaesque values.)

The style of Zola's fiction also grows in large part out of his demiurgic ambitions — its powerful satirical qualities occasionally reminiscent of Juvenal or Voltaire, its baroque colors, exaggerations, and oppositions recalling at times Agrippa d'Aubigné, its Hugolian lyrical and epic traits transforming everything into complex, all-embracing visionary symbols, its affinities in *Germinal* and elsewhere (e.g., the passages describing the Qurignon's Satanic munitions factory in *Travail*) with Van Gogh, Munch, Kollwitz, Grosz, and other Expressionists. A style marvelously well wrought, that is to say, for the task of world destruction and renewal in which Zola, along with Hugo and so many of his other great contemporaries, was engaged.

Moreover, Zola's fiction repeatedly reflects his ambition to be the prophet of the new religion of the future. Over and over again he proposes new faiths in his novels, just as he does in his journalistic articles or his speech to the AGE — the same faiths or different ones: for example, the pantheistic cult of Nature hymned in *La Terre*; Pascal's creed of science, work, progress, and life extolled in *Le Docteur Pascal* (6:1190, 1246); the scientific, socialistic humanitarian "religion of the future" outlined in the prophetic conclusion of *Les Trois Villes* by Pierre Froment (the rock, as his first name implies, on which an aging Zola dreamed of founding his own Church); and, of course, the immense gospels of fecundity, work, truth, and justice set forth through Pierre's sons, Zola's last fictional alter egos, Mathieu, Marc, and Luc, in *Les Quatre Evangiles*. Nor must we overlook in this respect all those many other novels in which Zola expressed one or another of the religious or pseudoreligious doctrines, reveries, and visions, real or imaginary, competing for predominance in his mind — *La Faute de l'abbé Mouret, Germinal* or *L'Œuvre*. Not only in his early poems, his nonfictional writings, and the long, fiery-eyed fictions of his old age, but also in the evangelical novels of his maturity, Zola struggled, like so many earlier nineteenth-century figures, to become the Buddha, the Moses, the Christ, of tomorrow — or, at least, if that were impossible, his forerunner or progenitor.

But in his fiction, too, as well as his nonfictional writings, he turns out to be, all things considered, an extraordinarily strange prophet. More like Renan, let us say, than Taine, Michelet, Fourier, or most other nineteenth-century prophets, he is constantly contradicting himself, erasing with one hand what he writes with the other, a mercurial prophet proclaiming not just one new faith, but multiple clashing faiths, a prophet alternately or simultaneously dejected and ecstatic, a prophet habitually torn between belief and doubt, hope and despair. Even *Les Quatre Evangiles*, the final flowering of Zola's old Messianic dream, proclaims not just one new faith, but a whole series of largely disparate new faiths, each with a different supreme value, each with a different vision of the shape of things to come.

As for *Les Rougon-Macquart*, it would be futile to seek here, either, any single consistent underlying philosophy. Certainly the vaguely Tainian materialism that Zola cautiously adopted in his preliminary notes for this series does not fill this role. Nor does the pure philosophical positivism that he embraced with such fanfare in *Le Roman expérimental*. Nor even the vision of things, reminiscent of Renan's creed as summarized by Melchior de Vogüé, expressed in *Le Docteur Pascal*, the series' intended "philosophical conclusion." What philosophical or religious system could possibly accommodate novels with such diverse world views as, for example, *La Faute de l'abbé Mouret, La Joie de vivre, La Terre, Le Rêve, La Bête humaine, La Débâcle*, and *Le Docteur Pascal?* Sometimes the old romantic humanitarian in Zola surges to the fore, sometimes the anti-anthropocentric, scientistic inventor of a new faith based on geology, sometimes the black poet, the nihilist, the quasi-Schopenhauerian pessimist, sometimes the irrational, erotic pantheist, sometimes the proponent of salvation through faith in science, work, and life. Again we seem to hear, as in a cavernous echo chamber, the clashing voices of Renan, Taine, Michelet, Hugo, Cuvier, Darwin, Bernard, Schopenhauer, and a host of other nineteenth-century thinkers. Furthermore, not only the series as a whole, but also more than one of the individual novels in it are remarkable for their extreme philosophical and religious ambiguity. This is true, certainly, of *L'Assommoir* or *La Joie de vivre* — not to mention *Germinal*, with its myriad different, philosophical or religious interpretations, all of them mirage-like, ranging from the most optimistic to the most pessimistic, the most positivistic to the most idealistic.

In short, the more deeply we penetrate into the eye of the fiction writer in Zola, the more obvious it becomes that we are plunged, here too, into what is not so much a cosmos as a chaos. A dark chaos illuminated by flashes of lightning, the red glow of flowing lava. A chaos dreaming of the new reality, the new truth, to which it is struggling, with infinite pain, to give birth.

Notes

1. *Correspondance*, ed. B. H. Bakker (Montréal: Les Presses de l'Université de Montréal, 1978–) 1:169–70. (This edition will hereafter be referred to as *Corr.*)

2. *Œuvres complètes*, ed. Henri Mitterand (Paris: Cercle du Livre Précieux, 1966–69), 10:147–48. Unless otherwise indicated, subsequent references to Zola's writings will be to this edition.

3. *Les Rougon-Macquart*, ed. Henri Mitterand, Bibliothèque de la Pléiade (Paris: Gallimard, 1960–67), 5:1739.

4. *Les Rougon-Macquart*, Pléiade ed., 3:1826.

5. Carl Jung, "God, the Devil, and the Human Soul," *Atlantic Monthly* 200 (November 1957):63.

6. See P. Walker, "Zola et la lutte avec l'ange," *Les Cahiers naturalistes*, no. 42 (1971):70–94.

7. See P. Walker, "Prophetic Myths in Zola," *PMLA* 74 (September 1959):444–52.

8. *Corr.*, 1:182–83.

9. Paul Bourget, *Essais de psychologie contemporaine*, 5th ed. (Paris: Lemerre, 1889), 198.

10. See P. Walker, *"Germinal" and Zola's Philosophical and Religious Thought*, Purdue University Monographs in Romance Languages (Amsterdam: John Benjamins, 1984), 87–96.

11. *Corr.*, 1:206.

12. *Corr.*, 1:223.

13. *Corr.*, 1:117.

14. See P. Walker, "*L'Assommoir* et la pensée religieuse de Zola," *Les Cahiers naturaliste*, no. 52 (1978):70–71.

15. See *Les Rougon-Macquart*, Pléiade ed., 5:1586: "If he has told it all, the dark side of things and the abominable, he has done so as a teacher who demonstrates with a human cadaver, as a healer also. . . ."

Check-List of English Titles of Novels by Emile Zola

Zola's novels are listed in chronological order with (1) the French title and date of publication of the first French edition and (2) the various titles of English translations of each novel in alphabetical order. For fuller details see chapter 22 of Graham King, *Garden of Zola* (London: Barrie and Jenkins; New York: Barnes and Noble, 1978); the bibliography by Angus Wilson, *Emile Zola* (London: Secker and Warburg, 1952); and David Baguley, "Les Œuvres de Zola traduites en anglais (1878–1968)," *Les Cahiers naturalistes*, no. 40 (1970):195–209.

EARLY NOVELS

La Confession de Claude (1865)
  Claude's Confession

Le Vœu d'une morte (1866)
  A Dead Woman's Wish

Les Mystères de Marseille (1867)
  The Mysteries of Marseilles

Thérèse Raquin (1867)
  The Devil's Compact
  Nemesis
  Theresa
  Thérèse Raquin

Madeleine Férat (1868)
  Fatal Intimacy
  Madeleine Férat
  Magdalen Ferat
  Shame

THE *ROUGON-MACQUART* NOVELS

La Fortune des Rougon (1871)
  The Fortune of the Rougons

The Girl in Scarlet
The Rougon-Macquart Family
Wedded in Death

La Curée (1872)
  In the Whirlpool
  The Kill
  Renée, the Crime of the Family
  The Rush for the Spoil
  Venus of the Counting House

Le Ventre de Paris (1873)
  La Belle Lisa
  Fat and Thin
  The Fat and the Thin
  The Flower and Market Girls of Paris
  The Markets of Paris
  Savage Paris

La Conquête de Plassans (1874)
  The Conquest of Plassans
  A Fatal Conquest
  A Mad Love
  A Priest in the House

La Faute de l'abbé Mouret (1875)
  Abbé Mouret's Transgression
  The Abbé Mouret's Sin
  The Abbé's Temptation
  The Sin of the Abbé Mouret
  The Sin of Father Mouret
  The Sinful Priest

Son Excellence Eugène Rougon (1876)
  Clorinda
  His Excellency
  His Excellency Eugène Rougon
  The Mysteries of the Court of Louis Napoleon
  The Mysteries of Louis Napoleon's Court

L'Assommoir (1877)
  L'Assommoir
  The 'Assommoir'
  The Dram Shop
  Drink
  Drunkard
  Gervaise
  The Gin Palace
  Nana's Mother

Une Page d'amour (1878)
  Hélène
  A Love Affair
  Love Episode
  A Love Episode
  A Page of Love

Nana (1880)
  Nana

Pot-Bouille (1882)
  Lesson in Love
  Piping Hot
  Pot-Bouille
  Restless House

Au Bonheur des Dames (1883)
  Ladies' Delight
  The Ladies' Paradise
  Shop Girls of Paris

La Joie de vivre (1884)
  How Jolly Life Is!
  The Joy of Life
  Joys of Life
  The Joys of Life
  Life's Joys
  Zest for Life

Germinal (1885)
  Germinal
  Nana's Brother

L'Œuvre (1886)
  Christine the Model
  His Masterpiece
  The Masterpiece

La Terre (1887)
  Earth
  The Earth
  The Soil
  La Terre

Le Rêve (1888)
  The Dream
  A Dream of Love
  Le Rêve

La Bête humaine (1890)
  The Beast in Man
  La Bête humaine
  The Human Beast
  Human Brutes
  The Monomaniac

L'Argent (1891)
  Money

La Débâcle (1892)
  La Débâcle
  The Debacle
  The Downfall

Le Docteur Pascal (1893)
  Doctor Pascal

THE *TROIS VILLES* SERIES

Lourdes (1894)
  Lourdes

Rome (1896)
  Rome

Paris (1898)
  Paris

THE *QUATRE EVANGILES* SERIES

Fécondité (1899)
  Fruitfulness

Travail (1901)
  Labor
  Work

Vérité (1903)
  Truth

Selected Bibliography of Works on Zola for Readers of English

BIBLIOGRAPHICAL SOURCES

Baguley, David. *Bibliographie de la critique sur Emile Zola. Vol. I: 1864–1970; Vol. II: 1971–1980.* Toronto: University of Toronto Press, 1976 and 1982. Both volumes contain a large number of references in English; the bibliography continues annually in the journal *Les Cahiers naturalistes.*

Hemmings, F. W. J. *The Life and Times of Emile Zola.* London: Elek; New York: (1956):97–122. Reprinted in *The Present State of French Studies. A Collection of Research Reviews,* edited by Charles B. Osburn, 586–623, 951–54. Metuchen, N.J.: Scarecrow Press, 1971.

Lethbridge, Robert. "Twenty Years of Zola Studies (1956–1975)." *French Studies* 31 (1977):281–93. Follows from the Hemmings article above.

Nelson, Brian. *Emile Zola. A Selective Analytical Bibliography.* London: Grant and Cutler, 1982. Indispensable reference work—in English.

Schor, Naomi. "Zola and *la nouvelle critique*." *L'Esprit créateur* 11 (1971):11–20.

BOOKS ON ZOLA AND HIS WORKS

Carter, Lawson A. *Zola and the Theater.* New Haven: Yale University Press, 1963.

Frey, John A. *The Aesthetics of the "Rougon-Macquart."* Madrid: José Porrúa Turanzas, 1978.

Furst, Lilian R., and Peter N. Skrine. *Naturalism.* London: Methuen, 1971.

Grant, Elliott M. *Emile Zola.* New York: Twayne, 1966. A general, historical introduction.

Hemmings, F. W. J. *Emile Zola.* Oxford, The Clarendon Press, 1953. Rev. ed., 1966. Indispensable reading.

Hemmings, F. W. J. *The Life and Times of Emile Zola.* London: Elek; New York: Scribner's, 1977. A fine, concise, eminently readable illustrated biography.

Kamm, Lewis. *The Object in Zola's "Rougon-Macquart."* Madrid: José Porrúa Turanzas, 1978.

King, Graham. *Garden of Zola. Emile Zola and His Novels for English Readers.* London: Barrie and Jenkins; New York: Barnes and Noble, 1978. An informative, readable book for the general public.

Knapp, Bettina L. *Emile Zola.* New York: Frederick Ungar, 1980. A straightforward introductory study.

Lanoux, Armand. *Zola*. Translated by Mary Glasgow. London: Staples Press, 1955. A slightly abridged translation of a *biographie romancée*.

Lapp, John C. *Zola before the "Rougon-Macquart."* Toronto: University of Toronto Press, 1964. A mainly thematic study of Zola's early works.

Levin, Harry. "Zola." In *The Gates of Horn: A Study of Five French Realists*, 305–71. New York, Oxford University Press, 1963. A perceptive general study.

Richardson, Joanna. *Zola*. London: Weidenfeld and Nicolson, 1978. A thorough, but somewhat ponderous survey.

Schor, Naomi, ed. *Zola. Yale French Studies* 42 (1969). Special issue. Contains ten articles in English on Zola's works, with an introduction by Schor.

————. *Zola's Crowds*. Baltimore: The Johns Hopkins University Press, 1978. A stimulating modern approach to Zola's texts.

Turnell, Martin. "Zola." In *The Art of French Fiction*, 91–194. London: Hamish Hamilton; Norfolk, Conn.: New Directions, 1959.

Walker, Philip. *Emile Zola*. London: Routledge and Kegan Paul; New York: Humanities Press, 1968. A useful introduction with excerpts from the novelist's works.

Wilson, Angus. *Emile Zola: An Introductory Study of His Novels*. London: Secker and Warburg, 1952. A lively general study with Freudian insights — numerous editions.

For a useful, edited anthology of theoretical and critical texts dealing with naturalism, see George J. Becker, ed., *Documents of Modern Literary Realism* (Princeton, N.J.: Princeton University Press, 1963).

INDEX